Affirmative Action

The Pros and Cons of Policy and Practice

Affirmative Action

The Pros and Cons of Policy and Practice

REVISED EDITION

Richard F. Tomasson, Faye J. Crosby, and Sharon D. Herzberger

ROWMAN & LITTLEFIELD PUBLISHERS, INC.
Lanham • Boulder • New York • Oxford

ROWMAN & LITTLEFIELD PUBLISHERS, INC.

Published in the United States of America
by Rowman & Littlefield Publishers, Inc.
4720 Boston Way, Lanham, Maryland 20706
www.rowmanlittlefield.com

12 Hid's Copse Road
Cumnor Hill, Oxford OX2 9JJ, England

British Library Cataloguing in Publication Information Available

The 1996 edition of this book was catalogued by the Library of Congress as
follows:

Tomasson, Richard F.
    Affirmative Action : the pros and cons of policy and practice /
Richard F. Tomasson, Faye J. Crosby, and Sharon D. Herzberger.
        p.   cm.—(American University Press public policy series)
    Includeds bibliographical references and index.
    1. Affirmative action programs—United States.   I. Crosby, Faye J.
    II. Herzberger, Sharon D.   III. Title.   IV. Series.
HF5549.5.A34T66   1996
331.13'3'0973—dc20   96-24714 CIP

ISBN 0-7425-0210-4

Printed in the United States of America

∞ ™ The paper used in this publication meets the minimum requirements of
American National Standard for Information Sciences—Permanence of Paper for
Printed Library Materials, ANSI/NISO Z39.48–1992.

Contents

Part Two
Against Affirmative Action
Richard F. Tomasson

Preface

> The clash over affirmative action is a clash between two deeply valid principles. The first is a procedural ideal: color-blindness. (Because race is a morally irrelevant trait, people should be treated without regard to it.) The second is a moral outcome: racial equality. (Since our history is marred by racial injustice, we should try to reduce racial inequalities in wealth and power.)
>
> Glenn C. Loury[1]

Affirmative action has made many twists and turns in the four decades it has been around. In the 1960s it was a policy singularly devoted to improving the employment and educational opportunities for American Negroes—the universally accepted designation at the time. It was "soft" affirmative action, a policy of outreach that wasn't very controversial. In the 1970s three big changes occurred. First, additional categories came to be covered by affirmative action, mainly Hispanics/Latinos, Asians, and women; it became a policy for "women and minorities." Second, there was a move toward "hard" affirmative action with an emphasis on employers meeting numerical goals and quotas, targets and timetables, in the hiring and promotion of women and minorities. Third, it became a controversial public policy. These changes became institutionalized in the 1980s and first half of the 1990s. In the second half of the 1990s, however, a number of court decisions, popular initiatives in several states and cities, and decisions by governmental agencies resulted in a national pullback from "hard" affirmative action. There was a shift from jobs to higher education occupying center stage.

Affirmative action did not come about from any legislation. Rather, it grew out of a 1961 executive order of President John F. Kennedy in which the term *affirmative action* was first used in one of its contemporary mean-

ings, "outreach." It is best understood as the most recent (final?) phase of
the increasingly inclusive civil rights movement, central to the domestic
history of America since Word War II. The star players in the affirmative
action movement have been government bureaucracies, corporations, the
universities, and, above all, the courts.

There, in three hundred words, is a summary history of four decades of
affirmative action. One of the tasks of this book is to fill in the details of
the unfolding of this controversial public policy issue, one surpassed in
capacity to arouse passion only by taxes and abortion.

This book can be viewed as two books. The first, by Crosby and Herzberger, is a strong defense of the policy and practice of affirmative action.
The second, by Tomasson, is an equally strong statement in opposition to
that policy and practice. The two "books" use different sorts of evidence,
emphasize different value orientations (sometimes different interpretations
of the same value), and employ different kinds of language and terminol-
ogy to make their opposing arguments. It could not be otherwise. For
example, proponents of affirmative action usually call it just that, affirmative action, while opponents commonly refer to it by the single word *preferences*. The pro and con arguments presented here clarify not only the two
sides of the public debate but also the different definitions of those big
ideas in the debate: fairness, equality, equity, diversity, democratic.

Historically, this book is current through 1996, up to the passage in
November of that year of the California Civil Rights Initiative, famously
known as Proposition 209. It outlawed the use of race and gender as factors
in admission to the state's colleges and universities, in public employment,
and in state contracting. The wording of the initiative, based on the wording of the Civil Rights Act of 1964, is this:

> Neither the State of California nor any of its political subdivisions or
> agents shall use race, sex, color, ethnicity, or national origin as a criterion
> for either discriminating against, or granting preferential treatment to, any
> individual or group in the operation of the state's system of public employ-
> ment, public education or public contracting.

The passage of Proposition 209 was a watershed event in the recent
history of affirmative action, deplored by its advocates, celebrated by its

opponents. Beyond that, it had at least four consequences: (1) It began a national trend of state and local initiatives to outlaw race- and gender-based preferences similar to Proposition 209. (2) It put the focus of affirmative action on higher education because of the extraordinary publicity given to the demise of preferential treatment and the decline in enrollments of underrepresented minorities—African Americans, Hispanics/Latinos, and American Indians—in the University of California system.[2] (3) With the focus of affirmative action on the universities, gender, though always included, became largely irrelevant because females of all racial categories do better in school than their male counterparts. (Gender has not, however, become irrelevant in the employment sector.) (4) It led to new plans and programs to enhance the presence of minorities in selective public universities without considerations of race. Private higher education everywhere continues free to practice race-based affirmative action.

Two years after the passage of Proposition 209, in November 1998, the Washington State Civil Rights Initiative (Initiative 200), using the same language, was passed by a vote of 58 to 42 percent.[3] It was a remarkable victory for a grassroots movement opposing race- and gender-based affirmative action. It was energetically and expensively opposed by "the establishment"—government, big business, big labor, the media, the NAACP, the Urban League, the American Civil Liberties Union, and numerous liberal church groups—united in a campaign called No!200. Popular Democratic governor Gary Locke publicly opposed Initiative 200 and worked behind the scenes for its defeat as did the big employers in the state such as Boeing, Costco, Eddie Bauer, GTE, Hewlett Packard, Kaiser, Microsoft, Starbucks, US Bank, and Weyerhaeuser. The *Seattle Times,* the state's largest newspaper, relentlessly denounced the initiative on its editorial page and in full-page advertisements; most of the other newspapers in the state also opposed the initiative.

CNN and *Seattle Times* exit polls showed who supported the Washington Civil Rights Initiative: women, 50 percent; independents, 56 percent; liberals, 35 percent; Republicans, 79 percent; self-described conservatives, 78 percent; voted for President Clinton in 1996, 40 percent; union members, 54 percent; supporters of the legalization of "medical marijuana," 53 percent; younger voters (age eighteen to sixty-four), 57 percent; and older voters (sixty or older), 57 percent.

In several states, most notably Florida, plans are afoot to get an initiative such as those passed in California and Washington on the ballot. The opponents of these initiatives regard them as a kind of anti–civil rights movement reversing the gains made by minorities and women since the 1960s. Furthermore, they argue that if the language of these initiatives were different and affirmative action were defined in terms of outreach to minorities and women, they would not have been successful. At worst, they regard them as manifesting a resurgence of racism in America.

A number of court decisions since 1996, though none as yet from the Supreme Court, have applied a doctrine of "strict scrutiny" to public affirmative action programs. What this means in practice is that the courts tend to see any program that uses quotas, requires employers to hire women and minorities in specified numbers, or is intended to promote diversity as being constitutionally suspect. One example is *National Association of Broadcasters v. Federal Communications Commission* (1998).

The FCC for many years had been a vigorous practitioner of preferences in the hiring of women and minorities in the broadcast industry. The National Association of Broadcasters, the trade association that represents most of the nation's radio and TV broadcasters, opposed the close monitoring of their hiring practices and claimed they forced quota hiring of women and minorities. They went to federal court. In April 1998 the United States Court of Appeals for the District of Columbia Circuit ruled that the equal employment policies as practiced by the FCC were unconstitutional. The court said that "the program amounted to a 'soft quota' because hiring records were scrutinized and, if broadcasters had been hiring minorities or women at a level less than 50 percent of the total population, they came under special scrutiny."[4] The FCC responded to the court's decision by deciding not to appeal to a higher court and to revise its rules on the hiring of women and minorities in accordance with the court's ruling.

In the 6-to-4 decision the judges divided largely along political lines. Judges appointed by a Democratic president dissented; those appointed by a Republican president supported the decision. This is not an unusual pattern in recent court decisions dealing with affirmative action, and it reflects an ideological difference between the parties.

The outlawing of race-based affirmative actions in California through Proposition 209 and in Texas as a consequence of the *Hopwood* decision (see pp. 161–162) has compelled some states to seek ways to prevent major declines in the enrollment of blacks and Hispanics at their selective universities without resorting to race preferences. They are seeking color-blind alternatives. This is an enormous challenge because blacks and Hispanic students, on average, have SAT and ACT scores substantially lower than white and Asian students. The average black or Hispanic high school graduate reads at a level well below the average white high school graduate.

The most notable color-blind systems adopted so far are those of California, Texas, and Florida. Let's call them the "Top Percent Plans." In California the plan is to guarantee a slot in the University of California system to any graduate in the top 4 percent of any high school graduating class in the state. This plan has had some success, increasing the presence of black and Hispanic undergraduates on the nine campuses of the system after a sharp drop in 1998 following the elimination of preferences mandated by Proposition 209. The Top 4 Percent Plan has also focused attention on the quality of the state's public school system, particularly on heavily minority schools. This plan, because the percentage is so small, does not seem to have resulted in lower test scores or grade-point averages of incoming freshmen. However, some *cascading* has occurred, a decline from the pre–Proposition 209 year of 1997 compared with 2000 in the number of blacks and Latinos at the most selective campuses—Berkeley, UCLA, and San Diego—but an increase at other campuses—Irvine, Riverside, and Santa Cruz—of the University of California system.[5]

Texas has a "10 Percent Plan" that guarantees admission to the top 10 percent of graduates from all Texas high schools to any of the state's public universities without regard to scores on standardized admission tests. After a federal appeals court eliminated race-based admissions in 1996, black and Latino admissions dropped on the Austin campus. But after the introduction of the 10 Percent Plan, black enrollment in the fall of 1999 reached precisely where it had been in prepreference days: 4.1 percent. Hispanic enrollment was at 13.8 percent, just below what it had been four years earlier: 14.5 percent.[6]

In November 1999 Governor Jeb Bush of Florida announced his "One Florida Initiative," similar to the Texas plan introduced by his brother, George W. Bush.[7] The difference is that his plan guarantees admission to one of the state's public universities to the top 20 percent, rather than the top 10 percent as in Texas, of each public high school's graduating class. Financial aid will be increased to help poor students. The figure of 20 percent was chosen because it was believed it would generate a higher level of racial diversity than a 10 or 15 percent plan. How many minority high school graduates will be able to take advantage of the "Talented Twenty" plan is uncertain because of the limited offerings of many of the high schools they attend. This plan may, and was intended to, take the wind out of the sails of Ward Connerly's movement for a Florida Civil Rights Initiative (FCRI) similar to those passed by the voters in California and Washington. If Connerly is successful in getting the wording of the initiative approved by the Florida Supreme Court and collects a sufficient number of signatures to get the FCRI on the ballot in 2002, even its opponents concede it will pass. The polls and the success of the California and Washington initiatives show a majority of Americans oppose race and gender preferences when the language is phrased in the manner of Proposition 209.

These Top Percent Plans have given rise to much debate. On the positive side, the plans are heralded for getting rid of race-based affirmative action. In a sense they can be regarded as a new form of affirmative action in that their intent is to maintain a reasonable presence of blacks and Hispanics on selective campuses without considerations of race.

These plans force the universities to deal with the intractable problem of the condition of public education, particularly the schools with large black and Latino enrollments. They also aid talented rural and poor white youth to have a chance at attending the selective public universities in their state, a career path many have never even dreamed of.

There is criticism of these Top Percent Plans. From the pinnacle of selective universities, the source of the most articulate defense of race-based affirmative action, comes Frank H. T. Rhodes, president emeritus of Cornell University.[8] He claims these plans are deserving of "an S.S.W. award." The initials stand for "swift, sure and wrong." He writes:

> For all its simplicity and attractiveness, the 10 percent solution [the Texas solution] is race-blind at the price of being individual-blind. A quota system, however well-intended, and a numerically based admissions system, however well-conceived, deny the significance and priority of individuality, in all its bewildering complexity. This is a terrible price to pay. . . .

Why not base admissions decisions on an assessment of the student as a whole person, with honest regard for race and ethnicity as two attributes among many others?

Some specific criticisms leveled at these Top Percent Plans are these:

1. Good students from good high schools not in the top percentage category of their high school graduating classes are discriminated against compared to graduates in the top category from poorer schools and who are less well equipped for college.
2. When students are guaranteed automatic admission based on class standing, they will have an incentive to take easy courses to maintain or improve their class standing.
3. Universities will be forced to engage much more in remedial education to bring the top graduates of poor high schools up to minimal standards to compete. Remedial education is expensive. It is "a recipe for the destruction of America's great public universities," claimed an editorial in the *New Republic*.[9]
4. The Top Percentage Solution does nothing for enhancing minority enrollments in graduate, law, medical, and other professional schools.
5. Fundamental to these plans intended to bring about substantial black and Hispanic enrollments in selective public universities is an acceptance of the continuation of segregated high schools, not their elimination. If California, Texas, and Florida had integrated high schools, automatic admission by class rank would fail to result in black and Hispanic enrollment in acceptable numbers.

"Why is that the case?" asks philosophy professor Carl Cohen, the University of Michigan's most vocal opponent of affirmative action.[10] "Presumably because the academic performance needed to rank among the top 10 percent is one for which minority students have not been prepared. Is it not time to turn away from programs devised to circumvent inadequate preparation and attend instead to the preparation itself?"

In the spring of 2000 the United States Commission on Civil Rights issued a strongly negative critique of these Top Percent Plans.[11] It is a ringing defense of traditional race-conscious affirmative action. The six Democrats on the commission approved the statement; two members, a Republican and one who describes himself as an independent, wrote an equally strong dissenting statement. And so the controversy continues.

Two plans from nongovernmental sources have recently come forth to enhance minority educational achievement as a consequence of the national pullback from race-based affirmative action. One is from the National Task Force on Minority High Achievement of the College Board, the testing agency responsible for the SAT.[12] The other is from the National Alliance of Black School Educators (NABSE).[13]

The problem, as stated by the College Board Task Force Report entitled "Reaching the Top," is this: "(F)ar too few Black, Hispanic, and Native American students are reaching the highest levels of educational achievement. . . . Until many more underrepresented minority students from disadvantaged, middle class, and upper-middle class circumstances are very successful educationally, it will be virtually impossible to integrate our society's institutions completely, especially at leadership levels." It proposes "an extensive array of public and private policies, actions, and investments" from preschool through college and university. This commitment is called *affirmative development*. It is affirmative action defined as "outreach," subsuming a limitless variety of programs to enhance the upward educational mobility of underrepresented racial and ethnic categories of the population. The subtext of the report is that all the programs from preschool through graduate school to promote "high achievement" should be "especially" for blacks, Hispanics, and Indians.

Even the most ardent opponents of affirmative action would be sympathetic to the general aim of the College Board's Task Force, even if dubious about its means. Its formation was a direct response to the pullback from affirmative action that began with the passage in 1996 of California's Proposition 209.

The report avoids mention of any legal or constitutional difficulties in establishing programs to enhance high achievement among underrepresented minorities. It is peppered with phrases such as "disadvantaged and minority students." These imply that the programs proposed are not only for "minority youngsters." Still, the central concern of the task force is unambiguously with blacks, Hispanics, and Native Americans. The emphasis on "disadvantaged" or "underrepresented" minority youth is to eliminate Asians from the target categories.

The bottom line for the task force is that African Americans, Hispanics, and Native Americans are to reach "overall educational parity" with whites or Asians at the highest levels of academic achievement. The report does not provide any time frame, only suggesting that it occur "eventually." To accomplish this goal, "ways must be found to improve academic outcomes for *all of their social class segments*" (emphasis added). Much concern is expressed over the magnitude of the white–black and white–Hispanic gaps in reading scores of twelfth graders. Reading and the use of language is the single most important factor in the low academic achievement of some sectors of America's minority populations.

A more pragmatic call for "closing the education gap" with no talk of reaching "the highest levels of academic achievement" comes from the National Alliance of Black School Educators (NABSE), found in the January 2000 *Atlantic Monthly* in the form of a twenty-seven-page "Special Advertising Section" sponsored by a number of American corporations. Its summary statement of purpose at the beginning reads, "Forge a corps of dedicated, highly trained black educators who wield influence from kindergarten through city hall, and you can help bridge the gap that persists in the United States between far too many black youngsters and their white counterparts." It concludes with seventeen proposals as to how individuals, corporations, and institutions can get involved with NABSE projects. No suggestion is made here that NABSE programs are "especially" for blacks, even if they are.

The College Board's Task Force's report is rooted in the common, but erroneous, American faith that the schools are the answer to achieving ethnic and racial equity. Certainly the schools are important, but not nearly as decisive as the subcultures of the "disadvantaged" minorities and the poor. There certainly is a reciprocal relation between the schools adapting to these subcultures and they, in turn, adapting to the schools. But the emphasis must be on the subcultures adapting to the schools, and not the other way around, as the report has it. It says that pedagogy and the curriculum should be changed "in ways that are more consistent with the cultures of their students." No specifics are given. There are big doses of underclass culture—high rates of teen pregnancy, alienation, nonstandard language, machismo, low levels of general knowledge, individual and social disorganization—in our ethnic subcultures that are inimical to success in school, particularly so among the males. These problems are given almost no attention in the debate on school achievement of minorities.

The report recognizes that male achievement problems are "especially acute for underrepresented minorities" and that "negative outcomes for males are more pronounced at low socioeconomic levels." This is a very important observation. It is that males adapt more than females to the underclass elements in some minority subcultures.

The teen birthrate, I propose, is the single best measure of the extent of underclass culture within a racial or ethnic category in contemporary America. Furthermore, there is a high inverse correlation between the teen birthrates of such categories and (particularly male) success in school. Chinese Americans, followed by Japanese Americans, record the lowest teen birthrates; blacks, Mexican Americans, Hawaiians, and Indians, the highest rates. Whites, with much internal variation, fall between these extremes. I realize that correlation does not prove causation, but this is an intriguing relationship and should receive much more attention than it does from all those concerned with the low educational achievement of some minorities.

My guess is that any changes that result in lowering the extraordinarily high teen birthrates found in many sectors of our minority populations will reverberate into higher levels of school achievement. Here is how the vicious cycle works in the modern education society: Teenage mothers, with their low level of social capital relative to the needs of the education society, have babies who are, consequently, at a disadvantage from birth, and, they, in turn, out of their disadvantaged position, have babies as teenagers, and the cycle is repeated. The great paradox of this social pattern is that it is more dysfunctional for the male babies than for the female babies.

A defection from the ranks of the major intellectual opponents of affirmative action occurred in the late 1990s when Nathan Glazer, a professor of education and sociology at Harvard, changed his mind. He is the author of *Affirmative Discrimination* (1975, reprinted 1987), as the title suggests, a work critical of affirmative action. In 1998 he wrote, "In recent years I have become uneasy with the position that we should eliminate all racial and ethnic preferences in college, university, and professional school admissions."[14]

Glazer had believed since the 1960s that blacks would follow the path of European minorities and become assimilated into mainstream American society. He claimed he had been wrong. And there is "nothing that concentrates the mind on an issue more sharply than discovering one has been wrong about it."[15] He writes that Americans "never found a way to properly include African Americans in the great project that called for and fostered assimilation," and we "cannot ignore the remarkable and unique degree of separation between blacks and others."[16] He points to the high degree of school and residential segregation and the low rates of intermarriage of blacks compared with the much higher rates for Asians, Latinos, and American Indians. Glazer makes a telling observation that reveals the castelike status of African Americans in the American mind: We regard the children of black–white (or black–Asian) intermarriage as black, while, at the same time, we regard the children of white–Asian intermarriage as "mixed." "We do not recognize partial or loose affiliation with the group, or none at all, for blacks, as we do for all other ethnic and racial groups."[17]

His position, reluctantly assumed, is that race preferences for blacks are the best means around for accomplishing the uncompleted task of their assimilation or—to use a softer term—their integration. Glazer might have pointed to Latin America, which has been more successful than we have in assimilating the descendents of their slave populations.

Glazer argues race preferences should exist only for African Americans, not for Hispanics—they will follow the path to assimilation of other immigrant groups; not for American Indians—there are many special programs, schools, and colleges just for them; not for women—they can make it on their own as they have shown; and not for the poor or "disadvantaged"— most of them are not blacks so they will not particularly benefit.

Glazer advocates preferences in the admission and retention of African Americans to highly selective colleges, universities, and professional schools for several reasons. First, affirmative action was conceived and intended only for American Negroes. It was never originally intended for women and other minorities. They were just bureaucratically included later. Second, blacks have the greatest academic deficiencies of all racial and ethnic groups in American society as a consequence of bad schools and a history of enforced segregation. Without race preferences the numbers of blacks in elite universities would drop precipitously. The most commonly accepted estimate is that with a color-blind admissions policy, blacks would decline to 1 or 2 percent from the present 6 or 7 percent. Third, he opposes the view of most opponents of affirmative action that blacks, like whites, will be most successful if they attend institutions best suited to their academic abilities. He answers that to argue in this way "is to underestimate the hold that the most selective institutions have on the public mind and on the mass media, and to underestimate the significance of entry into these

institutions by blacks as a measure of how America is fulfilling its obligations to achieve greater equality and integration for blacks."[18]

The most publicized book, by far, to deal with affirmative action in recent
years is *The Shape of the River* (1998), by William C. Bowen and Derek
Bok; the former is president emeritus of Princeton and the latter, president
emeritus of Harvard.[19] The authors, like Frank Rhodes, the president emeritus of Cornell who criticized the Top Percent Plans discussed earlier, are
members of the category, above all categories, most supportive of "racially
sensitive" admissions to selective colleges and universities. The subtitle
of Bowen and Bok's book explains what the study is about: "Long-term
Consequences of Considering Race in College and University Admissions."

The Shape of the River brings hard numbers to the debate on race preferences, here limited to African American preferences. It uses a data set of
ninety thousand first-year students at twenty-eight selective colleges and
universities for 1951, 1976, and 1989. To these data has been added a
survey of their life experiences since their graduation. The detailed analysis
of Bowen and Bok, and a staff of associates, shows that the blacks were an
outstanding group to begin with. Yet in spite of having been admitted
with somewhat lower SAT scores than their white counterparts, they had
successful and prosperous careers and claimed they benefited from their
experience at these selective colleges and universities. They did, however,
have a lower graduation rate than did the whites.

Reactions to this study are most predictable. For an adulatory review
of Bowen and Bok's book, let us again turn to Nathan Glazer.[20] For a
correspondingly negative critique of the study, I turn to Martin Trow, a
professor of sociology and public policy at the University of California,
Berkeley.[21]

Glazer finds that Bowen and Bok analyze and present the "hard numbers" on which *The Shape of the River* is based "with perspicacity, insight,
thoroughness, and balance." He concludes his nineteen-page review with
this paragraph:

From the evidence presented in this important book. It is hard to see the
harm that has been done to the students benefited, to the institutions that
have adopted this consensus [on racially-sensitive admissions], to the few
[white and Asian] students that have had to settle for their second or third

[college] choice, or to the society. And it is possible to see much good. Considering the alternatives, which one must always do in public policy, this arrangement is the best we can now hope for.

Now to Martin Trow's even longer review of Bowen and Bok's treatise (twenty-two pages). Unlike Glazer, his concern is not mainly with African Americans but with all racial and ethnic categories, and he is opposed to preferences for any of them.

Indeed, I find the book mildly embarrassing in its intense focus on the ability of a small group of elite universities to cream off a disproportionate number of academically able black students, and then to demonstrate that the students thus preferred are advantaged thereby, that they make friends with people of other races, do not resent their having been preferred, and do very well occupationally and financially after graduation. . . .

Very briefly put, my sense is that the book has less concern for the stock of well educated black people in our population, or the welfare of the society in which those people take their place, than in their own institutional pride, and in the trophy minority students they can enroll in fierce competition for the status attached in some circles to the numbers and percentages of students in preferred categories they can enroll. And in all this, inevitably, whatever disclaimers they make, they must suggest that black students who do not go to their most selective institutions, or would not go under a race neutral regime, would be greatly disadvantaged thereby. They do not make that case, and I don't believe it for a second. Nowhere can they demonstrate, in their piles of survey data, that a black student who is admitted on his/her own merits to UC, Riverside, or indeed to CSU San Diego, is significantly disadvantaged in relation to an affirmative action admit to Princeton or Harvard. More important, it does not persuade me that black citizens or the country are injured thereby.

The notion that you have to go to one of these most selective universities to fulfill your potential, and become a leader in American life, is a survival of an elitist conception of American life that does not recognize how widely dispersed power and influence are, how diverse the origins of our institutional leaders. I accept that graduation from one of these selective institutions gives graduates advantages through their networking and their reputation as elite universities. That kind of advantage is built into the status system of the society and its universities, and minorities who are admitted to those institutions have as much right to that advantage as anybody else. But it is simply true that now and for the future the overwhelming majority of blacks in leadership positions will come from other institutions which they enter without race preferences. And the costs to blacks and to American society as a whole of the racial/ethnic preferences defended by Bowen and Bok far outweigh the marginal advantage to the small number of highly qualified black students who are assured entry to any number of first rate colleges and universities without any preferred advantage.

Affirmative action is an issue about which sociologists feel strongly for and against. The large majority personally favor affirmative action, though a small percentage are intense opponents of it. The preponderance of support for affirmative action has been so pervasive in the American Sociological Association (ASA) that in 1998, the ASA was able to publish, advertise, and support in its monthly newsletter, *Footnotes,* a piece of advocacy research supporting affirmative action and its greater implementation. This was regarded as a grossly improper activity of the ASA by many of its members. It resulted in a statement signed by thirty-nine sociologists of vastly different views on affirmative action.[22] Supporter Nathan Glazer and opponent Martin Trow were both among the signers. This statement can be regarded as a statement of the proper role of a social science organization in dealing with a deeply divisive social issue about which people feel strongly:

> The purpose of the American Sociological Association is the promotion and the protection of the discipline of sociology.
>
> In a celebration of the publication and ASA sponsorship of Barbara Reskin's *The Realities of Affirmative Action in Employment,* ASA executive officer Felice J. Levine has written that the association has "a special opportunity to bring social science knowledge to bear on important issues of social concern and social policy" (*Footnotes,* September–October 1998, p. 2).
>
> There is a long and respectable tradition of advocacy research in sociology and the social sciences. We do not mean to question it. But the practice and sponsorship of advocacy research by the American Sociological Association is improper and contradicts the purpose of the Association.
>
> It is inappropriate for the American Sociological Association to take an

advocacy role on affirmative action. To do so damages the integrity of the Association as a nonpolitical scientific professional association.

The results of the ASA-sponsored study, in Levine's words, "led to the inextricable (*sic*) conclusion that employment discrimination is alive, that affirmative action programs are often not understood in popular depictions, and that *more, not less, affirmative action is needed*" (emphasis added). Were the "inextricable conclusion" otherwise, it would make no difference to our argument here.

Affirmative action is a public policy on which the American population as well as the members of the ASA are divided. That a majority of the active ASA membership is probably supportive of the pro side is irrelevant. Affirmative action at its core is an issue of the definition, means, and ends of equality on which equally thoughtful and knowledgeable people disagree. It is a prototypical hot button issue on which the American Sociological Association, but not its individual members, must be officially neutral if it is to be an association of scientific professionals.

The great debate on affirmative action will continue. And it should. And it should proceed with arguments, studies, analyses, and interpretations of research findings by sociologists and other social scientists. But this should be done without partisanship from the American Sociological Association.

What are the views of college faculty in general toward affirmative action? Their opinions are enormously varied. A question from the 1999 American Faculty Poll asked a representative sample of 1,511 faculty to agree/disagree with the following statement about affirmative action at "your college or university"[23]: "Affirmative action programs have made your institution a better place for teaching and learning." The responses were these:

20.6 percent	Strongly agree
42.7 percent	Somewhat agree
18.2 percent	Somewhat disagree
7.9 percent	Strongly disagree
10.6 percent	Don't know, not applicable

Now read the two sides of the great debate on affirmative action—or, if you like, preferences. You probably now have a predilection for the one side or the other, but try to temporarily suspend judgment and enter into the values and assumptions of the two sides. My guess is that when you finish, you will have a commitment to one side or the other. But maybe not the side you started with.

Notes

1. Glenn C. Loury, "Admit It. TRB from Washington." *New Republic,* 27 December 1999, p. 6.

2. However, in 1995 the Board of Regents of the University of California barred the use of racial or gender preferences, a policy that was not to take effect until 1998.

3. From the *Egalitarian,* newsletter of the American Civil Rights Institute, December 1998.

4. Neil A. Lewis, "F.C.C. Revises Rule on Hiring of Women and Minorities," *New York Times,* 21 January 2000.

5. Barbara Whitaker, "Minority Rolls Rebound at University of California," *New York Times,* 5 April 2000; Jeffrey Selingo, "U. of California Sees Increase in Minority Applicants Admitted," *Chronicle of Higher Education,* 14 April 2000. In September 2000, the University of California proposed expanding offers of admission to the top 12.5 percent of every high school graduating class in the state if they complete two years at a community college with at least a 2.4 grade-point average.

6. "The Diversity Project in Texas," *New York Times* editorial page, 27 November 1999.

7. Rick Bragg, "Florida Plan Would Change Admissions Based on Race," *New York Times,* 11 November 1999; and Peter T. Kilborn, "Jeb Bush Roils Florida on Affirmative Action," *New York Times,* 4 February 2000.

8. Frank H. T. Rhodes, "College by the Numbers," *New York Times,* 24 December 1999, p. 23.

9. "Admitting Error," *New Republic,* 27 December 1999, p. 9.

10. Carl Cohen, "Diversity by Numbers," Letters, *New York Times,* 29 December 1999.

11. Jeffrey Selingo and Patrick Healey, "U.S. Civil-Rights Panel Blasts Statewide Admissions Policies on Class Rank," *Chronicle of Higher Education,* 21 April 2000.

12. Downloaded October 1999 from www.collegeboard.org.

13. The *Atlantic,* January 2000, center section.

14. Nathan Glazer, "For Racial Dispensation in Admissions," *Academic Questions* (Summer 1998): 22–31.

15. Nathan Glazer, *We Are All Multiculturalists Now* (Cambridge, Mass.: Harvard University Press, 1997), p. 122.

16. Glazer, *We Are All Multiculturalists Now,* pp. 20, 158.

17. Glazer, *We Are All Multiculturalists Now,* p. 158.

18. Glazer, "For Racial Dispensation in Admissions," p. 27.

19. William C. Bowen and Derek Bok, *The Shape of the River* (Princeton, N.J.: Princeton University Press, 1998).

20. Nathan Glazer, "The Case for Racial Preferences," *Public Interest* (Summer 1999): 45–63.

21. Martin Trow, "California after Racial Preferences," *Public Interest* (Summer 1999): 64–85. The paragraphs quoted here are from an earlier version of this article, downloaded from www.acri.org.

22. *Footnotes* (March 1999): 9 (newsletter of the American Sociological Association).

23. A. Sanderson, V. C. Phua, and D. Herda, *The American Faculty Poll* (Chicago: National Opinion Research Center, 2000), p. 52. The specific percentages were supplied to me by Dr. Voon Chin Phua at TIAA-CREF; e-mail: vcphua@tiaa-cref.org.

Part One

For Affirmative Action

To MVP, for being so actively affirming.—FJC

To David.—SDH

Acknowledgments

I would like to thank Liz Graham, Suzanne Chan, Kristin Heydenberk, Laura Shannon, and Joanna Durso for their help with researching sources. To Heather Golden I am extremely indebted, for her help with research and with manuscript preparation. The students in my Social Psychology class deserve a round of applause for their unflagging and critical interest in the topic of affirmative action. Kathy Bartus and Beth Muramoto both deserve recognition for their help in the process. So does Marilyn Patton, who helped at every step. Finally, I am grateful to the Committee on Faculty Development at Smith College for the financial and moral support they gave to the research and writing.

— FJC

I would like to acknowledge many people who assisted me throughout the process of writing this book. First, I would like to thank Celeste Kingston for many months of meticulous research and Dawn Zorgdrager for her timely and patient help with manuscript preparation. Elizabeth Zalinger helped with reference checking. People from the following organizations took time to gather information for me: Gerald Parks of General Electric, John Bowman of Organizaiton Resources Counselors, Inc., and Dave Grindberg of the EEOC Above all, I want to thank Tom Gerety, the former president of Trinity, who gave me the opportunity to learn how to practice affirmative action.

— SDH

Chapter 1

The Issues

Picture it. The month is June. It's a sunny day, but you are shuffling papers across your desk. Your job as a manager for a medium-sized utility company keeps you inside when you'd rather be out playing golf.

Your company is like many others in your region. Most managers—and indeed most employees in the company—are white. About ten percent of the total workforce in the company can be counted as African-American or Hispanic. Another five percent are Asian American. No Native Americans work for the company.

Sitting at your desk, pencil in hand, you hear a knock at the door.

"Come on in," you shout without looking up. The door opens, and through it enters Alvin, the company's model black employee. Alvin works in a different division than you, but you've always known who he was because of his "high visibility." You two have become friends at the company's fitness center, where both of you run laps around the track.

As soon as you look up, you know there is a problem.

"What's up?" you ask.

"Ah, geeze," says Alvin, rubbing the back of his neck as if he had a very sore muscle. "I have got to talk to someone. I've been with the company for fifteen years, and today, for the first time in all those years, I think I have to say this place is racist."

You listen.

Alvin describes the situation. He has just learned that a white man named Jacob, and not he, will be receiving the promotion he had expected.

"Jacob," continues Alvin "got better ratings from his superior last year; but I've been with the company longer, I've got stronger endorsements from my subordinates, and I had the best performance rating in the entire company five years ago. Now you tell me: isn't there something fishy here?"

What do you think? Is there "something fishy?" Are you certain from what he has told you that Alvin has been the victim of antiblack discrimination? Are you convinced that the company is racist?

Now switch channels.

This time you are a professor, tenured at a large state university in America's heartland. Pouring over your books in the central reading room of the campus library, you glance out the window and see your best friend, chair of the English Department, walking in a dejected fashion toward the faculty club. You stick a pencil in the book to mark your page and dart out into the autumn.

"Hey! Marc!" you shout as you move toward your friend. No response. And so you shout a little louder: "Yo, Marcus!"

"Oh, hi," he replies, "don't mind me. I'm in a daze."

Marc explains his predicament. A few years ago his department had hired a young woman named Jane. When Jane was up for reappointment last year, the department had voted not to offer it to her. Marc has just found out this morning from the administration that Jane brought a grievance against the department. She claims sex discrimination.

"What bothers me most," confides your friend to you, "is how vindictive Jane seems. We are all honorable men, and we all liked Jane. We didn't think her work would warrant tenure when the time came, and so we severed ties now, while she is still very junior. What we have done was really done out of consideration for Jane. And now she claims we are all bigots and male chauvinist pigs."

You know your friend harbors no prejudice against women, but are you sure that no element of sex discrimination crept into the decision of the English department? Are you certain that Jane would have been treated just the same way if she were a man? Can you tell beyond a reasonable doubt that her claim is without merit?

Affirmative Action and the Soul of the Nation

When it comes to issues of discrimination, uncertainties abound. America today seems obsessed with questions of gender and of color. Accusations and counter-accusations fill the media. Among the contending realities, the truth can be hard to discern.

Centrally situated in many contemporary discussions of discrimination is the debate over affirmative action. For some, affirmative action is a divisive policy and one that seeks to replace old-fashion racism and sexism with new reverse-racism and reverse-sexism. For others affirmative action is a good and necessary part of the struggle to diminish discrimination.[1]

Gallup polls conducted over the last year have also shown a marked instability in Americans' attitudes toward affirmative action. A Gallup poll conducted in February, 1995, showed that 50 percent of those questioned approved of affirmative action for women, but only 40 percent approved of affirmative action for racial or ethnic minorities. In that same survey, only 41 percent of the population answered yes to the question of whether affirmative action programs are still needed today for women or for minorities. In contrast, 86 percent thought that affirmative action was needed when it was introduced 30 years ago, and approximately three quarters of the respondents thought that affirmative action programs over the last 30 years have helped women and minorities.[2]

One month after the first survey, another survey conducted by the Gallup organization for CNN and *USA Today* showed more support for affirmative action. Fifty-five percent of the respondents favored affirmative action; 31 percent thought we need to increase affirmative action programs in this country; and 57 percent thought affirmative action laws ought to apply to all businesses, not just those with a proven history of discrimination.[3]

By July, 1995, after months of hammering from the political right, Americans had undergone a dramatic shift in opinion. In that month a Gallup poll showed that nearly a quarter of those surveyed thought affirmative action discriminated against whites and nearly half thought affirmative action programs are not "needed today to help women and minorities overcome discrimination."[4]

Divided opinion about affirmative action signifies American ambivalence about a number of issues. The issues surrounding affirmative action touch the core values of our nation. With affirmative action, questions arise not only about how best to enact our values, but also about how to cope with priorities among values.

It is because of the tangle of different issues and values that connect to affirmative action, as well as the general lack of clarity about what affirmative action entails, that divisions among the supporters and the opponents of affirmative action do not always cut tidily along gender, ethnic, or ideological lines.[5] Although women or people of color tend in many surveys to endorse more strongly than men or whites some aspects of affirmative action, the divisions are often blurred.

Unless conducted responsibly, debates over affirmative action further polarize citizens. You could almost feel the heat of rhetoric in California where Governor Pete Wilson recently locked horns with liberal politicians. Wilson seemed to be trying to use his new opposition to what he calls affirmative action as a stepping stone to the White House; and Jesse Jackson seemed loath to let pass an opportunity for a well-publicized confrontation. Too often, disagreements about affirmative action have resulted in each side vilifying the other.

The urgent need for calm and respectful, as opposed to inflammatory, considerations of affirmative action has been noted by several national leaders. On July 19, 1995, President Bill Clinton began his highly publicized speech on affirmative action delivered at the National Archives by noting "our fate and our duty to prepare our Nation" to live in a diverse and changing world.

> ...we must reach beyond our fears and our divisions to a new time of great and common purpose.
>
> Our challenge is twofold: first, to restore the American dream of opportunity and the American value of responsibility, and second, to bring our country together amid all our diversity into a stronger community, so that we can find common ground and move forward as one.
>
> More than ever these two endeavors are inseparable. I am absolutely convinced we cannot restore economic opportunity or solve our social problems unless we find a way to bring the American people together.

> To bring our people together, we must openly and honestly deal with
> the issues that divide us. Today I want to discuss one of those issues,
> affirmative action.[6]

We would like our book to have a part in the great national debate on
affirmative action. The first half of the volume, written by Faye Crosby
and Sharon Herzberger, presents arguments in favor of affirmative action.
The second half of the book, written by Richard Tomasson, argues against
affirmative action. It is for the reader to decide which aspects of each side
of the argument make the most sense.

The pro-affirmative action portion of the book takes as fundamental a
distinction between principle and practice. A policy can look magnificent
on paper and yet be implemented in bad ways. Some have claimed that
affirmative action is such a policy. Therefore, people can endorse the
policy but reject the practice.[7] Our discussion details why the *policy* is
needed, is fair, and is effective, before considering the factors that affect
the efficacy of any *plan* that instantiates the policy.

But first of all, we define affirmative action. Defining what exactly is
meant by affirmative action is not something that occurs in every discussion. Indeed, one analysis of the news media has revealed that newspapers rarely specify what they have in mind when they print either opinion
or news pieces on affirmative action.[8] In this regard, furthermore, the *New
York Times* and the *Washington Post* differ not at all from *U.S.A. Today:*
none of the papers is more informative than the others. It is small wonder
then that—even as survey respondents express strong opinions to poll-
sters—the majority claim little knowledge of the definition and the work-
ings of affirmative action.[9]

If nothing else, we hope that we will let people know what affirmative
action is and what it is not. If you are to decide about the merits of the
policy, you need to know what the policy is and how it operates. It may
well be that after reading our arguments in support of affirmative action,
you nonetheless dislike the policy; but at the very least, you will know
what it is in the actual policy—and not in some mischaracterization of the
policy—that displeases you. Of course, it is our belief that to know affirmative action is to appreciate its value and, indeed, its necessity.

Chapter 2

Defining Affirmative Action

A ffirmative action is not a spanking new policy. Nor has it been around since the signing of the Constitution. Most authorities date the inception of affirmative action to 1965, when President Lyndon Johnson signed Executive Order 11246. This means that for only 14 percent of the length of the time-chart of the American nation affirmative action, in one form or another, has been the law of the land. Income tax has existed three times as long as affirmative action. Some of the confusion about affirmative action may come from the fact that it is a relatively new concept as far as national policies go.

Confusion may also result because all three branches of the federal government have played and continue to play a significant role in the formulation and regulation of a national affirmative action policy. Many state governments and numerous local governments have also developed affirmative action plans. Affirmative action has been treated somewhat differently in the hands of the president, of Congress, and of the Supreme Court. As everyone—foe and friend alike—admits, the current tangle of laws and regulations can be hard to arrange in an orderly display.

Our general definition of affirmative action is this: affirmative action exists whenever an organization goes out of its way (i.e., exerts an effort) to help realize the goal of true equality among people. While our general definition does not match what Richard Tomasson offers in the second half of this book, ours is the one common to many social scientists. [1] Ours is also the same as the definition that occurs in official materials published by the Department of Labor, like Fact Sheet 95-17, which specifies that certain employers must "take affirmative action to insure that equal opportunity is provided in all aspects of their employment."[2]

To explicate the policy of affirmative action, we distinguish between classical affirmative action and other laws and regulations that have been tagged with this label but were not intended under the presidential decree. The latter include quota systems for hiring and programs that mandate a certain arbitrary percentage of funds be set aside for contracts and grants with minority educational institutions or for minority or women-owned businesses. For expository clarity, we first describe classical affirmative action policy established by Executive Order 11246. We then look at the newer forms of affirmative action through the lens of two government documents, one of which was prepared for Senator Robert Dole and another for President Clinton. What we call classical affirmative action is what Richard Tomasson calls "the self examination type." His other categories of affirmative action do not conform to the parameters of classical affirmative action.

Executive Order 11246

President Lyndon Johnson wished to build the Great Society. No matter how disastrous his foreign policy, Johnson's domestic programs are generally acknowledged to have been crucial for the civil rights movement. Johnson is also known to have been a strategic pragmatist, a wheeler-dealer.

In September, 1965, Johnson signed Executive Order 11246. Just fifteen months had passed since he had signed the Civil Rights Act. One section of the Civil Rights Act permitted courts to order "such affirmative action as may be appropriate" to end discrimination and to establish restitution in cases where *de jure* or *de facto* discrimination had been found.[3] The executive order went further.

The amended Executive Order 11246 requires every federal contractor above a minimum size to function as an affirmative action employer. Contractors who do more than $10,000 in government business in one year are covered. Organizations that hold contracts in excess of $50,000 and who employ at least fifty people must develop written affirmative action plans.

What does an affirmative action plan entail? What does it mean to be an affirmative action employer according to Executive Order 11246, as amended, with its related laws and regulations? To be an affirmative action employer is to make sure that the organization imposes no artificial barriers to persons in certain targeted categories. Today the targeted categories are derived from considerations of gender and ethnicity.[4] White women, ethnic minority women, and ethnic minority men make up the categories by the regulations that flow from Executive Order 11246 as amended. To these have been added qualified individuals with disabilities by the Rehabilitation Act of 1973 and Vietnam-era veterans by an act in 1974. The only individuals who are not presumed, under the order, to face barriers are able-bodied white men who did not serve during the Vietnam war. In all cases, the elimination of artificial barriers for some groups of people is considered to be tantamount to assuring true equal opportunity for all individuals.

Given that an affirmative action employer is one who makes sure the barriers are down, the question arises: How does one demonstrate that no artificial barriers exist? The code of federal regulations delineates the method by which an organization can make sure that barriers do not exist. The method is simple and results-oriented. If an organization employs (or, in the language of the law "utilizes") people of various designated groups in proportion to their availability in the relevant labor market, then the organization has *prima facie* evidence that there is no discrimination, either in terms of disparate treatment or disparate impact.[5]

With classical affirmative action, all that an organization has to do is to demonstrate a match between utilization and availability. This simple definition lies behind the impassioned language of the president in his July, 1995 speech to the nation about affirmative action: "Let me be clear," said Clinton,

about what affirmative action must not mean and what I won't allow it to be. It does not mean and I don't favor the unjustified preference of the unqualified over the qualified of any race or gender. It doesn't mean and I don't favor numerical quotas. It doesn't mean and I don't favor rejection or selection of any employee or student solely on the basis of race or gender without merit... Quality and diversity go hand-in-hand, and they must.[6]

What if an organization finds that it underutilizes women, minority men, or disabled white men? Then, according to affirmative action regulations, the organization must devise a plan—with goals and a timetable—that specifies how the problem might be remedied. The organization might develop a timetable and specify its goals for various points along the timetable. As long as it can demonstrate that it is making good faith efforts to follow its own plan, the federal government cannot withdraw its contract.

From a legal point of view, Johnson's executive order is well constructed. The order does not intrude into the lives of private citizens: Only those organizations that wish to receive federal dollars for their goods or services need play by the government's rules. Yet, the lure of business is strong, and to gain business, many organizations are willing to try to please the customer, even when the customer is the federal government. In fact, though, as we shall discuss in Chapter 7, what started out as an effort by businesses to comply with federal regulations in order to secure contracts has become a much broader commitment to diversify workplaces for the overall benefit of the company.[7]

From the point of view of organizational development and design, Johnson's order shows him to have been a keen observer of human nature. The classical affirmative action policy that Johnson initiated with Executive Order 11246 turns out to be consistent with the major principles of contemporary social psychology.[8] Essentially, classical affirmative action operates as a self-monitoring system. No one's prejudices or attitudes—public or private—need be assaulted or even assessed. There is no presumption of intentional wrongdoing or evil intent. Incentives, rather than punishments, are the order of the day.

Office of Federal Contract Compliance Programs

Perhaps because of the beauty of its design, classic affirmative action is a policy that operates with relatively small resources. These resources reside in the Office of Federal Contract Compliance Programs (OFCCP). OFCCP functioning is built upon Executive Order 11246, as amended, and the two similar statutes that extend coverage to qualified Vietnam-era veterans and individuals with disabilities.

Currently, there are estimated to be over a quarter of a million organizations that have developed affirmative action plans. According to the Employment Standards Administration, one out of every four American workers is employed by an affirmative action firm. And yet, if you count all the people working at all the district and regional branches of the OFCCP, you will arrive at a number under one thousand. Approximately 800 people work for the OFCCP nationwide. That's one OFCCP staff member for every 31 companies. Given that some of the companies that report to the OFCCP must employ small armies of lawyers and accountants, one can hardly charge the OFCCP with featherbedding.

Nor does it seem as if the government has sufficient forces to engage in the predatory behaviors that some people imagine occur with affirmative action. OFCCP agents work hard to be responsive to companies that ask for technical assistance, especially in the preparation of an initial affirmative action plan. District offices also respond to directives from the ten regional offices or from headquarters in Washington to conduct periodic compliance reviews. Not much time is left over for witch-hunts.

Of course, the OFCCP is not the only government office to concern itself with issues of discrimination. The Equal Employment Opportunity Commission (EEOC) handles complaints of discrimination that have been reviewed by state or local agencies for fair employment practices. Meanwhile, the Office of Personnel Management makes sure that federal employees are treated in accordance with affirmative action and antidiscrimination laws.

Affirmative Action and Equal Opportunity

Affirmative action, as delineated by Executive Order 11246, "is," in the words of President Clinton "simply a tool in the pursuit of that enduring national interest, equal opportunity."[9] Yet, being an equal opportunity employer is not necessarily the same as being an affirmative action employer. Around these words there has been much confusion.

The fact is that an organization can, in theory, achieve an outcome of true and measurable equal opportunity through a policy of equal opportunity employment or through a policy of affirmative action in employment. For some organizations, passive equal opportunity employment practices suffice to achieve true equality of opportunity in hirings, retentions, promotions, training, and compensations. For other organizations, the same results can only be achieved through more active involvement.

The same holds for educational institutions. Sometimes policies that appear on the face of things to be neutral really are neutral; but sometimes equal treatment has disparate impact. Consider the question of "neutral" and need-blind admissions to private colleges and universities. Americans of color, except for Asian-Americans, have lower household incomes than white Americans.[10] The median income of Asian-American households was $42,500 in 1992, while for white, Latino/a, and black households the figures were approximately $38,900, $24,000, and $21,000, respectively. Suppose now that College A uses ability to pay full tuition as one criterion for admission; then students from African-American or Latino-American households will be penalized in securing admission. The resulting discrepancies in the student body may be inadvertent and not the result of either overt or covert racism; but the practice has disparate impact.

Imagine College B, in contrast, admitting students without regard to ability to pay and then committing itself to providing funds for those admitted who are discovered to need financial aid. College B is less likely than College A to discriminate, albeit unintentionally, through its admission process. College A might profess equal opportunity, but only College B would provide real, not just slogan, equality of opportunity.

The difference between apparent and real equal opportunity is profound. In a briefing to congressional staffers, one of us delineated the differences between the policy of affirmative action and the policy of equal opportunity employment.[11] The policies differ in five respects:[12]

1. Affirmative action requires positive action, while equal opportunity is reactive;
2. Affirmative action is a race-conscious and gender-conscious policy, while equal opportunity purports to be usually "race blind" and "gender blind";
3. Affirmative action is predicated on the recognition of continuing injustices (with or without attitudinal prejudice) in our system, while equal opportunity assumes that opportunities are, in fact, equal for all citizens;

4. Affirmative action downplays the significance of intentions in the course of affairs, while equal opportunity envisions that good intentions automatically result in good effect;
5. Affirmative action draws attention to the system, while equal opportunity allows attention to be focused on individuals.

As a policy, classical affirmative action looks like a routine standard business practice. Corporations love numbers, and they are in the habit of having goals and timetables. They regularly monitor their assets and liabilities and devise plans to achieve specific goals in specific ways by specific times. Corporations would rather foresee problems and circumvent them than remedy deficiencies or recover losses.

Organizations with affirmative action plans expect their managers to be planful rather than reactive. In the case of affirmative action, the planning involves people rather than products or finances. Planfulness is a large part of American business.

Some people contend that planning or foresight is no longer needed in American business. Conservative ideologue Charles Murray has quipped, "The civil rights movement did its job."[13] According to Murray, the few qualified white women or people of color who are barred by discrimination from opportunities can simply sue. We contend that such an outlook smacks of poor management skills especially because, as we shall demonstrate, Murray's quip is, alas, not as true as one might wish.

The passive equal opportunity approach does not always yield equal treatment. Affirmative action functions to help keep grievances at a minimum by identifying and reducing problems before they result in discontent. This is why, as we shall see, affirmative action can enhance worker satisfaction. Happy organizations are stable and productive organizations.

The Place of Preferential Treatment in Classical Affirmative Action

Over the years, vast numbers of organizations have discovered through self-monitoring that their utilization of people in the targeted categories has not matched the availability of such people in the labor force. The organizations have devised corrective plans, complete with timetables and quantified goals. In the process they have sometimes, say, hired qualified individuals from the underrepresented groups in preference to qualified individuals from the overrepresented group.

One famous instance of corrective preferential hiring occurred in Santa Clara County. An internal review had shown underutilization of women in the transportation agency. While women constituted 36 percent of the local labor pool, they comprised only 22 percent of the workers at the transportation agency. None of the 238 skilled craft workers were women. A voluntary affirmative action plan included corrective measures. Civil service rules allowed the hiring official to take any of seven qualified candidates. The official selected the one female candidate for the job, and Paul Johnson—who had received the recommendation of the selection board—sued for sex discrimination. Johnson won in district court, but the decision was reversed on appeal. In 1987 the Supreme Court upheld the finding of the Ninth Circuit Court of Appeals and thereby made it legal to use gender as a "plus factor" in employment decisions.[14]

The legality of using demographic characteristics as a plus factor when devising corrective affirmative action programs had already been established before *Johnson*. In 1978 the Supreme Court had "squarely addressed" affirmative action in the famous *Bakke* case.[15] The University of California at Davis had denied medical school admission to Bakke, who was white, while admitting less highly qualified minority applicants through a special set-aside program. Bakke sued. The Supreme Court of the State of California had ruled that Bakke's constitutional rights were violated and forbade the university to use race-conscious admission policies. The United States Supreme Court upheld the finding that the university had violated the rights guaranteed Bakke by the Fourteenth Amendment. The Court also ruled that it was constitutional—not unconstitutional—for schools to employ race as a factor in admissions.

While most educated Americans have heard of *Bakke* and many have also heard of *Johnson v. Transportation Agency*, it is a rare individual who follows all the legal intricacies of the cases. And intricate they are. Legal experts note that opinions among the Supreme Court justices have been more divided about affirmative action than about most other issues that appear before them.[16] The distinction between quotas and plus-factor policies, for example, is one that lawyers and judges would readily glean from *Bakke*, but it is not one that most lay people noticed.

You should not be surprised, then, to find that in the minds of even many sophisticated observers, affirmative action has become equated with arbitrary preferential treatment. While it is true, as we shall see, that some new statutes and regulations do involve set-asides, the U.S. Department of Labor expressly forbids the quarter million organizations over which it has authority to use quota systems. Says the Department of Labor program information sheet entitled *Highlights on Executive Order 11246*:

> Affirmative action...does *not* mean that unqualified persons should be hired or promoted over other people. What affirmative action *does* mean is that positive steps must be taken to ensure equal employment opportunity for traditionally disadvantaged groups.[17]

To equate affirmative action with arbitrary preferential treatment or quotas is, thus, to misconstrue seriously the nature of the classical affirmative action policy; but it is a misconstruction that is quite common.

Typical of such a misconstruction is the much cited, early work of Professor Madeline Heilman of New York University. Heilman has become known as an expert on women's employment issues, and particularly on issues of sex discrimination. Heilman has conducted a series of experiments in which women are told that they are being selected for a position (or reward) either because they are well qualified or because they are needed to fill a quota. Her data show beyond any shadow of doubt that women both feel undermined and are undermined when they are selected *without attention to merit*. Heilman then concludes from her research program that affirmative action can undercut the very people whom it is intended to benefit.[18] Note that Heilman's conclusion is warranted if and only if you equate affirmative action with preferential treatment of the quota variety.[19]

Even more widely read is the work of noted black authors like Shelby Steele and Thomas Sowell. In his highly acclaimed book, *The Content of Our Character*, Steele perpetrates the view that affirmative action is nothing but blind preferential treatment and argues that preferential treatment only engenders self-doubt and lack of purpose among black youth. Says Steele:

> The effect of preferential treatment—the lowering of normal standards to increase black representation—puts blacks at war with an expanded realm of debilitating doubt, so that the doubt itself becomes an unrecognized

preoccupation that undermines their ability to perform, especially in integrated situations.[20]

If we extrapolate from Madeline Heilman's experimental work, we must conclude that Steele seems entirely justified in claiming that blacks (and whites) are undercut when standards have been lowered. Even so, we have to note that Steele is wrong to link affirmative action with the lowering of standards.

Shelby Steele and his twin brother, Claude Steele, are both university professors. Both live and work in the state of California. It is perhaps emblematic of life in California that while Claude Steele's writings guide us in developing effective affirmative action programs, Shelby Steele is publishing his beautifully written but sometimes ill-informed essays against affirmative action.[21]

California is also the state of Glynn Custred and Thomas Wood, two middle-aged white men who have been college professors and now are political activists. Self-styled "angry white men," they have spearheaded a movement to place an item on a statewide ballot. The wording of their initiative reads:

> Neither the State of California nor any of its political subdivisions or agents shall use race, sex, color, ethnicity or national origin as a criterion for either discriminating against, or granting preferential treatment to, any individual or group in the operation of the State's system of public employment, public education or public contracting.[22]

Most commentators describe the Custred-Wood initiative as an anti-affirmative action one. Certainly, it is intended to assert the rights of the dominant group. But would the referendum change the operation of those systems put in place through classical affirmative action?

The danger is less than you might imagine. Consider this slightly reworded version of their initiative:

> The State of California, its political subdivisions and its agents shall be able to demonstrate they do not use race, sex, color, ethnicity or national origin as a criterion for either discriminating against, or granting preferential treatment to, any individual or group in the operation of the State's system of public employment, public education or public contracting.

And now consider: one tried-and-true method for demonstrating that an organization is not, in fact, granting preferential treatment to any group is to monitor the organization's employment practices and to make sure that all groups are hired and promoted in proportion to their availability among the designated workforces. Depending on how it is implemented, the Custred-Wood initiative, if passed, could give a boost to, not be the bane of, classical affirmative action.

Scrutiny from the Right

Echoes of California have reverberated in the U.S. Congress. On March 3, 1995, Senator Jesse Helms introduced what he called "An Act to End Unfair Preferential Treatment." The bill had two major provisions. The first was that the federal government may not use race, color, gender, ethnicity, or national origin "as a criterion for either discriminating against or granting preferential treatment to any individual or group." The second was that the federal government may not use race, color, gender, ethnicity, or national origin "in a manner that has the effect of requiring that employment positions be allocated among individuals or groups; with respect to providing public employment, conducting public contracting, or providing a federal benefit for education or other activities."[23] In his remarks, Helms noted, "This bill's principal difference with the California legislation is that I am proposing to eliminate the same kinds of discriminatory, expensive, and counterproductive programs on the federal level as California is attempting on the state level."[24] Helms offered "a few examples of government-sponsored affirmative action programs that are so counterproductive and divisive they make me wonder how much more of this we can swallow."[25] Included in his examples was the famous case of the Viacom scandal in which a mass media corporation attempted to defer over a billion dollars in taxes by selling its cable operations to an African-American buyer. Helms went on to claim to "have it on good authority that there are more than 160 such preference programs in place today in the federal bureaucracy."[26]

The "good authority" to which Helms was referring was certainly a document prepared by Charles V. Dale of the Congressional Research Service (CRS) at the request of Senator Dole, who was about to initiate his campaign for the Republican presidential nomination.[27] In his speech Helms referred to Dole several times, always as a sign of solidarity. Given the delivery date of February 17, 1995 stamped on the document, Helms must certainly have had access to the report commissioned by Dole.

What then was the Dale report? Dole had requested:

> a comprehensive list of every federal statute, regulation, program, and executive order that grants a preference to individuals on the basis of race, sex, national origin, or ethnic background. Preferences include, but are not limited to, timetables, goals, set-asides, and quotas.[28]

The list was compiled in a two-step process. First key words were searched in several legal databases. Second, staffers from the CRS examined the several hundred citations individually to determine which of the citations met the criteria set out by Senator Dole. The ones that seemed apposite were then grouped, as much as possible, according to the relevant federal agencies or the general subject matter. From "acquisitions" through "energy" and "transportation" to "veterans affairs" over twenty agencies had regulations listed in either the U.S. Civil Service code or the Code of Federal Regulations that pertained to affirmative action or preferential treatment.

What did the CRS report say? Was it filled with "counterproductive and divisive" preference programs? In fact, it was not. No regulation or law uses the word "quota." The majority of the regulations and statutes cited are of the classical affirmative action mold and involve no set-asides or mandated preferential treatment aside from extra vigilance. Under the heading "Banking," for instance, only one of the ten citations involves anything close to a set-aside.

Most of the programs that do use terms such as "set-aside" or "preference," furthermore, do so in general terms and attach no numbers to the exhortations. For example C.F.R. §2301.3 (1994) directs a branch of the Department of Commerce to "give special consideration to applications that foster ownership and control of, and participation in public telecommunication entities by minorities and women." But nowhere is the "special consideration" tied to quotas or arbitrary preferences.

Table 2.1 reproduces the text of the CRS report pertaining to the Department of the Environment. In it you can clearly see that the programs

Table 2.1

Environment

P.L. 101-549, 104 Stat. 2399, 2708, § 1001 (1990): "In providing for any research relating to the requirements of the amendments made by the Clean Air Act Amendments of 1990 which uses funds of the Environmental Protection Agency, the Administrator of the Environmental Protection Agency shall, to the extent practicable, require that not less than 10 percent of total Federal funding for such research will be made available to disadvantaged business concerns," defined to mean any concern with 51% of the stock owned by Black Americans, Hispanic Americans, Native Americans, Asian Americans, Women or Disabled Americans.

40 C.F.R. § 33.240 (1994): Environmental Protection Agency (EPA) procurement requirements provide that "[it] is EPA policy to award a fair share of subagreements to small, minority, and women's businesses. The recipient must take affirmative steps to assure that small, minority, and women's businesses are used when possible as sources of supplies, construction, and services."

40 C.F.R. § 35.936-7 (1994): Grantees of EPA state and local assistance grants "shall make positive efforts to use small business and minority owned business sources of supplies and services. Such efforts should allow these sources the maximum feasible opportunity to compete for subagreements to be performed using federal grant funds." See also 40 C.F.R. Part 35 APPENDIX C-1 (14.) (consulting engineering agreement).

40 C.F.R. § 35.3145(d) (1994): State Water Pollution Control Revolving Fund requirement "for the participation of minority and women owned businesses (MBE/WBEs) will apply to assistance in an amount equaling the grant. To attain compliance with MBE/WBE requirements, the [regional administrator] will negotiate an overall 'fair share' objective with the State for MBE/WBE participation on these SRF funded activities. A fair share objective should be based on the amount of the capitalization grant award or other State established goals." See also 40 C.F.R. § 35.4066(g) (1994) (grants for technical assistance).

40 C.F.R. § 35.6580 (1994): Recipients under Cooperative Agreements and Superfund State Contracts for Superfund Response Actions "must comply with six steps...to insure that MBEs, WBEs, and small businesses are used whenever possible as sources of supplies, construction, and services," including establishment of "an annual 'fair share' objective for MBE and WBE use."

Source: Dale (1995).

are race- and gender-conscious and that they emphasize merit and fair process.

Scrutiny from the Left

Republicans are not the only ones to have ordered in-depth studies of preferential treatment and affirmative action. On March 7, 1995, President Clinton requested an in-depth review of all federal affirmative action initiatives and programs; and in July, 1995, George Stephanopoulos and Special Counsel Christopher Edley, Jr. delivered to the President their affirmative action review.[29]

The president had set the framework for the investigation by asking for information to determine two fundamental issues:

1. Is affirmative action fair? and
2. Is affirmative action effective?

In order to address these questions, Stephanopoulos and Edley divided their report into eleven sections. After providing an overview, they gave the history and rationale of affirmative action and presented the research documenting the persistence of discrimination and showing how affirmative action plans have helped diminish racism and sexism. They then reviewed the programs, including classical affirmative action, in the military, federal procurement policies, and educational policies.

Stephanopoulos and Edley's review of affirmative action was extremely even-handed. Most practices appeared to function effectively and fairly; but some practices appeared questionable. Stephanopoulos and Edley, accordingly, advised that the President order the Justice Department to review the operation of affirmative action in all branches of government. That review has been going on since the summer of 1995. While the vast majority of programs reviewed to date have been found to conform to the current standards set by the Supreme Court, the Justice Department has eliminated two programs in the Department of Defense.[30]

In Sum

The average citizen may feel uncertainty about what affirmative action is, and in recent years a number of programs have come under the label even though they are not of the kind started by Lyndon Johnson in 1965. Classical affirmative action, which affects one in every four American workers, is simply an auditing system that is mandated for the federal government and for firms that do business with the federal government. The audit alerts the organization to discrepancies between the availability of groups of qualified candidates and their utilization, and then encourages the organization to correct any deficiencies. A person can endorse or reject the policy of classical affirmative action without endorsing or rejecting other programs such as arbitrary set-asides or preferences.

Being clear about what affirmative action is and what it is not should help defuse much of the rhetoric that surrounds the issue. Differences of opinion will, of course, continue to exist; but the extremity of volatility of the debate need not persist. With clarity may, we hope, come a certain calmness.

Chapter 3

Underlying Issue of Need

G iven the existence of equal opportunity employment practices, why does the country need a policy that requires organizations to exert efforts to assure the just and equal treatment of people? The question is reasonable, and it is one that has occurred to many reasonable citizens.

Our answer proceeds along logical lines. Specifically, we propose:

1. Americans dislike unfairness generally and specifically dislike unequal treatment according to ethnicity or gender.
2. Yet, categorical unfairnesses still exist.
3. To uproot disliked unfairness, one must first notice it.
4. In the absence of systematic information, the only unfairnesses that are noticed are those that involve dramatic misfirings of justice.
5. If an organization waits until the unfairness is dramatic to correct it, it potentially faces explosive situations.
6. Explosive situations are much more costly, in human and financial terms, than nonexplosive situations and are, hence, to be avoided.

All six parts of the answer seem unexceptional and even self-evident except for the second and the fourth. Yet systematically collected data show that our second and our fourth propositions are as true as the self-evident ones. Let us consider the evidence in order.

Systematic Unfairnesses

People like social commentator Charles Murray claim that affirmative action is an outmoded policy because categorical unfairnesses no longer exist.[1] Gallup polls also show that many citizens believe that affirmative action was needed in the past but that it has now served its purpose.[2] The question arises: are women still systematically disadvantaged relative to men and are people of color still systematically disadvantaged relative to white people?

Hard numerical data show that, unfortunately, the playing field is not yet level. To be sure, great strides have been made because of the civil rights movement and the women's movement.[3] But disparities in education and employment still abound. The disparities can be linked to insensitive, stereotyped thinking, and persistent prejudices by those who are in positions of authority or who are already part of the power structure.

One study by James Johnson, Elisa Bienenstock, and Jennifer Stoloff looked at job applicants in the Los Angeles area.[4] Race and skin color were found to affect the probability of obtaining employment by as much as 52 percent. While whites and light-skinned African-Americans were relatively likely to find employment when searching for a job, dark-skinned men were not. In fact, dark-skinned men were twice as likely as others to remain unemployed.

Perhaps the most compelling evidence of discrimination comes from "tester" studies in which comparable individuals of differing ethnic or gender groups are shown to receive different treatment from each other.[5] One study, conducted by the Fair Employment Council of Greater Washington Inc. and cited in Stephanopoulos and Edley's review for President Clinton, found that whites were treated significantly better than equally qualified blacks in almost one-quarter of job searches. Whites were treated better than Latinos one-fifth of the time.[6] Table 3.1 reproduces for you other examples found by Stephanopoulos and Edley.[7]

The prejudices which come out in behaviors are not always admitted by those who hold them. Consider in this regard a study by John Dovidio, Geoffrey Mann, and Samuel Gaertner.[8] The researchers found that whites were loath to admit to racial bias and tried to avoid communicating any differential feelings toward other white or black people. When white students were presented with information about a person and asked to make

Table 3.1

In their *Affirmative Action Review: Report to the President,* prepared in July, 1995, George Stephanopoulos and Christopher Edley, Jr. cite many examples of disparate treatment. Here are a few excerpts from pages 21 and 22 of the report:

Two pairs of male testers visited the offices of a nationally-franchised employment agency on two different days. The black tester in each pair received no job referrals. In contrast, the white testers who appeared minutes later were interviewed by the agency, coached on interviewing techniques, and referred to and offered jobs as switchboard operators.

A black female tester applied for employment at a major hotel chain in Virginia whre she was told that she would be called if they wished to pursue her application. Although she never received a call, her equally qualified white counterpart appeared a few minutes later, was told about a vacancy for a front desk clerk, later interviewed, and offered the job.

A black male tester asked about an ad for a sales position at a Maryland car dealership. He was told that the way to enter the business would be to start by washing cars. However, his white counterpart, with identical credentials, was immediately interviewed for the sales job.

A suburban Maryland company advertised for a typist/receptionist. When a black tester applied for the position, she was interviewed but heard nothing further. When an identically qualified white tester was interviewed, the employer offered her a better position that paid more than the receptionist job and that provided tuition assistance. Follow up calls by the black tester elicited no response even though the white tester refused the offer.

A GAO audit study uncovered significant discrimination against Hispanic testers. Hispanic testers received 25 percent fewer job interviews, and 34 percent fewer job offers than other testers. In one glaring example of discrimination, a Hispanic tester was told that a "counter help" job at a lunch service company had been filled. Two hours later, an Anglo tester was offered the job.

The Urban Institute's Employment and Housing Discrimination Studies (1991) matched equally qualified white and black testers who applied for the same jobs or visited the same real estate agents. Twenty percent of the time, white applicants advanced further in the hiring process than equally qualified blacks. In one in eight tests, the white received a job offer when the black did not. *In housing, both black and Hispanic testers faced discrimination in about half their dealings with rental agents.*

ratings, they judged whites and blacks equivalently on negative characteristics. But when rating positive characteristics, the white students judged
whites more favorably. The white students, furthermore, saw themselves
as only slightly better than the average white student at their university
but as much more qualified than the average black student there. In indirect and subtle ways, prejudice was affecting the students' ability to make
neutral decisions.

The tendency to make biased evaluations is not limited to undergraduate students in college. Careful studies conducted since the early 1990s
reveal that women are typically held to a higher standard than men in
corporations.[9] Were women and men evaluated equitably, the wage gap
would be half its present size, shrinking to 9 percent, according to economists.[10] Similar biases have been found to stymie the progress of African-
Americans.[11]

Nor are college students the only ones to imagine themselves to be less
hampered by stereotypes than they actually are. The dynamics can be
quite complex, especially when the inclusion of ethnic minority people or
white women causes dislocations in traditions or norms. The Federal Glass
Ceiling Report includes an illustrative case of one Hispanic woman. Says
the woman:

> I have all the credentials and I have been assigned the job of writing copy in
> English which they run with no corrections. However, in staff reviews they
> always mention that I speak with an accent. When I ask them if they have
> difficulty understanding me, they say, "No, but you know how it is upstairs.
> Accents make them nervous...." [12]

Sometimes our practices rely on old habits of thought so that seemingly
neutral programs put the underdog at a further disadvantage. Reliance
upon wages as the criterion for divorce settlements has, for example,
ensured that women suffer economically from divorce. As the psychologist Sandra Bem strongly asserts, setting salaries by prevailing market rates
is another way that old imbalances are perpetuated.[13] A practice may have
a rationale that appears neutral, but if the impact of the practice is disparate, we are left to wonder: In what sense is the practice truly neutral?

If Charles Murray were correct, we would not find the kinds of examples cited here. Nor should we find that discrimination complaints are

widespread. Yet, the Equal Employment Opportunity Commission received over ninety thousand discrimination complaints in the fiscal year 1994.[14] Between 1990 and 1994, furthermore, in the federal courts, over three thousand cases were decided at either the district court level or in courts of appeal.[15]

Detecting Unfairness

You might think that having the right attitude and a fairly clear mind is all that is needed to notice unfairness or discrimination. But reasonable though it seems, our confidence in the powers of observation is misplaced. In this section, we show why.

During the 1960s, while Congress was passing civil rights legislation and Johnson was signing affirmative action into law, researchers around the country were busy documenting the extent of and the effects of racial and gender prejudice and discrimination. One of the researchers, named Philip Goldberg, devised an ingenious test of prejudice against women that could be considered a precursor to the tester studies discussed in the last section.[16] He asked subjects to read and evaluate a set of short essays. Half of the time, the subjects were led to believe that the essay had been written by a woman and half of the time by a man. Subjects who read an essay, which they supposed to have been written by a woman, rated the essay less favorably than other subjects who supposed the same essay was written by a man.

One aspect of Goldberg's study that was especially remarkable was that his subjects were all female. Goldberg drew a conclusion from his study that antifemale prejudice was not limited to men. Although subsequent studies—especially those in recent years—have often failed to replicate Goldberg's findings,[17] the original experimental results became conventional wisdom in the 1970s, when it was assumed that women had internalized their oppression.

It came as something of a surprise, therefore, a little more than a decade later to discover—as one of us did in a survey study—that employed women had a well-developed recognition of and felt measurable anger over the issue of sex discrimination. In 1978, three samples of white adults living in a suburb of Boston, Massachusetts, were interviewed face-to-face by professional interviewers concerning their feelings about their jobs, their home lives, and the job situation of employed women. Over 400 people were in the study.[18]

Great care had been taken in sampling. All towns in the Commonwealth of Massachusetts have what are known as "street lists" telling the name, age, and profession of people residing at every address. Women and men between the ages of twenty-five and forty were selected from the accurate street list of the town of Newton. Then, with the help of rating guides published by the National Opinion Research Center, the employed men and women were classified into two categories: those with high-status jobs and those with low-status jobs. People with jobs of middling status (e.g., nurses and school teachers) were excluded from the sample so as to avoid what some analysts dubbed the issue of the female-dominated semiprofessions. Housewives were classified according to their husbands' jobs.

Equal attention was paid to the construction of an elaborate interview schedule. Some 120 questions were developed to measure people's feelings of entitlement, satisfaction, and resentment as well as their expectations and desires concerning their home lives, own work lives, and the work lives of women in America. It was because of the elaborate nature of the survey that an important discovery was made.

We found that although women gave no evidence of the kinds of internalized negative view of their own gender that Goldberg had found, the employed women in the survey were extremely reluctant to observe that they themselves were victims of the sex discrimination that they knew to be in force in the marketplace. We knew, from our tabulations, that the employed women in Newton were earning only 80 percent of what the employed men earned in jobs that were exactly comparable. We also knew that the gender gap in pay could not be accounted for by differences in training or other qualifications. Nor were the men more psychologically invested in their jobs than the women. By any objective measure, the employed women in the Newton study were being discriminated against.

Despite their own victimization, which we measured objectively, and despite the employed women's accurate assessment of the extent of sex discrimination generally, the employed women expressed as much job satisfaction as did the employed men on eight different scales. Each scale included a component of satisfaction with compensation. On these scales, as on the others, few women in the study gave recognition of the fact that they personally were likely to be paid less well than a man with their qualifications. For the vast majority of the employed women in the study, it was as if each person saw herself as the one lucky female to have escaped discrimination. The tendency, which we called "the denial of personal disadvantage," was equally strong among women with high-status jobs and among women with low-status jobs.

The discovery of the denial of personal disadvantage in the Newton study has raised two questions. First, several scholars, ourselves included, have wondered whether the phenomenon would be found in other studies, with other samples, on other issues. A number of different studies have now shown that, yes, indeed, the tendency is widespread.[19] Strong group identifications reduce the tendency to see oneself as exempt from the disadvantages of one's group. But even people with well-developed allegiances to their membership groups can fall prey to the illusion that their circumstances are somehow better than the circumstances of those around them.

The second question is: What are the components of the denial phenomenon? From the outset, it seemed logical to assume that one component was emotional. A recent empirical study of Nyla Branscombe has shown that denial tends to help people maintain a high self-esteem.[20] It is uncomfortable for people to imagine that the self is vulnerable to the same forces that can and do damage others.

Along with the emotional component is a cognitive one. Unless the dimensions are simple or the discrimination is flagrant, it is extremely difficult to perceive imbalances or unfairnesses when the data consist of individual comparisons. To get a sense of the problem, think of the scenes with which we opened the book. Can you be sure that Alvin is the victim of antiblack discrimination when you compare him to Jacob, the white man who won the promotion that Alvin had wanted? And what about the situation of Jane, the English professor?

Examples such as Alvin and Jane came to mind when we looked, years ago, at the information we had gathered in Newton, Massachusetts. First, we reflected on how we, with some eighty pounds of computer print-outs and with access to a large array of data, were able to perceive that a group of employed women in the Boston suburb received only eighty cents for every dollar received by an exactly comparable group of employed men. And then we asked ourselves how much discrimination affected any one individual among the 145 employed women. Being unable to answer the second question, we noticed that any one individual woman would be no better situated than we to know if her individual talents and training were being rewarded to the extent that they are rewarded in men. Like Alvin or Jane, the woman might have an intuition or a point of view, but hard, incontrovertible proof would be difficult to muster.

The fundamental insight of the Newton study, then, was that information about the situations of individuals is—*and must be*—processed differently than information about the situations of groups.[21] When you are looking at sets of people, you can perceive patterns that you simply cannot see when you look sequentially at each person or each pair of people. With any one comparison, individual idiosyncrasies can be used to explain differential outcomes, but across groups, the idiosyncrasies can be averaged away.

Soon after publication of the Newton findings, one of us had occasion to be speaking with an administrator at a prestigious Eastern university where only 3 percent of the tenured faculty at that time were women. The administrator had responsibility for encouraging various academic departments to think about promoting women from untenured to tenured positions, but he was not the affirmative action officer of the university. Upon hearing the thrust of our analysis, the administrator commented on two departments that were of special interest for his purposes. In both departments all of the tenured faculty were male, and in both there was a promising young woman who might be considered for tenure within a few years.

"The problem" said the administrator, "for Department A is that they are a fairly small department and the young woman's line of research—excellent though it is—overlaps with an area that is already covered by a senior male colleague. Everyone in Department A likes the young woman and thinks very highly of her abilities, but they don't know if they can afford to have two faculty with similar interests. Until today, this sounded very reasonable."

What made the administrator less sympathetic to Department A's excuse for not promoting the young woman was his newly formed plan to gather information systematically across all departments. It was in the systematic mapping of all the data that the administrator noticed how Department B, which had more faculty in it than Department A, was thinking that it might not tenure the promising young woman there because her research was *too distinct* from that of her senior colleagues.

In isolation, Department A's reasoning sounded plausible. In isolation, Department B's did too. Only when they were seen in conjunction did the arguments of the two departments sound more like feeble excuses than rational bits of policy.

Less dramatic, but ultimately more pervasive, than the kind of incident that occurred with the administrator are data that a number of investigators have collected in a series of carefully designed and meticulously conducted experiments.[22] Subjects in the experiments were presented with materials which had measurable but complicated unfairnesses built into them. The subjects were asked to make decisions about whether any discrimination existed. The question was: Would subjects be better able to detect discrimination when they encountered information in aggregated form than when they were presented with the same information in small packets?

To gain a sense of what the subjects encountered imagine that Company Z is in the process of comparing men's and women's salaries. Salary is supposed to be determined by four and only four factors: a) level in the company (from first-line supervisor, called level 8, to president, called level 18); b) years seniority; c) education; and d) impartial motivational ratings (where 3 means outstanding, and 1 means adequate). There are ten divisions in the company, each with its own pay range. For the company as a whole, the top managerial salary is $52,500. For the bottom it is $15,000.

Imagine further that you are presented with the information shown in Table 3.2. Is there discrimination? Is it easy to see?

How about in Table 3.3? What does the comparison say now?

Now look at Table 3.4 in which information about all departments is brought onto one sheet. What conclusion do you now draw? If you are like our subjects, you can see the discrimination when the information is aggregated as in Table 3.4, but detection eludes you if you only make individual comparison, even if you make the individual comparisons in rapid succession.

In three separate experiments, conducted with three different subject pools and using three sets of procedures that differed slightly from each

Table 3.2 Division E—Average qualifications and salaries for female and male managers in the division

| | Inputs (Qualification) | | | | |
	Level	Seniority	Education	Motivation	Salary
female managers	12	15	B.A.	2	$48,000/yr
male managers	13	20	B.A.	3	$70,000/yr

Note: Levels 8–18 are management (8–14 = middle management); seniority means years with the company; B.A. means Bachelor's degree; motivational ratings are assumed to be fair, and they are 1 = adequate; 2 = good; 3 = excellent.

other, the results of the studies were clear, strong, and consistent.[23] *In all cases, subjects could detect the unfairness that had been built into the materials when and only when they encountered the information in aggregate form. When they were presented with all the very same information sequentially by division, the subjects could not perceive the unfairness.*

The subjects in the experiments were highly intelligent; some attended Yale, some attended Smith, and some attended Stanford. If such intellec-

Table 3.3 Division D—Average qualifications and salaries for female and male managers in the division

| | Inputs (Qualification) | | | | |
	Level	Seniority	Education	Motivation	Salary
female managers	13	20	B.A.	3	$56,000/yr
male managers	13	20	some grad	2	$60,000/yr

Note: Levels 8–18 are management (8–14 = middle management); seniority means years with the company; B.A. means Bachelor's degree and "some grad" means that the person did some graduate work beyond the B.A.; motivational ratings are assumed to be fair, and they are 1 = adequate; 2 = good; 3 = excellent.

Table 3.4 Statistics for male and female managers in hypothetical Company Z

Division	Level	Seniority	Education	Motivation	Salary
		Randomly Selected Female Managers			
A	14	25	B.A.	3	$60,000
B	13	20	some graduate	2	$28,000
C	13	20	B.A.	3	$60,000
D	13	20	B.A.	3	$56,000
E	12	15	B.A.	2	$48,000
F	12	15	some college	3	$46,000
G	10	5	graduate degree	1	$40,000
H	10	2	some college	1	$34,000
I	10	5	B.A.	2	$24,000
J	10	2	B.A.	3	$22,000

Division	Level	Seniority	Education	Motivation	Salary
		Randomly Selected Male Managers			
A	13	25	graduate degree	2	$70,000
B	9	20	high school	1	$20,000
C	13	20	high school	3	$60,000
D	13	20	some graduate	2	$60,000
E	13	20	B.A.	3	$70,000
F	13	10	graduate degree	3	$64,000
G	8	5	high school	1	$32,000
H	11	2	graduate degree	2	$56,000
I	10	2	some college	1	$26,000
J	14	1	graduate degree	2	$58,000

Note: Levels 8–14 are middle management; seniority means years with the company; motivational ratings are 1 = adequate, 2 = good, 3 = excellent.

tually able people could not detect unfairness, the reason could not be that they were too dull.

Nor did the subjects' attitudes make a difference in their powers of observation. While the format of the information mattered a great deal, the political orientation of the subjects mattered not at all. Pro-feminists were not more likely than others to detect unfairnesses. Furthermore, men were not more or less likely than women to be insensitive to gender discrimination in the piecemeal condition; nor were men more or less likely than women to be sensitive to the same amount of discrimination in the aggregated-information condition.

The effect was not limited to inflammatory issues like sex discrimination. In one of the experiments, half of the young women were presented with materials that dealt with sex discrimination and half were presented with materials that dealt with Plant A and Plant B. The subjects who encountered the information about Plants A and B reported that the experiment was boring; but in all other ways they behaved in their judgments just like the subjects who were learning about sex discrimination.

The situation is similar to what happens with a visual illusion. It doesn't matter whether you are among the world's great art connoisseurs or an artistic Neanderthal. Everyone falls prey to illusions such as the one you see in Figure 3.1.

When judging sizes, a ruler works better than the eye. When judging fairness, systematic assessment works better than impressions. Many people—especially those who have brought home a piece of outsized furniture that had looked so good on the showroom floor and so bad in the living room—have had direct experiences that teach them to use a ruler. Few people have had similar experiences with judgments of fairness.

Classical affirmative action policy centers around the monitoring of employment practices. To have an affirmative action plan, whereby utilization is measured against availability, is analogous to having a ruler. A well-designed affirmative action plan is one that allows people to make decisions and to implement plans on the basis of accurate information. Just as a ruler can help you to decorate your house according to your tastes, so can affirmative action help to insure that you create and maintain fair employment practices.

Parting Thoughts

To see the necessity for affirmative action does not automatically predispose a person to like each and every affirmative action plan. Some plans function better than others. Some plans incorporate more elements of fairness than do others. Support for the policy does not lead inexorably

Figure 3.1 Which is larger?

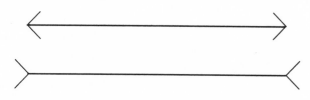

to a blanket endorsement of everything that is done in the name of affirmative action.

All this is true. Yet it is also true that your reaction to any imperfection
in the system will be conditioned by whether or not you believe affirmative action to be a necessary policy for our society. If you are led by the
studies we described to see the need for affirmative action, then your
reaction to problems in policy or practice will be to seek corrections. But
if you conceive of affirmative action as unneeded, then your reaction to
problems will likely be to jettison the policy.

Like George Stephanopoulos and Christopher Edley, Jr., we acknowledge that some types of affirmative action are better than other types, and
we acknowledge the existence of problems in the implementation of all
types of affirmative action, including classical affirmative action. We do
not know if affirmative action is riddled with more problems than any
other aspect of life in a democracy, including such aspects as voting and
taxation. But just as an instance of voting fraud would not make us wish
to reestablish government by monarchy, neither would isolated abuses of
affirmative action make us wish to return to so-called equal opportunity
employment practices. The best course is, as President Clinton has said,
to "mend it, don't end it."[24]

As a democracy, we need voting; as a society, we need affirmative
action. No other American policy promotes the proactive detection of
unfairness in the same way as affirmative action. Without affirmative action, practices that are unfair tend to be detected only if they are blatant or
if they are litigated. Peace comes only with justice; to abandon our practices of monitoring ourselves would be to erode, sooner or later, the
stability of the American socio-economic and political community.

Chapter 4

Fairness and Affirmative Action

A mericans dislike unfairness; but, like every other society, ours is one in which numerous interwoven practices have systematically put some individuals at a disadvantage in ways and to degrees that have only become obvious in hindsight. Slavery appeared normal—at least to slave owners and slave dealers. Suffrage for women was hard won, and for many years it seemed fair and right that half the adult population should participate in our democracy in ways denied the other half. For Americans, as for humans around the globe, what "is" in our society has come to be seen as "what ought to be."[1]

Any attempt at creating a fair system is, of necessity, both aided and hampered by our devotion to justice. Our very need to believe in a just world can make us defensive about recognizing the ways in which current practices and policies fail at fairness. Especially when we have had a stake in the system, an acknowledgment of corruption can be painful.

Hotly debated is the fairness of affirmative action. Our position is that classical affirmative action is fair. Given the degree of interpretation in many situations, the fairness of affirmative action may not always be immediately evident to reasonable citizens. But reflection allows one to move beyond first impressions.

We see classical affirmative action as more fair than passive equal opportunity employment practices. Without denying that problems of implementation can introduce unfairness into some affirmative action plans, we hold that, in principle, the policy treats both groups and individuals justly.

We also maintain that the newer policy of set-asides is less just, and hence less justifiable, than classical affirmative action.

We argue our case by considering the grounds on which affirmative action has been defended and attacked in the national media. We start with issues of retributive justice, move to the justice of turn-taking, and then consider the case for true equity. We end by considering the ways in which the current debate puts into high relief two issues of fundamental importance for justice theorists and a related question for policy-makers.

Retributive Justice

The basic concept of retributive justice is that we are entitled to inflict injury on individuals and groups in equal measure to the injury that they have inflicted on us. To some the idea is outrageous, but the impulse toward retribution is both old and strong. An eye for an eye; a tooth for a tooth—so goes the biblical rendition of the idea.[2] The Hatfields and the McCoys made an occupation of retribution. Any divorce lawyer must have story upon story of the role of revenge in human affairs.

Some citizens seem to object to affirmative action because they understand the policy to be a retribution against mean-spirited whites of previous generations and because they think retribution ineffective or inappropriate. As black novelist and commentator Bebe Moore Campbell told a *New York Times* reporter, she can sympathize with the angry white males who feel rage over affirmative action. "I understand where they're coming from... They're saying 'My parents didn't own slaves. Let's get on with it.'"[3]

In fact, neither classical affirmative action nor the other programs established in the name of affirmative action have ever been conceived of by their proponents as retributive justice. The policy of monitoring employment to make sure that talented people from all groups are utilized in proportion to their availability is not seen by the U.S. Department of Labor as inflicting punishment on talented white men. Nor are governmental agencies enjoined to reserve a percentage of their business for specified groups for the purpose of punishing other, unspecified groups.

Why do some see affirmative action as retribution? It is possible that seeing affirmative action as punishment reflects subtle prejudice or, at least, preference for one's own group. Early studies on group identity revealed that we readily reward members of our own group more than members of different groups, even when group membership is assigned in an arbitrary way.[4] If three white men are vying for a job and only one gets it, the other two aren't likely to think of their nonselection as punishment. It is only when a member of a different group—a white woman or a person of color—gets the appointment that the idea of retribution comes to mind.

It is also quite possible that even nonsexist and nonracist people mistakenly equate affirmative action with retribution. Perhaps the misunderstandings arise from potentially confusing aspects of American law. In some instances, organizations have been ordered by the courts to develop and implement affirmative action plans. This is because when harm has occurred, the court can order corrective actions to "make whole" or restore the rights of the damaged parties. Typically, affirmative action plans are court-mandated when the organization has been found to discriminate against women or ethnic minorities. The most famous instance of a court-ordered affirmative action plan occurred in 1973 when AT&T was found to have discriminated against women.[5] Although no court has ever ordered affirmative action as a form of punishment, it is also true that courts can, under some circumstances, award punitive damages. In tort law, for example, punitive damages can be awarded to a harmed party when the harm that was done is socially reprehensible and should have been foreseen and could have been avoided.

Given the complexities of our legal system, it does not seem astonishing that members of the public might mistake one form of legal action for another. But the confusion need not persist. The facts are plain: in principle, affirmative action has nothing at all to do with retributive justice.

The Fairness of Turn Taking

Taking turns is fair play. Anyone who grew up with siblings knows this. Johnny got to play with the cat; now it's Nancy's turn. Norine chose her dessert first last time; now Freddy can.

Just as siblings, classmates, colleagues, and even competitors take turns sitting in the front seat, standing at the head of the line, having the right of first refusal, or teeing off first, so can women and men. So can people of color and white people.

Some commentators justify affirmative action by noting that white men have had the advantage in America for a couple of centuries. "Let women have a turn," they say. "Let people of color have a turn." Among the most articulate advocates of this position is Stanley Fish. Says Fish:

> [B]lacks have not simply been treated unfairly; they have been subjected first to decades of slavery, and then to decades of second-class citizenship, widespread legalized discrimination, economic persecution, educational deprivation, and cultural stigmatization.... The word "unfair" is hardly an adequate description of their experience, and the belated gift of "fairness" in the form of a resolution no longer to discriminate against them legally is hardly an adequate remedy.... When the deck is stacked against you in more ways than you can even count, it is small consolation to hear that you are now free to enter the game and take your chances.[6]

Giving preference to people from the targeted classes when they are neck-and-neck with white men is a practice that can occur not only with set-asides but also in classical affirmative action programs. Recall Santa Clara County. Administrators there reasoned, in essence, that they could not meaningfully distinguish between candidates who had met a set of criteria. Those who met the criteria were to be treated as equals. Then the rule was to select a woman over equally qualified men. Other things being equal, in other words, the woman was to receive the job.[7]

Turn taking was not the only possible selection procedure. The administrators could have declared everyone who met the criteria as equal and then tossed a coin.

Why not toss a coin? The answer, reasoned Santa Clara County, was that for years it seemed that men were selected over equally qualified women. The time had come to switch turns.

Clearly, there are circumstances that render turn taking among equals a more appropriate strategy and circumstances that render it a less appropriate strategy. When a situation permits absolutely unambiguous rankings among candidates, and when differences in the rankings predict meaningful differences on the job, it does not seem fair to invoke the turn-taking rule. Conversely, when the situation does not permit unambiguous ranking among candidates, or when all candidates above a given rank are predicted to perform well, the strategy seems appropriate.

Rankings can be ambiguous for a number of reasons. If complex combinations of qualities are needed for a job, it is likely that some candidates may excel when viewed from one perspective while others may excel from other perspectives. Alternately, there may be no truly reliable assessment techniques to predict who is the best and who is the worst. Or the assessment techniques may only allow for differentiations that are quite imprecise or broad-banded. When rankings are unstable, for whatever reason, it seems odd to insist that the prize, the admission, or the job go to the best-ranked candidate—for the person who ranks the best today may not be the one who ranks the best tomorrow.

Another relevant factor is the extent of bias. When there has been no hint of bias in the immediate past, then the need to take turns becomes redundant. Without bias, turns are taken spontaneously. Again, the converse is also true. Evidence of bias in the recent past argues that some mechanism, no matter how contrived, is needed to assure proper turn taking.

The practice of using contrivances to assure impartial turn taking is quite familiar to researchers of human behavior. When social scientists conduct systematic observational studies, experiments, or surveys, we use techniques such as approaching every fifth person who walks through the door, for example, to make sure that our sampling is random and not haphazard. Without such "tricks" our own unconscious desires (like the dread of approaching individuals with a certain look) could influence us and produce biased results.

Is turn taking between groups as fair as turn taking between individuals? In many realms of life, it is. The blue team was allowed to go first last week; now the orange team goes first. Manhasset High got the front row seats last year; so this year they go to Great Neck High. The boys' camp had morning swim at the raft yesterday; now the girls' camp does.

Perhaps some of the resistance to affirmative action, as a policy, derives from a discomfort in seeing women and men as separate groups or teams, or in seeing white Americans and Americans of color as separate groups or teams. Without denying that turn taking is fair play, the critics seem to object to the assumptions that women and men can be considered categorically and that whites and non-whites can be considered categorically—assumptions that are inherent in the justice-based principle of alternating access to scarce resources among categories of people.

And what is wrong with seeing people as members of categories? Clearly, in many circumstances, the answer is nothing. Indeed, group membership often enhances our sense of self. Think about the pleasure we feel when a team with which we identify does well.

But, when group identity is linked with a sense of grievance, tensions can mount. "Nothing," asserts Nathan Glazer, "is so powerful in the modern world as the perception of unfairness. Perhaps it is inevitable that wherever there are distinguishable groups, one group will feel it is unfairly treated in contrast to another."[8] The central objection to affirmative action by conservative commentators like Dinesh D'Souza and Shelby Steele is that it encourages various minority groups to climb "aboard the victim bandwagon." Continues D'Souza:

> With the encouragement of the university administration and activist faculty, many minority students begin to think of themselves as victims. Indeed, they aspire to victim status. They do not yearn to be oppressed, of course; rather, they seek the moral capital of victimhood.[9]

Policy leaders also grapple with the potential drawbacks of group categorization. Speaking to civil rights leaders in Boston six months after delivering his report to President Clinton, Christopher Edley, Jr. described some of the behind-the-scenes events and thinking at the White House as affirmative action was being reviewed. He indicated that at one end of the spectrum some advisors cautioned against color-conscious policies of any sort. No matter how great the potential gain of such policies, said those advisors, they represented a cost that could not be borne. At the other end of the spectrum were advisors who disbelieved color-conscious policies bear any cost at all. Somewhere in the middle were the President and his special counsels: they envisioned the color-conscious policy of affirmative action as worth the costs.[10]

Obviously, much depends on how institutions implement affirmative action. But even the most rational plan can irritate those whose own privileges or whose group's privileges are eroded. When monitoring reveals that targeted groups are not being utilized in proportion to their availability in the appropriate talent pool, plans like that of Santa Clara County provide a generally benign and innocuous way of correcting for the imbalance. Relying on the fairness of turn taking, such plans buy a great deal of social justice at the small price of inconveniencing—or rankling—a few individuals who had previously assumed that when rewards were being passed out, they had only to compete with "their own kind."

Treating Like Alike

Institutions of justice in the United States are built on the fundamental principle of treating like alike. So said H.L.A. Hart, the great legal scholar.[11] The concept, said Hart, may be more universal than national, but even if the concept is not key to other societies, it is at the core of ours.

In some ways, everyone is alike, at least in the eyes of the law. Some rights are taken to be inalienable, so that they apply equally to all citizens. The Declaration of Independence promises every citizen in our country "life, liberty, and the pursuit of happiness," and the Constitution guarantees the rights at least to the extent that the exercising of such rights does not trammel the rights of other citizens.

Recently the Supreme Court has reinforced the concept that unneeded distinctions among citizens are to be avoided. In the case of *Griggs v. the Duke Power Company*, for example, the Supreme Court ruled that employers cannot adopt criteria for hiring that adversely affect some groups and that are not related to job performance.[12] If a high school diploma is not shown to be related to success as a telephone repairperson, then the diploma cannot be used to sort among applicants. Similarly, driving a cab in New York City may require certain talents: a good memory, ability to plan, physical dexterity, and courage. Anyone who passes the threshold of qualification on these dimensions is eligible for hire. But you should not have to demonstrate an eidetic or photographic memory to obtain the job. Nor should a courageous and dexterous applicant with a doctoral degree be considered more eligible than one who exhibits the same characteristics but lacks a college education.

Treating people alike sounds simpler than it is. Sometimes equal treatment at a conceptually meaningful level means differential treatment at a more superficial level. If you want to treat a sister and brother the same, you might want to provide each with clothing that is comfortable. The suit that fits the brother is unlikely to fit the sister. So, to achieve a meaningful equality, different treatment is required. As Justice Blackmun said in the *Bakke* decision: "[I]n order to treat some persons equally, we must treat them differently."[13]

In many instances, the injunction to treat like alike means that distinctions are not just allowed but are in fact expected. For many issues in life, individuals are considered to be like some other people but yet unlike other people. A person who has met the requirements of an educational institution deserves to be granted the same credentialing degree as all others who have met the requirements. It is further presumed that the credential is conferred only on those who met the requirements and not on all people ever born.

That social justice is an intensively comparative matter is known to social scientists. A staple of social psychology is "the equity formulation" articulated decades ago by John Stacey Adams.[14] Written in algebraic form, equity exists when:

$$\frac{\text{A's outcomes}}{\text{A's inputs}} = \frac{\text{B's outcomes}}{\text{B's inputs.}}$$

When equity exists, satisfaction and peace reign. When A's outcomes, relative to A's inputs, exceed B's outcomes, relative to B's inputs, or vice versa, the imbalance provokes feelings of unfairness and dissatisfaction in the underbenefited party and of guilt in the overbenefited one. To the extent that your inputs are like mine—and only to that extent—your outcomes should also be like mine; this is the central claim of equity.

Equity theorists realize that actual situations can be more complicated than theoretical abstractions. Outcomes can be multidimensional. Knowing on which aspect of an outcome to focus is no small matter. Should I give all equal contributors to a project the same reward, even if that reward is more prized by some than others, or should I find rewards that are equally prized by them? If person X wants the status that comes with a certain job, and person Y wants the money, am I treating X and Y the same if I give them both fancy titles or give them both checks, or am I treating them the same if I give X the title and Y the check? Inputs too can pose problems of assessment. People are alike in some ways and different in others. How are we to select which dimensions are relevant inputs in the equity formula?

Those who see affirmative action as reverse discrimination imagine it as a violation of equity. Such critics note that, in the absence of a sufficient talent pool, quotas allow some individuals to enjoy outcomes out of all proportion to their legitimate inputs. They imagine all forms of affirmative action, including classical affirmative action, simply function as arbitrary and strict quotas.

But they imagine wrongly. As we have seen, classical affirmative action, established by Executive Order 11246 as amended, allows not for quotas but for goals, and those goals are to be established sensibly. Indeed, the whole point of monitoring how well utilization matches availability is to make sure via objective means that outcomes for all groups are, in fact, proportionate to inputs.

What about the issue of using gender or ethnicity as a plus factor when making allocations among candidates who are by and large comparable? Is this not a violation of equity? If we see the use of plus factors as compensating for possible deficiencies in the candidates, then their use is a violation of equity. Whether or not the short-term violation of equity can be justified by calling attention to the need to remedy historical imbalances is a matter of some dispute.

Much less doubtful is the fairness of using gender or ethnicity as a plus factor when they are seen as compensating for deficiencies in the *decision makers* rather than in the candidates. Decision makers are not always perfect. Even when we do not wish to discriminate against one group or another, old habits of thought and old sensibilities can perpetuate unfairnesses. We are all more comfortable with the familiar than with the unfamiliar, and comfort levels can influence perceptions.

Sometimes the comfort involves our use of old, familiar measures of assessment. The inappropriateness of habitual measures sometimes comes to light only when there is a legal challenge. Take a look, for example, at a recent charge made by women agents in the F.B.I.[15] The women pointed out irrelevant training practices that made it less likely that they could shine compared to male agents. In one test F.B.I. recruits were required to pull the trigger of a handgun twenty-nine times in thirty seconds. The women charged that they often had to use guns that were the wrong size for the typical female hand. The agents claimed that nothing about the trigger-pulling exercise related to what they would encounter as an agent and, hence, the test should not have been used as a predictor of the recruit's future success.

The people who devised the F.B.I. test probably considered it to be an objective, neutral way to assess a needed skill, but it was not. If merit were to be assessed on the basis of trigger pulls, then the F.B.I. needed either to provide guns of the appropriate size or, using the old outsize guns, to assign handicap points to women to compensate for the unfairness of the assessment procedure. To assign a handicap is to use gender as a plus factor.

While the use of plus factors among roughly comparable candidates seems entirely appropriate and fair, set-asides seem to be another matter. When a law specifies, for instance, that a certain percent of contract dollars is to be reserved for contracts with minority firms, perceptions of equity may be disrupted. This is especially true when the percent of dollars to be distributed bears no relationship to the capability or availability of minority- or woman-owned firms.

Consider in this regard the famous *Adarand* case of the summer of 1995.[16] In an attempt to comply with the Small Business Act's government-wide goal that 5 percent of government contracts and subcontracts be awarded to socially and economically disadvantaged individuals (with the further presumption that members of ethnic minority groups are disadvantaged), the Department of Transportation created a program that gave extra compensation to contractors if they hired minority subcontractors. In *Adarand*, a contractor had to choose between two bids, a very low bid from a nonminority firm and a somewhat higher bid from a minority firm. To receive extra compensation from the Department of Transportation, the prime contractor awarded the subcontract to the minority firm. The nonminority firm sued the department for denying it equal protection under the Fifth Amendment's Due Process Clause. Both the district court and the court of appeals ruled that the firm's rights had not been violated. But the firm carried the case to the Supreme Court, and there it obtained the ruling it sought.

In a 5–4 vote, the Supreme Court ruled that the Department of Transportation had acted unconstitutionally in the *Adarand* case. Overturning a previous ruling of the *Metro Broadcasting* case, the Court held that all federal affirmative action programs that use race or ethnicity as a basis for making decisions must apply the legal rule of "strict scrutiny." The programs must, in other words, serve a compelling national interest and must be narrowly tailored to achieving that interest. Even if ending ethnic discrimination is a compelling national interest, the Department of Transportation's means of serving that interest was not tailored narrowly to it.[17]

What does the Court mean by narrow tailoring? Consistent with notions of equity, the extent of the remedy must fit the identified problem. That is, the number of people who benefit from the remedy must roughly match the number of eligible candidates. In Birmingham white firefighters won their claim of reverse discrimination when the court ruled against the city's practice of hiring the highest ranking black person from the "black list" and then the highest ranking white person from the "white list" and so on to fill successive vacancies. Blacks constituted only 10 percent of the labor force in Birmingham, and the 50 percent hiring quota was deemed arbitrary and discriminatory toward whites.[18] Similarly, in *Croson* the Court ruled that a·30 percent minority subcontracting requirement was not justified, even though the population of Richmond was 50 percent African-American. The figure chosen for preferential treatment, according to the ruling, must bear some relationship to the pool of candidates with the qualifications necessary for the subcontracted job. Only when companies follow this requirement of narrow tailoring will "outcomes" seem reasonable given "inputs" and an equitable balance be achieved.

Once a company has achieved a diverse workforce, with roughly the proportions of qualified white women and people of color expected given their representation in the community, preferential consideration should no longer be employed. This does not mean that companies no longer have to worry about subtle or explicitly discriminatory practices that may reverse gains accrued during the affirmative action program. But it does mean that awarding favor to one group of qualified applicants over another group of qualified applicants should not be allowed. Continuing preferential treatment, after the group is part of the mainstream, inflicts an undue burden on other applicants.

When the *Adarand* decision came down, the media portrayed the decision as signaling the end of affirmative action.[19] In fact, the Court did curtail set-asides. But it did not rule against the kinds of monitoring-plus-correction programs that we have promoted. Indeed, Justice Ginsberg acknowledged Congress's authority "to act affirmatively, not only to end discrimination, but also to counteract discrimination's lingering effects."[20]

In March 1996, the 5th Circuit of the U.S. Court of Appeals rendered a decision in a suit that had been brought by four disgruntled and unsuccessful white applicants to the University of Texas Law School where applicants of color had been admitted with LSAT scores that were lower than those of the litigants. The court ruled against the University and prohibited the use of race-conscious admissions programs. Because the appellate court's decision is worded in a way that appears to contradict both *Bakke* and *Adarand,* observers are speculating that the case will be heard again, in due course, in the Supreme Court. In the meantime, controversy will continue.

Challenges

Like all but two members of the Supreme Court (Antonin Scalia and Clarence Thomas), we see affirmative action as a fair policy. The fairness of turn taking applies to classical affirmative action and to narrowly tailored set-aside programs.

We also acknowledge that—fair though it is—affirmative action is a disquieting policy. Close scrutiny of the issues surrounding affirmative action can prove challenging not only because it is uncomfortable to have to acknowledge the extent to which our practices fall short of our ideals, but also because the policy forces us to think about questions that defy simplistic answers. We believe that some of the controversy about affirmative action springs from its power to unsettle us.

One thorny issue, brought into high relief by affirmative action, concerns stability and change. Everybody knows that ours is a complex world. In such a complicated world, it often happens that we cannot easily gauge how systems will actually operate. We can imagine that certain practices will prove fair and equitable and then be surprised to discover that they are not.

How are we to handle situations in which people sign on to a project with one set of rules in place and then discover, in the middle of the project, that the rules which had appeared fair contain a bias? Do we change the rules in the middle of the process? To do so may seem unfair.[21] Or do we adhere to our original agreements, even though we now know them to be discriminatory?

Just such a dilemma presented itself to one of the telephone companies for whom one of us had done research in the 1980s. The company had been using a promotion system that rewarded seniority, especially in line (rather than staff) positions. The system had been in place for decades, and it was one of the elements that seem to inspire loyalty and dedication from the workers and managers. The system had been designed and refined with the goal of increasing company camaraderie and not as a means of keeping women out of management. Many managers were genuinely surprised by the realization—brought on them by a lawsuit—that the regulations had unfairly advantaged men. But even as they recognized the need for revision, a number of men in the company felt betrayed by the new directives. They had been planning their careers, playing by one set of rules, and making long-range decisions accordingly. After five, ten, or fifteen years with the company, they found their old credits counted for a lot less than they previously had. More than one man told our interviewers that he felt "as if the rug has been pulled out from under him."[22]

Not only can corrections appear to be betrayals, but they can also be costly and embarrassing for those who were in charge of the old systems.[23] Consider in this regard information given to us by a former Marine captain who had been involved in the issue of whether or not women should fly bombers. Mike, the Marine, told us that the G-suits are used to test people's recovery from a sudden loss of gravity. G-suits have long been worn by pilots of the very expensive aircraft, and their use in this simulation test is 100 percent appropriate. But the G-suit was fashioned for the male body, with its relatively short leg-to-torso ratio, and not for the female body, with its relatively long leg-to-torso ratio. Changing the design of the garment meant improved performance by women and, most would argue, a fair test. But change was expensive, and reputations were tarnished in the process.

A second thorny issue is that changing old systems and procedures does not suddenly reduce disparities in an organization. Opening up a new opportunity for today's women to be fairly tested for flight training, for example, does not mean that women will suddenly become available to fill the positions. We cannot ignore the effects of the chilling environment that discourages people from gaining the competence and experience necessary to be considered qualified for the newly opened positions. Ironically, in some cases only those with the gumption to prepare for a job that they were unlikely to get will now be eligible for consideration. Employers whose practices have discouraged people from obtaining the proper training are not held accountable under the rules of narrow tailoring for the consequences of abandoned hope.

Psychologists have long known about the effects of early encouragement or discouragement and how others' messages about one's competence can influence self-perceptions and behavior. For example, in recent years people have worried about the chilling consequences of alleged sex bias in aptitude tests such as the SAT and the PSAT.[24] Women consistently score about sixty points lower than men on the PSAT taken in the junior year, but they earn higher grades in school. Given that National Merit Scholarships and some other college scholarship funds are awarded on the basis of the PSAT, men obtain about 60 percent of the scholarships. Men thus derive an early benefit from listing an honor next to their name, and the early benefit may have long-term effects.

We have already concluded that it is not a good idea to hire unqualified people or admit unqualified students, and organizations cannot magically attract qualified people who do not now exist. What is a possible solution then? Organizations can offer training or engage in other activities that eventually will increase the pool of qualified applicants in the underrepresented groups. Exxon's and Procter and Gamble's internship programs, for example, enhance the diversity of the future pool of employees.[25] The Army operates a preparatory school for students nominated to West Point who possess the ability to develop into qualified candidates, but who at the time of nomination lack the credentials.[26] Voluntary and proactive approaches such as these create qualified pools of future employees or students.

Concluding Thoughts

Attempts to develop fair systems of affirmative action are complicated. What may seem fair to one party—already included in the organization or reaping the benefits of old procedures and rules—may seem unfair to the party currently on the outside. Thus, those who devise affirmative action programs might well take a hint from the equity theorists and concern themselves with spreading both the rewards and the costs around to all groups.

Even as perceptions of fairness are complicated and even as affirmative action raises uncomfortable issues, the fairness of the policy means that we ought not abandon it. For all the reasons we have articulated in the last chapter and this, affirmative action—and particularly classical affirmative action—is a policy that replaces apparent equity with real equity. Unlike more passive policies, affirmative action provides an objective numerical test for organizations of how well they have achieved in practice the equity which they desire to achieve. By looking at outcomes, in other words, affirmative action allows a gauge of how truly there has been equality of opportunity. Even more than passive "equal opportunity" employment practices, affirmative action thus safeguards the right of all individuals—no matter what their color or gender.

To say that the policy is fair in principle is not to say that every affirmative action plan is fair in practice. Affirmative action is not perfect. As *Adarand* and other Supreme Court cases show, some forms of affirmative action are of questionable constitutionality. Some mending—to paraphrase President Clinton—is needed.

Yet we should not exaggerate the problems of affirmative action. A few dramatic "reverse discrimination" cases such as *Bakke* or *Croson* or *Adarand* should not fool us into thinking that the justice system is groaning under the weight of suits brought by people from the "nontargeted" classes. Indeed, between 1 and 3 percent of the employment discrimination cases heard at either the federal district level or the federal appeals level were of the reverse discrimination type. None of the cases involved the OFCCP or what we have called classical affirmative action.[27] Of the ninety-one thousand discrimination claims filed with the Equal Opportunity Commission in 1994, only 4.9 percent alleged sex-based reverse discrimination and 2.8 percent alleged race-based reverse discrimination. Two-fifths of 1 percent of the claims were deemed meritorious by the EEOC.[28] Better statistics would be hard to find.

Chapter 5

The Effectiveness
of Affirmative Action

Even if you agree with us that affirmative action is a fair policy, you may contend that it is not an effective policy. Some very liberal commentators have deemed affirmative action ineffectual because, according to them, it is toothless. From the other side of the political spectrum, some conservatives see affirmative action as a policy whose benefits are not significant enough to justify the costs of developing and maintaining affirmative action plans.

The controversy has reverberated in Washington. When President Clinton ordered a comprehensive review of affirmative action in March of 1995, he specified that the review should pose two fundamental questions: 1) Is affirmative action fair, and 2) Does it work?[1] A policy that was fair but inefficacious would hardly be worth fighting for.

What are the elements of an effective policy? We believe effective policy produces positive results and does so at an acceptable level of cost. Pyrrhic victories are not successes.

Producing Positive Results

Essentially two techniques exist for demonstrating that affirmative action is an effective policy. First, you can look at specific instances in which it has made a difference to individuals. Second, you can look more generally at how affirmative action has affected either the economy as a whole or those firms which are federal contractors.

In a recent fact sheet pertaining to the Office of Federal Contract Compliance Programs (OFCCP), the U.S. Department of Labor has taken the first approach.[2] The four-page fact sheet poses a series of questions, largely aimed at the differences that the OFCCP has made in the lives of people. The questions are addressed by tracking specific cases of governmental action—cases which not only affect individuals, but have forced institutional change that will influence hundreds or thousands more. Table 5.1 reproduces part of the fact sheet and illustrates the types of changes brought about through affirmative action as monitored by the OFCCP. Looking at the examples, you can hardly fail to conclude that affirmative action is effective policy.

The second approach yields more controversial evidence for the effectiveness of affirmative action than the first approach. Alfred Blumrosen, a law professor at Rutgers University who specializes in labor issues, concludes that *equal opportunity* programs have worked well, perhaps contributing to the employment of as many as five million people of color—one-quarter of people of color in the 1992 labor force. Gains by women have been at least as strong.[3] Not all of these gains may be due to the programs we call "affirmative action," but the statistics are impressive. Two prominent economists who study affirmative action, Jonathan Leonard of the University of California at Berkeley and James Heckman of the University of Michigan, agree that federal contractors have employed a higher proportion of women and people of color than other companies in similar sectors of the economy.[4] But they regard the gains attributable to affirmative action as modest.

Stephanopoulos and Edley called President Clinton's attention to one of the reports prepared by Heckman and his colleague, John Donohue.[5] The White House report observed:

> There is near-unanimous consensus among economists that the government anti-discrimination programs beginning in 1964 contributed to the income of African-Americans. Nevertheless, it is difficult to draw conclusions about which specific anti-discrimination programs were most effective. And it may well be that the programs collectively helped even though no single program was overwhelmingly effective.[6]

Table 5.1

Some examples of OFCCP's successful efforts on behalf of American workers include:

- On September 16, 1994, OFCCP and Honeywell Corporation agreed to a 6.5 million settlement resolving a sex discrimination case that could affect up to 6,000 women. In addition to back pay, the company agreed to promote equal employment opportunity. Honeywell, a manufacturer of control products and systems, employs 51,000 employees in 95 countries.

- On September 14, 1994, OFCCP and Marriott International Corporate Headquarters in Washington, DC agreed to pay $112,000 in back pay and $55,000 in salary adjustments to 40 top-level women and minorities who were paid less than their minority male peers. In addition, Marriott agreed to review its compensation practices to prevent recurrence.

- On August 22, 1994, OFCCP negotiated a settlement on behalf of a visually impaired person. The settlement requires Kimberly Clark Corporation to pay the complainant back wages and allowances totalling $17,290 and to take remedial action to ensure that the hiring discrimination does not recur.

- On August 9, 1994, Canon Business Machines of Costa Mesa, California agreed to pay $633,000 to 30 qualified African-Americans, an Hispanic and a Caucasian female who were denied jobs. In 1992, Canon had 1,732 job applicants including 100 blacks. Of 96 new hires, none were black.

- Because of OFCCP's continuing affirmative action efforts in 1994-95, Native Americans, through Tribal Employment Rights Organizations (TEROs), are employed on federally assisted highway projects.

- On September 24, 1993, as a result of OFCCP's glass ceiling review of Fairfax Hospital, 52 women were paid $425,586 in back wages, and 44 of the women will receive $178,357 in salary increases. This was the first settlement for a glass ceiling compliance review.

Source: U.S. Department of Labor (1995).

Similarly, about gender-conscious programs they stated:

> The relative roles in this story of anti-discrimination laws and affirmative action, in education and the workplace, are unclear. The major equal opportunity laws covering women were passed in the mid-1960s, and the most rapid growth in women's earnings and occupational status did not begin for another decade. The lag between the change in law and the increase in earnings may be due to time it took for women to acquire education and training for traditionally male-dominated occupations. The rapid growth in the number of female graduates from professional schools coincided with increased anti-discrimination efforts.[7]

The experts can argue over whether the gains should be labelled "modest" or "impressive." But there is no argument that they are positive, and significant enough to support a claim that affirmative action is effective policy.

Avoiding Negative Effects

The effectiveness of any program must take into account not only the benefits reaped but also the costs incurred. Affirmative action has been criticized for two types of problems. First, some scholars have argued that affirmative action programs undermine the confidence of the intended beneficiaries. Second, some commentators claim that the policy of affirmative action causes those who are not direct beneficiaries (most often, white men) to stigmatize those who are. Let's take a look at these criticisms.

Self-Doubt

Most Americans do not like preferential treatment and tend to interpret it as an indication of personal inadequacy on the part of the recipient. If the intended beneficiaries of affirmative action also view preferential treatment in this way, they may feel devalued or compromised by it.

Some anecdotal evidence, reported in the popular press, illustrates the potential for detrimental self-perception stimulated by selection on the basis of preferential treatment. One news report talks of a bass player for the Detroit Symphony Orchestra who felt devalued when hired without the usual blind audition, due to pressure to hire African-Americans.[8] Stephen Carter talks of his dismay about being accepted to Harvard Law School only after the admissions officer learned that he was black.[9]

Systematically collected data also demonstrate the potential negative consequences of preferential treatment on self-esteem.[10] Remember the work of Madeline Heilman and her colleagues. In one study, women were told they had been selected for a leadership position on a two-person assignment either because the experimenter needed women leaders or because of their tested leadership skill. Those selected through arbitrary preferential treatment devalued their performance and reported less interest in continuing in the leadership role.

In a later study, women again were selected through preferential treatment or through merit, but this time those selected through preferential treatment were (1) informed before the task that they had scored better than the follower on a test of ability, (2) informed that they had scored worse, or (3) provided with no information about their relative competence. As predicted, women who believed that they had scored worse than their colleague and those provided with no feedback rated their leadership ability and their task performance relatively poorly. Those told, however, that they had good leadership potential rated themselves highly, almost as highly as those who had been selected through merit alone.

One of the fascinating findings in this research was that men did not respond in the same way. Only when men were selected through preferential treatment *and* informed before the task that their competence was in doubt did they devalue their leadership performance and ability. Those who were given no feedback perceived their leadership abilities similarly to those who had been told they were selected on the basis of merit.

Heilman and her colleagues suggest that confidence in one's ability to perform the task is crucial to counter any possible self-stigmatizing effects of affirmative action, particularly among women. In the absence of knowledge about one's ability to lead, women may assume they possess deficiencies, whereas men may assume they possess strengths.

Rupert Nacoste has conducted laboratory studies that look at ethnic as well as gender issues.[11] Nacoste's findings are basically the same as

Heilman's. To imagine oneself the recipient of unwarranted privilege is not happy or healthful.

Is there evidence to show that Heilman's and Nacoste's findings predict thoughts and feelings of people outside the psychological laboratory? No, there is not. In fact, the evidence all goes in the opposite direction. Let's start with an anecdote. *New York Times* writer Brent Staples admits, "When I was 17, the society spotted me a few points on the SAT's and changed my life."[12] He is grateful that someone looked beyond his test scores, saw promise, and gave him a break. He also thinks the break-giver was wise: "I became a writer—and a middle-class taxpayer—as many other black men went on to prisons, cemeteries, and homeless shelters. Sounds like a smart investment to me."

Polls offer more systematic evidence. In a poll reported in *The Gallup Poll Monthly* of July 1995, 708 white women and people of color were asked, "Have you ever felt that your colleagues at work or school privately questioned your abilities or qualifications because of affirmative action or have you never felt this way?"[13] Only 8 percent of white women, 19 percent of African-American women, and 29 percent of the African-American men replied in the affirmative.

Not only have surveys failed to show self-stigmatization; they have instead shown positive effects. Analyzing the 1990 General Social Survey, Marylee Taylor found that African-American workers employed by affirmative action firms expressed more ambition and less cynicism than African-Americans employed by other firms.[14] Similarly, surveys show that a small minority of African-American managers believes that affirmative action has hurt their careers and over half believe that it has helped blacks.[15] The same surveys show that half of well-educated blacks, compared to less than a third of similar whites, believe that they work harder than their peers and that their organization depends substantially on their contributions. Obviously, some people of color or women who have been helped by affirmative action would subscribe to the sentiment expressed by Cornell Professor Isaac Kramnick: "[I]t will take till eternity for the number of second-rate blacks in the university to match the number of second-rate whites."[16]

How can we explain the differences between the laboratory studies and real-world findings? First, as we said at the beginning of this volume, some of the laboratory research is set up to show that preferential treatment is detrimental. When Heilman pits arbitrary preferential treatment against selection on the basis of qualifications, no wonder preferential treatment fails.[17] Second, the contexts used in laboratory studies are uncharacteristic of real-world corporations and campuses in important respects. Selection in the real world does not immediately precede evaluation. Thus, selection procedures will not be as salient as in the experimental analogues. Furthermore, on campus and in the factory, people selected through preferential treatment have many opportunities to see other people's work; hence, they have many chances to see others' comparative strengths and weaknesses.

Nonetheless, laboratory findings can teach us important lessons. When we establish affirmative action programs, we must minimize the potential for self-doubt by reminding people of the qualifications that led to their selection. Of course, it also follows that affirmative action must be predicated first on qualifications—not arbitrary selection based solely on color or gender.

Provoked Hostility among Those
Who Are Not Direct Beneficiaries

The second problem that interferes with the effectiveness of affirmative action is others' hostility. Nacoste has shown that willingness to accept affirmative action programs to a large degree is tied to the emphasis placed on race, gender, or other "particularistic" characteristics as opposed to "universalistic" characteristics such as education and experience. For example, college admission procedures that weigh academic qualifications more heavily than group membership will be judged to be fairer than procedures that give predominant weight to group membership.[18]

The consequences of "unfair" decisions are many, and they are found in both educational and work settings. Students who are accepted to a college with a well-publicized affirmative action admissions policy may be perceived by fellow students as less qualified than those accepted into a non-affirmative action college.[19] Fellow students also may be less willing to interact with their "affirmative action" counterparts, or may assign lower salaries to "coworkers" whom they were pressured to hire.[20] Adult white males, surveyed in airports and other public settings, rated a co-worker hired under strong affirmative action pressure less competent, active, and effective, and with fewer positive interpersonal characteristics than those hired in the absence of strong affirmative action guidelines.[21]

Again, these are worrisome findings. But remember that they are largely generated in a lab or in a research context in which affirmative action has been made quite salient. It is not surprising, then, that other factors related to evaluation fade in significance.

Furthermore, let's be realistic. People of color and women suffered from suspicions about their competence long before affirmative action programs gave people an excuse for being suspicious. As Brent Staples notes, "It is absurd to argue, as many critics do, that affirmative action has placed African-Americans under suspicion of incompetence...."[22]

And remember also that fairness is in the eye of the beholder. When women and people of color perceive themselves to be deprived relative to equally talented members of other groups, they too can become frustrated, resentful, and even downright hostile.[23] So minimizing only the resentment of people who are already privileged to be members of the organization would indeed be a Pyrrhic victory.

The studies by Nacoste and Heilman and their colleagues do suggest, however, that we must be careful, first, to ensure that quality is a prerequisite for selection and, second, to publicize widely the criteria used in admissions or in the hiring process. Wise administrators create a supportive atmosphere by carefully communicating the criteria they use to select from a pool of applicants. They offer assurances that race, gender, veteran status, or any other personal characteristic will not be allowed to trump decision-making. The emphasis must be on quality, or else affirmative action may backfire to the detriment not only of the candidates but of the organization as well.

Final Words

Affirmative action is a steadily effective policy. Its accomplishments are measureable, if not dramatic. Its potential negative side effects, which loom large in the eyes of some pessimists and media gurus, are generally more apparent than real. To the extent that they are real, they are avoidable. Now we turn to a discussion of how to implement affirmative action policy effectively.

Chapter 6

Making Affirmative Action Work

Just as some types of affirmative action—notably classical affirmative action—seem to be fairer policies than other types, so too are some affirmative action plans more effective than others. True change is never easy, and those who have enjoyed privilege do not always yield it happily. But some affirmative action plans can achieve strong results with only weak protest. In this chapter, we will talk about how to implement such plans.[1]

Recruitment

The goal of affirmative action is the recruitment and retention of a diverse and well-qualified workforce or student body. Successful recruitment processes contain two elements: thought and action. Thought should precede action, and then the actions should continue to be thoughtful.

Thought before Action: Conceptualizing Recruitment

The recruitment process starts with an analysis of what attributes constitute success and what qualities predict it. Organizations must decide how to define success—what exactly constitutes acceptable performance on the job or in school? Organizations must also determine how successful performance can be predicted from the information available about an applicant.

Let's use college and graduate school admissions as an example of the kinds of issues to be explored when we define "successful performance." Colleges and universities appropriately define success as graduation, or completion of degree requirements. While they value and reward high achievement during the college years, students who "get by" also graduate, and these students fill a rather large subset of any graduating class. Thus, it is completion of the degree that most characterizes "success."

But colleges aspire to be more than just the setting where students pass from matriculation to graduation. Faculty recognize that colleges prepare students for life after college—a life that will require flexibility in an increasingly technological society and tolerance in an increasingly diverse one. Carefully crafted mission statements, therefore, incorporate these additional goals. Trinity College, for example, claims that its "paramount purpose is to foster critical thinking, free the mind of parochialism and prejudice, and prepare students to lead examined lives that are personally satisfying, civically responsible, and socially useful."[2]

If colleges and universities are not just mouthing platitudes in their mission statements, we would expect that the stated goals should be reflected in admissions criteria. Along with considering grades and achievement test scores, then, we should see admissions counselors considering additional factors. Counselors should select students who will enrich their colleagues because of their diverse talents, the experiences they have had, and the differing perspectives they are likely to bring to issues. Playing a tuba or football, living in Europe or in the Bronx, speaking Spanish or Chinese at home, and having African-American or Latino roots introduces variability to the campus that can foster personal and intellectual growth and can stimulate understanding of others.

The University of California at Berkeley exemplifies institutions that attempt to meet many goals through multivaried admissions criteria. Berkeley has so many high-achieving applicants that it could fill its first-year class with those who earned perfect high school grade point averages.[3] Yet, the university chooses to admit students who do not have perfect grades but bring other critically important qualities.

An example from the business world further illustrates the dilemmas of defining and then predicting success. When you hear the word "leader," what behaviors do you think of? Many would suggest a powerful person, one who commands respect and dispenses rewards or punishments to subordinates for services rendered. This view of a leader is what Judy Rosener calls "transactional," where the leader's performance is judged by the transactions between the leader and the subordinates.[4] In contrast to this view of leadership is one she calls "transformational." This leader also is powerful, but derives power from being charismatic, having good interpersonal skills, working hard, and motivating subordinates to transform their personal agendas into agendas that will benefit the organization as a whole. The transformational leader tends to reduce the organizational hierarchy by sharing power.

We may not think of a leader as one who readily gives away power; in fact, it is contrary to our view of corporations as exemplars of "survival of the fittest" mentality. But studies show that both types of leadership style can be effective.[5] Although the transformational and transactional styles characterize leaders of both genders, the transformational style is more prevalent among some groups of women. If we continue to define good leadership in the traditional way, we will exclude many women from consideration for posts in which they quite likely would have succeeded. They just would have used a different style of leadership.

Defining what is meant by success is only one part of an affirmative action recruitment plan. We also have to determine what predicts success. Again, let's start with a look at colleges and universities.

First, we need to realize that traditional academic credentials only partly account for success in college. High school grades correlate between .40 and .50 with first-year grades in college; SAT scores correlate between .30 and .35.[6] The measures are even less predictive of success in subsequent years. Thus, while traditional criteria significantly predict college success, the strength of the correlations suggests that other factors are even more predictive.

A study of graduates of Harvard over a thirty-year period complements this viewpoint. "Successful" Harvard graduates, defined as those who earn high incomes, are involved in their community, and report satisfying professional careers, are more likely to have come from blue-collar backgrounds and to have gained admission to Harvard despite SAT scores that are lower than other Harvard graduates.[7] Maybe this type of student is more "hungry" for success.[8]

Michael Charlot, dean of the law school at the University of Texas, also downplays traditional criteria and accepts students with a range of academic credentials. Among those accepted are some minority students with lower grades and test scores than their majority counterparts. But Charlot notes that all admitted applicants are capable of performing well and, like nonminority counterparts, almost all graduate and pass the bar exam.[9]

The key to these examples is that accepted students are *able* to do the necessary work; they have surpassed the threshold of academic competence considered predictive of success in the particular setting. Thus, to those who have set the admissions policy, it does not matter if others, who have been excluded from the organization, would have arrived with higher test scores or grades. They should not be considered "more qualified" for the positions available. This reasoning is consistent with our earlier discussion of the *Griggs* case.

Nothing we have said implies that a "low" threshold must be used. The threshold should be set at a point above which those selected are predicted to succeed in the job or in the school. Setting the threshold too high, however, will not result in higher proportions of people succeeding, but it will prevent many people who would have succeeded from having the opportunity to demonstrate their capability.

The examples above point to the misguided tendency to award extra points in the selection process to people who have more than sufficient skill or experience. A second misguided tendency pertains to using the wrong criteria. Stephen Carter talks about arbitrary barriers to the hiring of African-American law school professors.[10] Law faculties attempt to predict the success of applicants from their law-school grades, membership in the law review, and tenure as a judicial clerk. However, faculties are beginning to doubt whether these measures actually predict scholarly potential, the key criterion for success as a professor. As Carter says, the best way to predict whether someone is capable of performing a particular job is to see how well the person has already performed the job. Yet, most new assistant professors hired by law schools have no scholarly writings. Law faculties thus substitute indirect and questionable evidence for the missing direct evidence.

Similarly questionable criteria are used in other fields.[11] People are rejected from jobs because they reside in the city as opposed to the suburbs and are predicted to bring city problems (e.g., crime) into the work setting. And countless numbers of people are selected or rejected from positions based upon the personality characteristics they manifest during an interview, probably the least reliable and least valid predictor of performance in most settings.

This overview demonstrates how a thoughtful affirmative action program can avoid common pitfalls involved with prerecruitment efforts to define and predict success. Colleges, universities, and all employers committed to affirmative action will ensure that the criteria they use for selection are not arbitrary and that they will not exclude groups of people from consideration who would, given more appropriate criteria, be able to demonstrate their competence for the position.

Recruitment Practices

Once the qualifications for the job are determined, organizations can begin to develop procedures for advertising the position, screening applications, and rendering final decisions. While no single method of proceeding through these steps is to be recommended, some strategies seem to work well.

We often hear people say that they'd "like to hire a black person or a woman, but it's too hard to find them." They may even say, "As soon as a qualified Latina is available, she's scooped up." The shame is that employers often do not know how to look for employees that would bring diversity, or more likely they do not make the effort to look.[12]

In a nationwide survey of over four thousand employers, Braddock and McPartland found that instead of reaching out for a diverse sample, employers often rely upon less time-consuming informal methods of recruitment such as reviewing unsolicited applications or seeking referrals from current employees.[13] The drawback to these methods is that they may exclude minority applicants, since their social networks are likely to be different from the social networks of whites already employed in the organization. Braddock and McPartland's data suggest that employers who rely on informal methods are significantly more likely to hire a white college-educated applicant than an African-American with the same credentials. Furthermore, African-Americans who use "desegregated" social networks to obtain a job are hired at higher pay than those who use networks of people of their own race.

Consider an article from the *New York Times* which recounts failed efforts to integrate blacks into blue-collar union jobs. In poor economic times, not all union employees can work each day, and the predominantly white supervisors tend to call to work the people they know best. In New York blacks often were not called, not because of overt discrimination or prejudice, but merely because "in this union, family and friends come first."[14] As this article makes clear, when the jobs are handed out and people chosen for assignments, it is the person who comes to mind who is given the opportunity.

Some companies deliberately extend their recruitment efforts to minority organizations to avoid this pitfall. For example, Xerox has established formal ties to historically black colleges and universities and reaches out to women's groups and minority organizations, such as the Urban League.[15] Thus, although Xerox also has long encouraged employees to refer friends and relatives for employment, we presume that as the workforce became more diverse, the informal social networks of friends and relatives also became diverse. Thus, what might have been a problem could be turned into an effective affirmative action recruitment tool.

Other corporations use internship programs or other temporary hiring ventures to attract and screen potential employees from underrepresented groups.[16] Exxon has been cited by the Glass Ceiling Taskforce for its internship for women and minority high school students. Professional-level mentors offer engineering work experience, serve as role models, and counsel the students on career choices. Procter and Gamble provides internships to women and minority students to attract them to careers in engineering and science. Their commitment has succeeded, with 40 percent and 25 percent of the new hires in the last decade being women and minority men, respectively. Some companies specifically target people of color for seasonal or summer hiring and then offer regular employment to those who perform well.

Reliance upon formal networks is just as important for promotion processes within the corporation as with entry-level hiring. Braddock and McPartland criticize companies for not posting or circulating notice of promotion possibilities.[17] Companies that promote people following an open search within the company are significantly more likely to promote a minority employee than are companies that go directly to specific employees and encourage them to apply or offer them the job.

Many companies recognize the dangers of closed internal markets and have developed practices to avoid them. One company, SC Johnson Wax, employs an effective job-posting system and encourages managers to consider minorities and women for the jobs. Others consider high-potential employees across the company for promotions, rather than those just in the subdivision in which the opening occurs.[18] This practice prevents employees who have been side-tracked into low-profile positions from being ignored. Given that women and minorities are more likely to be hired into or steered towards low-profile positions,[19] efforts to get them back on track are essential.

Just because a company develops extraordinary methods of recruiting minorities and women for entry-level posts, we cannot assume that they pay the same attention to nurturing their employees and monitoring their career paths. Consequently, we often find companies that recruit from the outside for high-level posts. In contrast, some firms, such as Baxter Healthcare Corporation and 3M, deliberately promote from within, and thus commit themselves to planning for succession of management by developing the potential of their employees.[20]

The researchers Taylor Cox and Carol Smolinski report monumental costs associated with turnover of women and minority employees who leave after being bypassed for promotion in their companies.[21] As Texaco learned, the cost of settling or losing discrimination complaints is also quite high. Thus, corporate practices that develop and reward employees pay off economically.

Selection Practices

We have been talking about strategies for successful recruitment. Strategies for selection among the pool of candidates also affect the success of affirmative action. As we discussed in Chapter 3, it is the rare organization in which neutral decision-making procedures produce diversity. It is easy for stereotypes, personal biases, and favoritism to slip into the decision-making. All too often old habits of thought have hampered the ability to achieve equal employment opportunity. It is ironic, then, that deliberate consideration of group membership also is almost always needed to assure fairness in decision-making. Plus factors or preferential treatment are used in affirmative action programs to help members of different racial, ethnic, or gender groups achieve parity.

Let's discuss how to take group membership into account. First, organizations should assess the extent to which various groups are underrepresented in the institution as a whole or at the level at which the hiring or promotion will occur. Then, a review of candidates is conducted, paying special attention to people from the underrepresented groups, and identifying all people who meet the qualifications needed for the position.

Next, the organization should implement a system for selecting from among the qualified applicants. This practice often takes three different forms. The most commonly stated practice is to hire or promote a candidate from an underrepresented group when this candidate and others are deemed *equally* competent to do the job. This practice may work in situations where equal competence is obvious. For example, if you are hiring a telephone repair person and it is widely known that people with two years of experience and successful completion of several training courses are competent for the job, the applicant from the underrepresented group may get the nod.

For jobs where success depends upon performance across a number of arenas, though, it will be rare to find several applicants who are truly equal in competence. A manager must have the right kinds of experience and training, good social and communication skills, the ability to lead under various conditions, and a variety of other personal characteristics. Since it is difficult to find two people with exactly the same profile, other forms of preferential consideration must be available.

A second form of preferential treatment, which we and others have called the "value-added" or plus-factor system, allows race or gender or other particularistic criteria to have some weight in the selection decision. In this case, "extra points," so to speak, are added to the credentials of the person whose group is underrepresented. The value-added system might entail a quantitative approach to decision-making, wherein, for example, educational background counts for up to ten points, experience counts for ten points, work habits for five, and underrepresentation for another five. The system can also be implemented without explicit regard to numbers, as when a hiring committee decides that, although person X has slightly higher credentials than person Y, person Y brings diversity and thus is chosen. In some cases the "extra points" will suffice to ensure that the underrepresented applicant is selected; in other cases the strength of additional criteria may lead to selecting the majority group member.

In the third system, a more stringent variant of the value-added approach, a threshold again is set for what is considered minimal competence. Then all applicants who surpass the threshold are identified, and the top-ranked person from an underrepresented group is offered the position.

The latter approach may seem to push the limits of preferential treatment and disregard earlier admonitions to proffer measured credit for group membership. But remember that only qualified people are considered eligible for selection. Presumably, all applicants in contention at this point have been screened adequately and are predicted to perform well in the position.

Concern over the procedure should also dissipate when we think about a common occurrence in the selection process: our first- and, sometimes, second-choice candidates turn us down, and we make the offer to the next person on the list. At the time that the list is constructed, we make a judgment that all people on the list would be satisfactory. Why not, then, consider creating a preferential treatment system that avoids rank ordering of legitimate final candidates?

It makes further sense to adopt the approach when we consider the imperfect nature of selection processes. There is never 100 percent correspondence between our predictions about a selected candidate and the candidate's performance. Look around among your own peers. Is it rare to find examples of people predicted to perform superbly who now are performing only adequately? Is it hard to find examples of people who surprisingly have turned out to be good? Can you discern a difference in the performance of people who were the first choice of previous selection committees and those who were second or even third choice?

Finally, think also about the process that might lead us to attach more weight to differences among final candidates for a position than are deserved. Ranking final candidates creates distinctions that might well be exaggerated, especially if the rankings are not unanimous. Labelling someone as the top choice also sets in motion the process of cognitive dissonance, in which we affirm our decision by paying great attention to the advantages of the choice and downplaying perceived drawbacks.[22] This further distances the chosen candidate from others on the list.

Selection processes are not perfect, and we should not pretend that they are. We should not exaggerate our ability to predict how well any given person will perform once chosen. Selection committees are often faced with the consequences of making a "false positive" choice; thus we are aware of this type of error. We should occasionally remind ourselves of the "false negative" errors as well: rejected candidates may have performed superbly, had we given them the chance. We cannot ignore the possibility that personal biases, no matter how hidden or unconscious, affect judgments. When we approach selection decisions with the humility called for by recognition of these human limitations, preferential treatment processes seem not only reasonable, but wise.

Retention: Effectively Managing Diversity

Okay, we have begun to create an organization that is diverse. Now, can we sit back and let nature take its course? No. As Cox and Smolinski articulate well, organizational diversity offers a unique competitive advantage. The varying perspectives brought by a diverse group of people enhance the potential for creative problem-solving and innovation and may also stimulate connections to the myriad peoples of an increasingly interdependent world. But hiring a diverse workforce or admitting a diverse group of students does not in and of itself produce beneficial consequences. In fact, without subsequent attention to the organizational climate that greets the new people, the gains will disappear.[23]

The good news is that through the efforts of many organizations we have learned what works: how we can cope with the changes required on account of diversity, how to nurture new employees and students and ensure their success, and how to retain their loyalty. The bad news, according to the organization Catalyst, is that most organizations do not implement these ideas.[24] Even those with success in providing wider access to initial employment opportunities have not monitored the advancement and retention of the people of color and women that they hire.

A number of reports suggest that, largely due to benign neglect, women and minority group members may advance less rapidly in corporations than white male counterparts.[25] The slower pace may be due to the "informal culture" of the organization or to job assignment, evaluation, and benefit practices that create special hurdles for certain groups of people. These hurdles not only lead to poor advancement, but they translate into lower rates of retention. One company reported turnover rates in the 1980s for women and blacks at least twice the rate for white men.[26] Others, who "manage diversity" successfully, report much better retention.

The same problem exists on many college and university campuses. A task force at the University of Wisconsin found that the "complex, longitudinal challenges of diversifying have been reduced and externalized to the single problem of hiring 'our black' or 'our woman'.... It becomes the newly hired person's duty to find ways of 'getting along'..."[27] It may be even worse for students. One study of black students on white-majority campuses found that they were not as integrated academically (e.g., interacted less favorably with faculty) and experienced more discrimination than their counterparts at majority-black institutions.[28] High academic integration was found to be an important predictor of college grades.

These few examples demonstrate that attention to the post-selection environment rivals in importance attention paid to recruitment. In Cox and Smolinski's words, organizations must effectively "manage diversity" by giving "proactive attention" and by responding "effectively to the challenges posed by diversity in workgroups."[29]

Top-Down Commitment

One component necessary for sustaining initial affirmative action success involves commitment from the top of the organization. In fact, some studies suggest that such commitment may be the most important predictor of success.[30] Social scientists Hitt and Keats presented thirty simulated case studies of affirmative action programs to human resource and affirmative action employees of colleges and universities and asked them to judge the likely effectiveness of each program. Those programs with a "commitment from higher administration" and "receptive" attitudes held by key people in the organization were those rated most apt to succeed.

The recent White House report by Stephanopoulos and Edley touts the success of the Army in promoting qualified minority and women officers, success that is in part attributed to the "top-down priority" given to this program and the resultant clarity about the importance of achieving diversity.[31] Similarly, companies such as the Xerox Corporation and Procter and Gamble ensure that employees understand the institution's commitment.[32]

The CEO or college president cannot accomplish the goal single-handedly. Responsibility and accountability for the success of those newly brought to the company or the campus must be shared, and some companies have developed excellent programs to encourage shared accountability.[33] At IBM, Motorola, and Avon the evaluation of managers includes an assessment of their efforts to improve the representation of women and minorities at all levels of the corporation. Such assessment does not mean the automatic promotion of less-qualified people or the retention of unqualified ones. But it does mean ensuring that training is equitably offered, evaluation is veridical, and the climate is nurturing.

One caveat should be addressed here: to the extent that people perceive they are being forced by upper-level management to conform to affirmative action policies, the affirmative action program may backfire. In an experimental analogue of company hiring procedures, Nacoste and Hummels found that students would hire men and women equitably regardless of pressure to conform to affirmative action guidelines, but sometimes they would assign different salaries.[34] In comparison to other students, those who believed that preferential treatment programs provided more opportunities for women than they lost through discrimination penalized women in assigning salaries.

Given the student population of this experiment, we should be cautious about generalizing to the workplace. However, resistance, the tendency to rebel against imposed rules or procedures, is a frequent phenomenon in the real world. Consequently, the study reminds us that communication about management's commitment to affirmative action must be accompanied by education. When people in the organization know why management is so committed and they understand why affirmative action may benefit them, we would expect less activity to undermine affirmative action gains.

Addressing Stereotypes and Preconceptions

The climate for diversity has improved immensely over the last decades. But subtle and not-so-subtle bias still attenuates the potential of many people.[35] American Indians, Asian-Americans, and Latino/a-Americans are often seen by others as not "assertive" enough for management careers. Asian-Americans are similarly regarded as great for technical work, but not "people-oriented" enough to be leaders. The situation for women, at least Caucasian women, is less clear. Most CEOs believe that women are no longer subject to a "glass ceiling" when promotions are handed out. [36] Yet they still are often stereotyped as not willing to work hard, unable to make decisions, too emotional, and either not aggressive enough or, ironically given complaints about other groups, too aggressive.[37] In fact, more than half of all managers surveyed by one group of researchers believe that negative gender stereotypes still inhibit the advancement of women employees.[38]

Unfortunately, much stereotyping stems from the unmotivated, almost natural disinclination to differentiate individuals from the groups of which they are saliently a part. People of color and women often suffer from what Tom Pettigrew and Joanne Martin call "triple jeopardy": they are subject to racial or gender stereotyping, they are presumed to be less competent because of misconceptions about the organization's affirmative action program, and they are often "solos."[39] Solo status refers to the fact that in nondiverse organizations people of color and women are often isolated, one of only a few representatives of their demographic group.[40] Solos tend to be more salient, noticed more, and judged more extremely than their non-solo counterparts. Sometimes the judgments are more negative, but sometimes they are more positive, which can be just as harmful eventually because the exaggerated expectations are difficult to sustain.

What can be done about this problem? First, one of the keys to reducing dependence on stereotypical thinking is to provide enough individuating information to counter reliance upon stereotypes as the basis for judgment. When new people are brought into the organization, supervisors should ensure that information about their competence and experience is distributed widely. This information increases the chance that others will see the person as an individual, not as just a member of some socio-demographic group. The information also reminds others of the organization's commitment to hiring only qualified people and refutes the notion that the new person is a token appointment.

A second way to counteract the pressures of solo status and stereotyping is to provide extensive and meaningful opportunities for interdependent work assignments. Social psychologists have long known that contact itself between members of different social or ethnic groups does not obviate dependence upon stereotyping.[41] Consider the following illustrative anecdote. A man, hired as a professor, spoke of being identified first and always as a black person:

> I was educated in Europe, and I have traveled extensively in Europe and Russia, but when there's a conversation about Central Europe, at the lunch table or whatever, they never ask my opinion, but they never stop asking me about Jesse Jackson.[42]

For contact to be beneficial it must be extensive, cooperative, and based upon mutual contributions. For example, when students work on a joint research project over a number of weeks, they learn to think of each other as individuals, bringing strengths and weaknesses to the task. As long as all group members are qualified for work on the assignment, chances are that each will contribute a perspective, an idea, a solution, and members will begin to think of each other as a group rather than as representatives from diverse social, ethnic, gender, or racial groupings. We would expect then that the cognitive biases that work so often to divide one social group from another will dissipate.

Furthermore, positive relations engendered by close working relationships may spur more positive beliefs about other people in one's groupmates' social category.[43] In other words, if men work with women on an intense job assignment, they may begin not only to appreciate their women coworkers more and rely less on stereotypes when evaluating or predicting their behavior, but they may do similarly when they encounter other women in the organization.[44]

With the goal of promoting a healthy workplace, companies often establish deliberately diverse groups to work on a common goal or function important to the organization. In a variant of this technique, Dow Jones &

Company uses "mentoring quads" that promote interaction among people who differ in position and function within the company, as well as in race and gender.[45] The quads, composed of three mentors who work with one "protégé," meet twice a month for six months. Quads are explicitly designed to enhance promotional opportunities for women and people of color. Not only do quad members form more extensive and diverse networks as a result of this activity, but they develop familiarity and comfort with members of other social groups.

A final tactic is to confront stereotypes directly. The Bank of Montreal found that 75 percent of its employees in 1991 were women, but constituted only 9 percent of executives and 13 percent of senior managers.[46] When a task force set out to understand the discrepancy, they found preconceptions that interfered with women's advancement. Women were believed to be either too old or too young to compete with men for promotions, less committed to their careers because of motherhood demands, and not as well educated as men. The task force then analyzed employee personnel records, finding that none of the preconceptions was accurate. On all important characteristics, such as education, job performance, and dedication, women employees equaled or surpassed the men. The task force then sent a report to all employees refuting the preconceptions, thus encouraging the company to rethink the bases upon which judgments were made about competence for higher positions.

One company, GE, has adopted a "360-degree feedback" system of evaluation to ensure that employees at all levels understand how they are perceived by peers, supervisors, and people in lower-level positions in the organization.[47] This technique was designed as a tool to thwart biased judgments based on stereotypes or misunderstandings derived from interacting with people from differing cultural and gender backgrounds.

People can make judgments without relying upon stereotypes, but they must be motivated to do so. Motivation can spring from many sources: a desire to conform to the boss's wishes, one's own moral commitment to diversity, or knowledge that one's professional success depends on an ability to promote the careers of others. Organizations must find ways consistent with their structure and mission to create a healthy climate for all people, and motivating people to discard stereotypical thinking is one necessary component of this process.

Career Tracking

People of color and women often get on a career track that takes them away from the high-profile positions that most readily lead to advancement.[48] One study found that African-Americans in predominantly white organizations tend to be clustered in a few departments (e.g., human resources), and these departments produce few corporate officers, as opposed to departments related to finance or marketing.[49]

Some firms actively attempt to avoid career-tracking by rotating employees through career-enhancing assignments. Xerox, for example, sends high-potential managers overseas. Of the eighty managers on this assignment during the writing of the 1995 Federal Glass Ceiling Report, thirteen were women and twenty-three were minority group members.[50]

Other firms look across the organization when an assignment is made, trying to identify all people who are eligible for a job. This enlarges the pool of candidates, some of whom might be overlooked if less inclusive means of establishing a pool are used.

Mentoring

More than just tracking the progress of women and people of color, some organizations, such as Dow Jones & Co., have formal mentoring programs. Mentoring is believed by corporate insiders and experts in education to be one of the most important contributors to the success of people in the corporation and on the campus.[51] Mentoring helps the mentor as well as the one mentored. At IBM, for example, mentoring programs provide those giving counsel with opportunities to learn how to coach others—a particularly valuable training tool when the others come from different racial, ethnic, or gender groups.[52] For the new members of the organization, mentoring provides "penalty free" counsel, education about the organization's goals and norms, advice about performance and steps to success, and connections to experienced and respected leaders.

Mentoring also may serve the purpose of motivating people and enlarging their aspirations. One of us had quite a shock a few years ago when she asked an extraordinarily talented senior, someone with whom the author had worked for a year, whether she planned to attend graduate school. The woman said that she had not thought about it—no one had ever suggested she might be capable of obtaining a graduate degree. I was shocked to discover, first, that at no time before now, despite our close working relationship, did I make explicit my positive assessment of the student, and second, that such explicit communication was actually needed to evoke the student's exploration of her career potential. This encounter taught me to seek out and encourage high-ability students in their early years of college, to inform them about my evaluation, and to encourage them to consider wider options for career choices than they had previously.

Evidence is slim and tends to be anecdotal on the salutary benefits of role models and mentors with similar characteristics.[53] Despite the fact that women rate having a same-sex role model as more important and perhaps more satisfying than men do, opposite-sex role models can produce just as much gain in confidence and motivation as same-sex models.[54] Speizer's review in the early 80s noted this to be true in employment and college arenas, as well as in the home. Successful women, for example, may just as often cite their working fathers as role models as their working mothers. The point is that mentors may add much to a person's development, but it is probably through their professional qualities and connections, not demographic characteristics.

Critical Mass

Managing diversity, as you can see, refers to much more than just hiring a diverse workforce or bringing a diverse group of people onto a campus. It signifies more than just the desire to get a few Asian-Americans, Latinas, and handicapped people for the organization; it signifies commitment to change at the institutional level.

As the organization becomes more diverse, the change becomes easier and more self-perpetuating. Pettigrew and Martin suggest that organizations should aim for no less than 20 percent representation of members of each underrepresented group.[55] The 20 percent "critical mass" would mean that the majority would encounter and perhaps get to know underrepresented group members across a range of settings and would, accordingly, begin to see them as people with varying interests and talents. They also would be a force to be reckoned with. Presumably the institution would respond to and incorporate the minority's perspectives just as it had built the institution in response to the perspectives of the majority. Thus, instead of the minority always acceding to the norms and values of the institution, in truly diverse organizations, the institution shifts norms and values in response to the new members.

In some organizations women have effectively used their increased numbers to lobby for changes in practices that formerly disadvantaged them.[56] Sustained change is likely to be more difficult for less numerically prominent groups. While women have the numbers to achieve a critical mass, Latinos, African-Americans, and other groups will be more disadvantaged. This is especially true when we consider the special problems of subgroups of the larger demographic grouping. African-American men, for example, may suffer more harm from stereotyped images than African-American women.[57] In turn, the latter may need to combat more difficulties than their white counterparts.

Sometimes the amount of diversity in an organization is characterized as the proportion of people who are *not* nonwhite males. Thus, we may call an organization "diverse" if 60 percent of the organization is composed of white males, 20 percent of white females, and the remainder of much smaller percentages of people from other ethnic and gender groups. This thinking is fallacious. As noted above, each gender and ethnic group elicits different perceptions and reactions from colleagues. Furthermore, members of different groups, albeit all "minorities" relative to the white males within the organization, would be unlikely to see themselves as a homogeneous group. In fact, members of one minority group often adopt the same stereotypes as the majority about members of a different minority group.[58]

Therefore, a more accurate assessment of the organizational climate with respect to diversity will be derived from calculating the proportion of each recognizable underrepresented group. So, when Pettigrew and Martin suggest using 20 percent as the base for a critical mass, we can understand why organizations may not be fully successful in efforts to manage diversity.[59] Furthermore, even if organizations achieve a critical mass with respect to most ethnic and gender groupings, a highly compartmentalized structure will diminish the beneficial effects. Women or blacks or whoever is in the underrepresented group still may be a "solo" in their section of the organization. With a student body of 20 percent African-American, rarely a reality in majority-white schools, most African-American students may still be the sole member of their group in most classes. Furthermore, as members of underrepresented groups succeed and move up in the hierarchy of an organization, they often will become solos in their new positions, even though they were not isolated in their old ones. Organizations must be alert for times when isolation and its debilitating consequences may emerge.

Concern over isolation has led some people to examine the benefits of clustering, grouping the new people in certain sections rather than dispersing them throughout the organization. This has drawbacks too, and we do not recommend it. First, when people from some groups are already underrepresented, it is a shame to hire or admit only those with the experience or interest relevant to a subset of possible positions. Second, as has happened on some college campuses, clustering may only increase stereotypes about the group. Because it is relatively easy to hire Asian-Americans for positions in mathematics or engineering, clusters of Asian-Americans there may reinforce others' beliefs that all Asians are mathematically gifted but lack the verbal skills to succeed in other disciplines. Reliance upon hiring women in psychology and sociology promotes the stereotype that women are primarily interested in helping careers.

Reflections

Of course, true diversity is not a panacea for all ills. Greater prominence of some groups in the organization may bring problems to solve, as it becomes obvious to majority group members that resources and rewards will need to be shared and that the institution is changing.[60] Concerns over the changes are especially likely at first as people are getting to know their new colleagues and adjusting to the new organizational environment.

People who work or study in settings that are becoming more diverse should be informed that the benefits may not be forthcoming immediately. Heterogeneous groups tend to experience more process problems than homogeneous groups, especially when group membership varies along racial or nationality lines.[61] One test of this phenomenon was conducted by researchers Watson, Kumar, and Michaelsen.[62] They put together working groups of upper-level students in several sections of a management course. The groups analyzed case studies of business problems and generated lists of solutions for the problems and justifications for their recommendations. The working group membership was either all-white or culturally diverse (i.e., varying in nationality and racial-ethnic background). After five weeks culturally diverse groups attained worse scores on measures of both group process and problem solving than the homogeneous groups did. By seventeen weeks, however, the diverse groups generated better solutions to problems than the homogeneous ones, and the groups equaled each other on process dimensions. Studies such as this one provide support for the notion that, over time, cultural diversity may bring benefits not possible in homogeneous settings, but that the benefits may take time to be realized.

We did not begin this book asserting that affirmative action would be easy. In fact, we admit that the tasks involved in successful affirmative action are hard. Affirmative action means effort, much more effort than it takes simply to find people to fill positions. But the rewards, as we discuss in the next chapter, are many.

Chapter 7

The Promise of Affirmative Action

G reater than the challenges posed by affirmative action are the rewards it brings to individual organizations and to the nation as a whole. Some of the rewards are immediate and self-evident. Some emerge over time, often in surprising ways.

Organizational Benefits

The American workforce increasingly consists of people who are not white men.[1] Women currently represent 58 percent of the civilian workforce and are expected to comprise two-thirds of the workforce by the year 2000. Today African-Americans and Latin-Americans constitute 14 percent and 10 percent respectively, and these numbers are projected to rise to 16 percent and 14 percent by the turn of the century.

Companies that continue to select, retain, and promote only white males limit their possibilities for employing the best talent. When the monitoring process of classical affirmative action shows discrepancies between available talent and the utilization of that talent, we know that their workforce is less competitive than it might be. When a company adopts affirmative action goals and procedures, not only do previously excluded workers gain from having access to jobs; the organization gains from finding ways to have access to fresh talent.

Homogeneous organizations can unnecessarily curtail access to new markets. In contrast, attention to diversity can increase sales. The labor department's Glass Ceiling Commission Report tells of a Miami auto dealership that hired bilingual salespeople and held special events of interest to Hispanic clientele. Over a six-year period, the dealership increased sales by 400 percent and captured 50 percent of the Hispanic market.[2] Similar results were obtained by a California dealership where special training in Asian-American cultural patterns led to a five-fold increase in overall sales per month.[3]

Increased access to talented employees and expanded market access are only some of the benefits of diversity. As we have discussed before, enhanced creativity has also been documented in multicultural work groups, especially in groups that work together over a long period of time.[4] Finally, empirical research elucidates the connection between a company's financial success and diversity brought about by affirmative action. As Taylor Cox and Carol Smolinski reported to the Glass Ceiling Commission:

> Most of the research indicates that there is a strong positive correlation between performance on social responsibility goals (including equal opportunity) and performance on financial measures such as profits and market share. Research also indicates that investment funds which target companies with strong reputations on social responsibility goals have returns on investments which are among the highest in the world.[5]

Recognition of the benefits of affirmative action, especially in its classical form, is high among the business community. According to Nancy Krieter, director of research for Women Employed in Chicago, Illinois, the fiercest opposition to President George Bush's attempted assassination of affirmative action came from big business.[6] A recent survey of CEOs revealed that 94 percent believed that affirmative action improved their hiring and selection procedures, 41 percent attribute improved productivity to affirmative action, and 53 percent attribute improved marketing to their affirmative action program. While the majority of CEOs view some governmental requirements as unnecessary, over 70 percent plan to continue to track their progress on equal employment even if the government eliminates all affirmative action requirements.[7]

Are White Men Bearing the Costs?

One of the biggest hurdles to promoting affirmative action is the belief that the advances of white women and of people of color and the increased profitability of companies have all been paid for by white men. Glynn Custred and Thomas Wood, two self-proclaimed angry white men, have certainly advanced this view, and with vigor.[8]

How justified is this view? Not at all, in our opinion. Indeed, we maintain that affirmative action is a policy that benefits meritorious white men as completely as it benefits others.

Consider first of all men who seek jobs that are stereotypically given to women. The columnist Ellen Goodman wrote about the debilitating stereotypes that afflict men who seek jobs as day-care providers, even in this age when we expect them to be sensitive and caring fathers.[9]

Also imagine a white male native English speaker from Kansas applying for a professorship in a department of Spanish where men are the minority and native speakers of Spanish predominate.[10] If you sympathize with women who file suit against restaurants for discriminating against them because wealthy clients prefer the butler image, you must also sympathize with men who claim to have a hard time getting hired or promoted at a leading diet company ostensibly for difficulty relating to overweight women.[11]

None of the arguments we have made about affirmative action and none of the procedures we advocate exclude applicability to white men. We state loud and clear: affirmative action is for all people.

Let us also consider how men have benefitted from the changed norms about family-friendly policies. In keeping with the notion that managing diversity requires attention to the needs of all employees, you should learn about Eastman Kodak.[12] Their generous family leave policy is used by a large number of men, who take an average of twelve weeks of leave, compared to the thirteen weeks taken by women. A program probably initiated to benefit the burgeoning group of female employees worked to the benefit of all.

Sometimes the benefits to men, while quite pronounced, have been entirely unexpected. A couple of anecdotes, derived from our personal experiences, illustrate how affirmative action policies can have positive but serendipitous results for men.

The first anecdote concerns an exchange that took place five or six years ago. One of us had delivered a lecture on affirmative action. After the lecture, a pleasant-looking man approached the podium to recount something that had happened in the business he owned. At first it seemed that the man was going to present a brief against affirmative action. He said that a few years earlier his female employees had agitated for some changes. Some of the women wished to work in the warehouse, because wages there were higher than in the secretarial pool. The man had grudgingly allowed the women to try out the heavy work of lifting and transferring materials from the warehouse to trucks. Sure enough, within weeks the women were admitting that they did not like the heavy work and they were having a hard time keeping up with the men.

It was then that the women asked the businessman to invest in a forklift. Within six months the forklift had more than paid for itself, he said, because the men in the warehouse had fewer back problems, fewer days absent from work, and lower hospital bills for the company. To be sure, the business owner might have thought of getting a forklift all on his own; but it was the injection of new employees—and females ones at that— that led him to streamline his business.

A similar story was told to us in 1991 by the commandant of West Point. When West Point first went co-ed, with the famous Athena Project, the women cadets were treated essentially the same as the men cadets. By the end of their freshmen year, many of the women had put on a great deal of weight and the extra weight threatened to interfere with their ability to pass the second-year physical exam. A nutritionist was called in. When the nutritionist learned the diet of the cadets, she immediately perceived the problem. Simple changes were made so that the diet did not deposit fat on the women, and future classes of female cadets kept as slim and trim as they were on entry.

The most remarkable part of the story, said the commandant, was that the women were not the main beneficiaries of the action. In the opinion of the nutritionist, the traditional West Point diet had been dangerous to men. It was a poor-risk diet for coronary health. The changes might have immediate and visible benefits for the women, but for the men even greater benefits were to be expected in long-term health gains.

Anecdotes such as these illustrate a general principle. What may appear today to be a concession can prove to be in the best interest of the company and of all the talented white men in it. Some situations are indeed of the win-win variety.

The principle is not lost on all white men in the paid labor force. While the protests and the wimperings of some white men have garnered media attention, most white men do not appear to be suffering. If white men were bearing the brunt of affirmative action, we would expect a high percentage of their cases to reach the courts or the Equal Employment Opportunity Commission and to prevail. Yet, as we stated in Chapter 4, this is just not happening.[13]

Our Nation

What is true for individual organizations is also true for the nation. As Republicans were fond of saying in the Eisenhower years: "What is good for business is good for the country." When we exert efforts to assure ourselves that what appears to be equitable is in fact equitable, America reaps long-term as well as immediate gains.[14] To the extent that affirmative action arrests the trend toward bifurcated wealth in our nation, it contributes to economic and social stability.[15] Like Edmund Burke, we think that slow, steady, evolutionary change is far superior to revolutionary upheavals.

Affirmative action can help stabilize the country, even as it energizes the economy. During the 1963 March on Washington, A. Philip Randolph spoke of "social peace through social justice." Affirmative action is fair, both for groups of citizens and for individual citizens. Because it is fair, its continuation can contribute to the long-term harmonious functioning of our nation.

To emphasize the fairness of the policy is not to say that all organizations match in practice what is articulated in principle. When organizations fall short of putting fairness into play, adjustments need to be made. But these adjustments need not alter the basic and fundamental policy which we call classical affirmative action. On the contrary, adjustments are simply part of the process. This is why, as we've noted previously, we agree with President Clinton: when it comes to affirmative action, "mend it, don't end it."[16]

Notes

Chapter 1: The Issues

1. The popular media reports certainly show this diversity. For examples, see: "Action Still Needed" (June 2, 1995); Alter, "Affirmative Ambivalence"; Cohn, Morganthau, Smith, and Annin, "Battleground Chicago"; Cohn, Turque, and Brant, "What About Women?"; Cose, "The Myth of Meritocracy"; Fineman, "Race and Rage"; Kahlenberg, "Equal Opportunity Critics"; Klein, "Affirmative Inaction?"; Reed, Jr., "Assault on Affirmative Action"; Rosen, "The Color-Blind Court"; Thomas and Cohn, "Rethinking the Dream"; Wycliff, "Affirmative on Affirmative Action."

2. Moore, "Americans Today Are Dubious." See also Sniderman and Piazza, *The Scar of Race,* for an excellent discussion of Americans' changing opinions about many issues pertinent to race and social policy.

3. Moore, "Americans Today Are Dubious."

4. CNN/USA Today/Gallup Poll, Wave 2.

5. Crosby and Hinkle, "Goals, Quotas"; Kravitz and Platania, "Attitudes and Beliefs."

6. Clinton, "Remarks at the National Archives," p. 1256.

7. Winkelman and Crosby, "Setting the Record Straight." According to CNN/USA Today/ Gallup Poll, Wave 2: 67 percent of black respondents and 60 percent of white respondents endorsed the view that "it is good in principle but needs to be reformed," while only 11 percent of black respondents and 24 percent of white respondents endorsed the view that "it's fundamentally flawed and needs to be eliminated."

8. Crosby and Cordova, "Words Worth of Wisdom."

9. Kravitz and Platania,"Attitudes and Beliefs"; Goldsmith, Cordova, Dwyer, Langolis, and Crosby, "Reactions to Affirmative Action."

Chapter 2: Defining Affirmative Action

1. Murrell, Dietz-Uhler, Dovidio, Gaertner, Drout, "Aversive Racism"; Turner and Pratkanis, "Affirmative Action as Help"; Turner and Pratkanis, "Affirmative Action: Insights"; de Vries and Pettigrew, "A Comparative Perspective."

2. U.S. Department of Labor, *Program Highlights*, "Fact Sheet, No. ESA 1995-17."

3. Clayton and Crosby, *Justice, Gender*, Chapter 2.

4. The Executive Order 11246 did not originally include gender. Gender was added later. In 1973, Section 503 of the Rehabilitation Act extended affirmative action to qualified individuals with disabilities. The Vietnam Era Veteran's Readjustment Assistance Act of 1974 extended protection to certain classes of veterans.

5. "Disparate treatment" refers to intentional acts of discrimination; "disparate impact" means that some are adversely affected by what appears to be a neutral policy. Intent to discriminate need not be present for disparate impact to exist.

6. Clinton, "Remarks at the National Archives," p. 1259.

7. Robertson, "ORC Survey."

8. Zimbardo and Leippe, *The Psychology of Attitude Change.*

9. Clinton, "Remarks at the National Archives," p. 1265.

10. U.S. Bureau of Census, *Statistical Abstract.*

11. Heller, "Defining Affirmative Action."

12. Crosby, "Understanding Affirmative Action."

13. Murray, "Affirmative Racism," p. 206.

14. Newman,"Affirmative Action and the Courts," p. 89.

15. Ibid., p. 35.

16. Schlei and Grossman, *Employment Discrimination Law.*

17. U.S. Department of Labor, *Program Highlights*, "Fact Sheet No. ESA 1995-17," p. 1.

18. Heilman, "Unintended Consequences."

19. Crosby and Hinkle, "Goals, Quotas."

20. Steele, "The Content of Our Character," p. 118.

21. Watters, "Claude Steele."

22. Bunzel, "The California Civil Rights Initiative."

23. Congressional Record, Senate, "Proceedings and Debates," p. 1.

24. Ibid., p. 1.

25. Ibid., p. 2.

26. Ibid., p. 2.

27. Dale, *Compilation and Overview.*

28. Ibid.

29. Stephanopoulos and Edley, "Affirmative Action Review."

30. Katz Pinzler, "A Report on Presidential Reforms."

Chapter 3: Underlying Issue of Need

1. Murray, "Affirmative Racism."

2. Moore. "Americans Today Are Dubious."

3. Leo, "Our Addiction."

4. Johnson, Jr., Bienenstock, and Stoloff, "An Empirical Test." See also Johnson and Farrell, "Race Still Matters."

5. Neumark, Bank, and Van Nort, *Sex Discrimination*; Turner, Fix, and Stuyk, *Opportunities Denied.*

6. Stephanopoulos and Edley, "Affirmative Action Review," p. 21.

7. Ibid.

8. Dovidio, Mann, and Gaertner, "Resistance to Affirmative Action."

9. Cannings, "Managerial Promotion"; Olson and Becker, "Sex Discrimination."

10. Olson and Becker, "Sex Discrimination."

11. Greenhaus, Parasuraman, and Wormely, "Effects of Race."

12. Reich, *Good for Business*, pp. 121–122.

13. Bem, *The Lenses of Gender.*

14. Equal Employment Opportunity Commission, "Reverse Discrimination," and "Types of Reverse Discrimination."

15. Montwieler, "No Widespread Abuse."

16. Goldberg, "Are Women Prejudiced," pp. 28–30.

17. Swim, Borgida, Maruyama, and Myers, "McKay vs. McKay."

18. Crosby, *Relative Deprivation.*

19. Olson and Hafer, "Affect, Motivation."

20. Branscombe, "Defensive Denial." See also Alloy and Abramson, "Sadder but Wiser."

21. Nisbett and Ross, *Human Inference;* Nisbett and Ross, *The Person.*

22. Cordova, "Cognitive Limitations"; Crosby, Clayton, Hemker, and Alksnis, "Cognitive Biases"; Twiss, Tabb, and Crosby, "Aggregate Data."

23. When the contrasts involve flagrant breach, such as A has better qualifications, but B is paid more money, we can perceive unfairnesses in the single comparison. But perceptions become inaccurate when the contrast involves judgments of magnitude, such as when A has much better qualifications but is paid only slightly better than B. See Rutte, Diekmann, Polzer, Crosby, and Messick,"Organizing Information."

24. Clinton,"Remarks at the National Archives," p. 1263.

Chapter 4: Fairness and Affirmative Action

1. Homans, *Social Behavior.*

2. Deutsch, *Distributive Justice.*

3. Newkirk, "Expert," p. C1: 2–5.

4. Tajfel, *Human Groups.*

5. See Clayton and Crosby, *Justice, Gender.*

6. Fish, "Reverse Racism," p. 130. Essentially the same argument for the fairness of turn taking in a somewhat different guise is made by economist Barbara Bergmann and social psychologist Robyn Dawes. Bergmann and Dawes have been known to clash on a number of other points. For Dawes's point of view, see: Dawes, "Affirmative Action Programs." For Bergmann's point of view, see Bergmann, *Affirmative Action.*

7. Newman, "The Courts."

8. Glazer, *Affirmative Discrimination*, p. 195.

9. D'Souza, *Illiberal Education*, p. 242.

10. Edley, "Beyond the Rhetoric."

11. Hart, *The Concept of Law.*

12. Blumrosen, *Modern Law.*

13. Cited from *Regents of the University of California v. Bakke* (1978).

14. Adams, "Inequity."

15. Johnston, "FBI Hitting Snag," p. A18.

16. Dellinger, "Memorandum."

17. Ibid.

18. *In Re: Birmingham* Reverse Discrimination Litigation, 64 FEP Cases 1032 (11 Cir. 1994). See also the draft of a report on reverse discrimination commissioned by the U.S. Labor Department, published on March 23, 1995 issue of the *Daily Labor Record* (No. 56).

19. Holmes, "New Strict Tests."

20. *Adarand Constructors, Inc. v. Pena* (June 12, 1995), at 4543.

21. Rawls, *A Theory of Justice.*

22. Crosby, "Understanding Affirmative Action."

23. Crosby, "A Rose."

24. Owen, *None of the Above*; Rosser, *The SAT Gender Gap.*

25. Reich, *Good Business.*

26. Stephanopoulos and Edley, "Affirmative Action Review."

27. Montwieler, "No 'Widespread Abuse.' " For an interesting survey, see Hanson Frieze, Olson, and Cain Good, "Perceived and Actual Discrimination."

28. Equal Employment Opportunity Commission, "Reverse Discrimination."

Chapter 5: The Benefits of Affirmative Action

1. Stephanopoulus and Edley, "Affirmative Action Review."

2. U.S. Department of Labor, *Program Highlights.*

3. Montwieler, "No 'Widespread Abuse.'" See also Blumrosen, *Modern Law.*

4. Leonard, "The Impact of Affirmative Action;." Ashenfelter and Heckman, "Measuring the Effect;" Heckman and Wolpin, "Chicago Data."

5. Donohue and Heckman, "Continuous versus Episodic Change."

6. Stephanopoulus and Edley, "Affirmative Action Review," p. 16.

7. Ibid., p. 17.

8. Wilkerson, "Discordant Notes," p. 30.

9. Carter, *Reflections.*

10. Heilman, Lucas, and Kaplow, "Self-Derogating Consequences"; Heilman, Simon, and Repper, "Intentionally Favored?"

11. Nacoste, "Self-Evaluations," "Sources of Stigma," "Decision Makers."

12. Staples, "The Presumption of Stupidity," p. 14.

13. *Gallup Monthly* (1995, July), p. 10.

14. Taylor, "Beneficiary Groups."

15. Hochschild, "The Rumor of Black Inferiority."
16. Begley, "Henry Louis Gates Jr.," p. 50.
17. Heilman, Simon, and Repper, "Intentionally Favored?"
18. Nacoste "Decision Makers," "The Truth About Affirmative Action."
19. Garcia, Erskine, Hawn, and Casmay, "Minority Group Members."
20. Nacoste, "The Truth About Affirmative Action."
21. Heilman, Block, and Lucas, "Presumed Incompetent?" Interestingly, other research shows that white males devalue female managers whether or not the firm is said to be an affirmative action firm. See Summers, "The Influence of Affirmative Action."
22. Staples, "The Presumption of Stupidity," p. 14.
23. Clayton and Crosby, *Justice, Gender.*

Chapter 6: Making Affirmative Action Work

1. Retirement issues may become more and more salient, as those covered by affirmative action policies reach the age of sixty-five and as companies devise programs to encourage early retirement among younger employees. Virtually no one has yet devised good guidelines for affirmative action with respect to retirement.
2. *Trinity College Bulletin* (1995), p. 9.
3. Applebome,"Gains in Diversity," pp. 1, 22.
4. Rosener, "Ways Women Lead."
5. Landy and Trumbo, *Psychology of Work Behavior;* Rosener, "Ways Women Lead."
6. Murphy and Davidshofer, *Psychological Testing Principles.*
7. Shipler, "My Equal Opportinity," pp. 4-1, 4–16.
8. Christopher Small, Trinity College's vice president for enrollment management, communicated a similar message to us when he talked about admitting students of color whose academic records did not equal those of some white students. He stated that admissions officers would benefit from being able to spot students with "fight" in them. When combined with a motivating setting, this quality may predict perseverance and ultimate success more than the high school record.
9. Bernstein, "Racial Discrimination," p. B8.
10. Carter, "The Best Black."
11. Kirschenman and Neckerman, "We'd Love to Hire Them"; Wilson, "The New Urban Poverty"; Murphy and Davidshofer, *Psychological Testing Principles.*
12. Morrison, *The New Leaders.*
13. Braddock and McPartland, "How Minorities Continue To Be Excluded."
14. Uchitelle, "Union Goal," p.18.
15. Reich, *Good for Business.*
16. Morrison, *The New Leaders;* Reich, *Good for Business.*
17. Braddock and McPartland, "How Minorities Continue To Be Excluded."
18. Catalyst, *Cracking the Glass Ceiling.*
19. Collins, "Black Executives"; Reich, *Good for Business.*
20. Cox and Smolinski, *Managing Diversity;* Reich, *Good for Business.*

21. Cox and Smolinski, *Managing Diversity.*

22. Frey, "Recent Research"; Knox and Inkster, *Postdecision Dissonance.*

23. Cox and Smolinski, *Managing Diversity.*

24. Catalyst, *Cracking the Glass Ceiling.*

25. Ibid.; Woody, *Corporate Policy.*

26. Cox and Smolinski, *Managing Diversity.*

27. Spann, *Retaining and Promoting Women and Minority Faculty Members: Problems and Possibilities,* p. 7.

28. Nettles, "Black and White Students."

29. Cox and Smolinski, *Managing Diversity,* p. 6.

30. Hanna, "The Organizational Context"; Hitt and Keats, "Empirical Identification."

31. Stephanopoulos and Edley, "Affirmative Action Review."

32. Reich, *Good for Business.*

33. Ibid.

34. Nacoste and Hummels, "Decision Makers."

35. Morrison, *The New Leaders;* Reich, *Good for Business.*

36. Reich, *Good for Business.*

37. Catalyst, *Cracking the Glass Ceiling;* Morrison, *The New Leaders.*

38. Rosen, Miguel, and Pierce, "Stemming the Exodus."

39. Pettigrew and Martin, "Shaping the Organizational Context."

40. Kanter, "Some Effects of Proportions."

41. Hewstone and Brown, "Contact Is Not Enough."

42. Spann, *Retaining and Promoting Women and Minority Faculty Members: Problems and Possibilities,* p. 3.

43. Cook, "Cooperative Interaction."

44. Morrison and Von Glinow, "Women and Minorities."

45. Catalyst, *Cracking the Glass Ceiling.*

46. Ibid.

47. Parks, personal communication.

48. Buono and Kamm, "Marginality"; Collins, "Black Executives"; Morrison and Von Glinow, "Women and Minorities"; Reich, *Good for Business.*

49. Collins, "Black Executives."

50. Reich, *Good for Business.*

51. Cox and Smolinski, *Managing Diversity;* Morrison and Von Glinow, "Women and Minorities."

52. Reich, *Good for Business.*

53. Morrison, *The New Leaders;* Speizer, "Role Models."

54. Gilbert, "Dimensions"; Speizer, "Role Models"; Stake and Noonan, "The Influence of Teacher Models."

55. Pettigrew and Martin, "Shaping the Organizational Context."

56. Reich, *Good for Business.*

57. Johnson, Jr., Bienenstock, and Stoloff, "An Empirical Test"; Reich, *Good for Business.*

58. Bobo, Zubrinsky, Johnson, and Oliver, "Work Orientation"; Kirschenman and Neckerman, "We'd Love to Hire Them."

59. Pettigrew and Martin, "Shaping the Organizational Context."

60. South, Bonjean, Markham, and Corder, "Social Structure"; Wharton and Baron, "So Happy Together?"

61. Adler, *International Dimensions.*

62. Watson, Kumar, and Michaelsen, "Cultural Diversity's Impact."

Chapter 7: The Promise of Affirmative Action

1. U. S. Bureau of the Census, *Statistical Abstract.*

2. Reich, *Good for Business.*

3. Cox and Smolinski, *Managing Diversity.*

4. Watson, Kumar, and Michaelsen, "Cultural Diversity's Impact."

5. Cox and Smolinski, *Managing Diversity*, p. 34.

6. Kreiter, personal communication.

7. Robertson, "ORC Survey."

8. Bunzel, "The California Civil Rights Initiative."

9. Goodman, "Male Caregivers," p. B11.

10. Thurgood and Weinman, *Summary Report.*

11. Carton, "Muscled Out?," pp. A1, A11; but see also LaBonte, "Jenny Craig"; Richardson, "Caterer Favors a Butler Look," pp. B1, B3; Stephanopoulus and Edley, "Affirmative Action Review."

12. Reich, *Good for Business.*

13. Equal Employment Opportunity Commission, "Reverse Discrimination" and "Types of Reverse Discrimination"; Montwieler, "No 'Widespread Abuse.' "

14. Chemers, Oskamp, and Costanzo, *Diversity in Organizations*; Kirby, "Where Have We Been?"

15. William Julius Wilson, the noted African-American scholar, opposes affirmative action because it drives a wedge between middle-class and poor blacks. See Wilson, "The New Urban Poverty." He reasons that affirmative action helps only African-Americans in the paid labor force, and perhaps the benefits are actually limited to those who are well educated and already capable of securing good employment. Those helped, he asserts, tend to move out of the inner city as they gain economic prowess, leaving the cities a worse place for poor, under-educated blacks. While Wilson's argument is conceptually plausible, hard numbers refute it. Statistical analysis of census data show that the bifurcation of wealth among black citizens has been no less and *no greater* than among white citizens during the period since 1965 (see Crosby, Allen, and Opotow, "Changing Patterns"). Furthermore, we believe that, while affirmative action cannot cure all social ills, it can be used synergistically with other social programs, such as the economic development programs touted by Wilson "The New Urban Poverty," to benefit minority populations.

16. Clinton, "Remarks at the National Archives," p. 1263.

References

"Action Still Needed." *Commonweal*. 1995, June 2.

Adams, John S. "Inequity in Social Exchange." In L. Berkowitz, ed. *Advances in Experimental Social Psychology*, Vol. 2. New York: Academic Press, 1965.

Adler, Nancy J. *International Dimensions of Organizational Behavior*. 2nd ed. Belmont, CA: Wadsworth, 1991.

Alloy, Lauren B., and Lynn Y. Abramson. "Judgment of Contingency in Depressed and Nondepressed Students: Sadder but Wiser?" *Journal of Experimental Psychology: General*, vol. 108 (1979): pp. 441–485.

Alter, Jonathan. "Affirmative Ambivalence." *Newsweek* (March 27, 1995): p. 26.

Applebome, Peter. "Gains in Diversity Face Attack in California." *New York Times* (June 4, 1995): pp. 1, 22.

Ashenfelter, Orley, and James Heckman. "Measuring the Effect of an Antidiscrimination Program." In *Evaluating the Labor Market Effects of Social Programs*, edited by O. Ashenfelter and J. Blum, pp. 46–89. Princeton, NJ: Princeton University Press, 1976.

Begley, Adam. "Henry Louis Gates Jr., Black Studies New Star." *New York Times Magazine* (April 1, 1990): pp. 25–50.

Bem, Sandra L. *The Lenses of Gender: Transforming the Debate on Sexual Inequality*. New Haven: Yale University Press, 1993.

Bergmann, Barbara. *Affirmative Action*. New York: Basic Books, in press.

Bernstein, Richard. "Racial Discrimination or Righting Past Wrongs?" *New York Times* (July 13, 1994): p. B8.

Birmingham Reverse Discrimination Litigation. 64 FEP Cases 1032. 11 Circuit (1 994).

Blumrosen, Alfred. W. *Modern Law: The Law Transmission System and Equal Employment Opportunity.* Madison, WI: The University of Wisconsin Press, 1993.

Bobo, Lawrence, Camille L. Zubrinsky, James H. Johnson, Jr., and Melvin L. Oliver. "Work Orientation, Job Discrimination, and Ethnicity: A Focus Group Perspective." *Research in the Sociology of Work,* vol. 5 (1995): pp. 45–85.

Braddock II, Jomills H., and James M. McPartland. "How Minorities Continue to be Excluded from Equal Employment Opportunities: Research on Labor Market and Institutional Barriers." *Journal of Social Issues,* vol. 43, no. 1 (1987): pp. 5–39.

Branscombe, Nyla. "Defensive Denial." Paper presented at Nag's Heart Conference on Collaboration and Competition. Amherst, Massachusetts, July, 1995.

Bunzel, John H. "The California Civil Rights Initiative." Speech delivered to the Commonwealth Club. San Francisco, California, March 24, 1995.

Buono, A. F., and J. B. Kamm. "Marginality and the Organizational Socialization of Female Managers." *Human Relations,* vol. 36, no. 12 (1983): pp. 1125–1140.

Cannings, Kathy. "Managerial Promotion: The Effects of Socialization, Specialization, and Gender." *Industrial and Labor Relations Review,* vol. 42, no. 1 (1988): pp. 77–88.

Carter, Stephen. "The Best Black, and Other Tales." *Reconstruction* (Winter, 1990): pp. 6–9, 26–48.

Carter, Stephen. *Reflections of an Affirmative Action Baby.* New York: Basic Books, 1991.

Carton, Barbara. "Muscled Out? At Jenny Craig, Men Are Ones Who Claim Sex Discrimination." *Wall Street Journal* (Nov. 29, 1994): pp. A1, A11.

Catalyst. *Cracking the Glass Ceiling: Strategies for Success.* Washington, D. C.: U. S. Department of Labor, 1994.

Chemers, Martin M., Stuart Oskamp, and Mark A. Costanzo, eds. *Diversity in Organizations: New Perspectives for a Changing_Workplace.* Thousand Oaks, CA: Sage, 1995.

Clayton, Susan D. and Faye J. Crosby. *Justice, Gender, and Affirmative Action.* Ann Arbor: The University of Michigan Press, 1992.

Clinton, William J. "Remarks at the National Archives and Records Administration." In Administration of William J. Clinton (July 19, 1995): pp. 1255–1264.

CNN/ *USA Today/* Gallup Poll. "A CNN/USA Today/Gallup Poll: July Wave 2." July 20–23, 1995.

Cohn, Bob, Tom Morganthau, Vern E. Smith, and Peter Annin. 1995. "Battleground Chicago: Report from the Front: How Racial Preferences Really Work—Or Don't." *Newsweek* (April 3, 1995): pp. 26–33.

Cohn, Bob, Bill Turque, and Martha Brant. "What About Women?" *Newsweek* (March 27, 1995).

Collins, S. M. "The Marginalization of Black Executives." *Social Problems*, vol. 36, no. 4 (1989): pp. 317–331.

Congressional Record. "Proceedings and Debates of the 104th Congress. First Session." (March 3, 1995).

Cook, S. W. "Cooperative Interaction in Multiethnic Contexts." In *Groups in Contact: The Psychology of Desegregation*, edited by N. Miller and M.B. Brewer, pp. 155–185. New York: Academic Press, 1984.

Cordova, Diana. "Cognitive Limitations and Affirmative Action: The Effects of Aggregate Versus Sequential Data in the Perception of Discrimination." *Social Justice Research* 5 (1992): pp. 319–333.

Cose, Ellis. "The Myth of Meritocracy." *Newsweek* (April 3, 1995), p. 34.

Cox, Taylor Jr. and Carol Smolinski. *Managing Diversity and Glass Ceiling Initiatives as National Economic Imperatives*. Ann Arbor: The University of Michigan, 1994.

Crosby, Faye J. "A Rose by Any Other Name." In *Affirmative Action: Quotas and Equality*, edited by K. Arioli. Zurich, Switzerland: Swiss National Science Foundation, in press.

Crosby, Faye J. *Relative Deprivation and Working Women*. New York: Oxford University Press, 1982.

Crosby, Faye J. "Understanding Affirmative Action." *Basic and Applied Social Psychology* vol. 15, nos. 1 & 2 (1994): pp. 13–41.

Crosby, Faye J., Brenda Allen, and Susan Opotow. "Changing Patterns of Income among Blacks and Whites Before and After Executive Order 11246." *Social Justice Research*, vol. 5 (1992): pp. 335–341.

Crosby, Faye J., Susan D. Clayton, Kathryn Hemker, and Olaf Alksnis. "Cognitive Biases in the Perception of Discrimination: The Importance of Format." *Sex Roles* 14 (1986): pp. 637–646.

Crosby, Faye J., and Diana Cordova. "Words Worth of Wisdom: Towards an Understanding of Affirmative Action." *Journal of Social Issues* (in press).

Crosby, Faye J., and Steve Hinkle. "Goals, Quotas, and the Monitoring Process." Paper delivered at the Fifth International Conference on Social Justice Research. Reno, Nevada (June 26, 1995).

Dale, Charles. *Compilation and Overview of Federal Laws and Regulations Establishing Affirmative Action Goals or Other Preference Based on Race, Gender, or Ethnicity*. Washington, D.C.: Library of Congress, Congressional Research Service, 1995.

Dawes, Robyn M. "Affirmative Action Programs: Discontinuities between Thoughts about Individuals and Thoughts about Groups." In *Applications of Heuristics and Biases to Social Issues*, edited by L. Heath, R.S. Tindale, J. Edwards, E. J. Posavac, F. B. Bryant, E. Henderson-King, Y. Suarez-Balcazar, and J. Myers, pp. 223–239. New York: Plenum Press, 1994.

Dellinger, Walter. "Memorandum to General Counsels." Washington, D.C.: U. S. Department of Justice, Office of Legal Counsel, June 28, 1995.

Deutsch, Morton. *Distributive Justice: A Social Psychological Perspective.* New Haven: Yale University Press, 1985.

de Vries, Sjiera, and Thomas F. Pettigrew. "A Comparative Perspective on Affirmative Action: Positieve Aktie in The Netherlands." *Basic and Applied Social Psychology* vol. 15, nos. 1 & 2 (1994): pp. 179–199.

Donohue, John and James Heckman. "Continuous versus Episodic Change: The Impact of Federal Civil Rights Policy on the Economic Status of Blacks." *Journal of Economic Literature,* vol. 29 (1991): pp. 1603–1643.

Dovidio, John F., Jeffrey Mann, and Samuel L.Gaertner. "Resistance to Affirmative Action: The Implications of Aversive Racism." In *Affirmative Action in Perspective,* edited by F.A. Blanchard and F.J. Crosby, pp. 83–102. Published under the auspices of the Society for the Psychological Study of Social Issues. New York: Springer Verlag, 1989.

D'Souza, Dinesh. *Illiberal Education: The Politics of Race and Sex on Campus.* New York: The Free Press, 1991.

Edley, Jr., Christopher. "Affirmative Action: Beyond the Rhetoric." Speech delivered at John W. McCormack Institute of Public Affairs. Boston, Massachusetts (December 8, 1995).

EEOC Office of Communications and Legislative Affairs. "U.S. Equal Employment Opportunity Commission Charge Resolution Statistics—Reverse Discrimination (Race), FY 1987–FY 1994" (March, 1995).

EEOC Office of Communications and Legislative Affairs. "U.S. Equal Employment Opportunity Commission Charge Statistics Reflecting Types of Reverse Discrimination (Race), FY 1987–FY 1994" (October, 1995).

Fineman, Howard. "Race and Rage." *Newsweek* (April 3, 1995).

Fish, Stanley. "Reverse Racism or How the Pot Got to Call the Kettle Black." *Atlantic Monthly* (November, 1993): pp. 128–136.

Frey, D. "Recent Research on Selective Exposure to Information." *Advances in Experimental Social Psychology,* vol. 19 (1986): pp. 41–80.

Garcia, Luis T., Nancy Erskine, Kathy Hawn, and Susanne R. Casmay. "The Effect of Affirmative Action on Attributions about Minority Group Members." *Journal of Personality* 49:4 (December, 1981): pp. 427–437.

Gilbert, Lucia A. "Dimensions of Same-Gender Student-Faculty Role-Model Relationships." *Sex Roles,* vol. 12, nos. 1/2 (1985): pp. 111–123.

Glazer, Nathan. *Affirmative Discrimination: Ethnic Inequality and Public Policy.* Cambridge, MA: Harvard University Press, 1987.

Goldberg. Philip. "Are Women Prejudiced Against Women?" *Transaction* (April. 1968): pp. 28–30.

Goldsmith. Nancy, Diana Cordova, Karen Dwyer, Bergen Langlois, and Faye Crosby. "Reactions to Affirmative Action: A Case Study." In *Affirmative Action in Perspective*. edited by F.A. Blanchard and F. J. Crosby, pp. 139–146. Published under the auspices of the Society for the Psychological Study of Social Issues. New York: Springer Verlag, 1989.

Goodman, Ellen. "Male Caregivers Are Getting Mixed Messages." *Hartford Courant* (March 1, 1994): p. B11.

Greenhaus, Jeffrey H., Saroj Parasuraman, and Wayne M. Wormley. "Effects of Race on Organizational Experiences, Job Performance Evaluations, and Career Outcomes." *Academy of Management Journal*, vol. 33, no. 1 (1990): pp. 64–86.

Hanna, Charlotte. "The Organizational Context for Affirmative Action for Women Faculty." *Journal of Higher Education*, vol. 59, no. 4 (July/ August, 1988): pp. 390–411.

Hanson Frieze, Irene, Josephine Olson, and Deborah Cain Good. "Perceived and Actual Discrimination in the Salaries of Male and Female Managers." *Journal of Applied Social Psychology* 20:1 (1990): pp. 46–67.

Hart, Herbert L.A. *The Concept of Law*. Oxford: The Clarendon Press, 1961.

Heckman, James, and Kenneth Wolpin. "Does the Contract Compliance Program Work? An Analysis of Chicago Data." *Industrial and Labor Relations Review*, vol. 29 (1976): pp. 544–564.

Heilman, Madeline E. "Affirmative Action: Some Unintended Consequences For Working Women." *Research in Organizational Behavior* 16 (1994): pp. 125–169.

Heilman, Madeline E., Caryn J. Block, and Jonathan A. Lucas. "Presumed Incompetent? Stigmatization and Affirmative Action Efforts." *Journal of Applied Psychology*, vol. 77, no. 4 (1992): pp. 536–544.

Heilman, Madeline E., Jonathan A. Lucas, and Stella R. Kaplow. "Self-Derogating Consequences of Sex-Based Preferential Selection: The Moderating Role of Initial Self-Confidence." *Organizational Behavior and Human Processes*, vol. 46 (1990): pp. 202–216.

Heilman, Madeline E., Michael C. Simon, and David P. Repper. "Intentionally Favored, Unintentionally Harmed? Impact of Sex-Based Preferential Selection on Self-Perceptions and Self-Evaluations." *Journal of Applied Psychology*, vol. 72, no. 1 (1987): pp. 62–68.

Heller, Scott. "Defining Affirmative Action: What You Think It Is Affects How You Feel About It." *Chronicle of Higher Education* (November 17, 1985): pp. A8, A15.

Hewstone. Miles, and Rupert Brown. "Contact is Not Enough: An Intergroup Perspective on the 'Contact Hypothesis.'" In *Contact and Conflict in Intergroup Encounters*, edited by M. Hewstone and R. Brown, pp. 26–29. New York: Basil Blackwell, 1986.

Hitt, Michael A. and Barbara W. Keats. "Empirical Identification of the Criteria for Effective Affirmative Action Programs." *The Journal of Applied Behavioral Science*, vol. 20., no. 3 (1984): pp. 203–222.

Hochschild, Jennifer L. "Affirmative Action and the Rumor of Black Inferiority." *Journal of Blacks in Higher Education* (Summer, 1995): pp. 64–65.

Holmes, Steven A. "U.S. Issues New, Strict Tests for Affirmative Action Plans." *New York Times* (June 29, 1995): A1: 4–5 and A16: 4–6.

Homans, George C. *Social Behavior: Its Elementary Forms.* London: Routledge and Kegan Paul, 1961.

Johnson, Jr., James H., Elisa J. Bienenstock, and Jennifer A. Stoloff. "An Empirical Test of the Cultural Capital Hypothesis." *The Review of Black Political Economy* (in press).

Johnson, Jr., James H. and Walter C. Farrell, Jr. "Race Still Matters." *Chronicle of Higher Education* (July 7, 1995): p. A48.

Johnston, David. "F.B.I. Hitting Snag in Talks about Bias." *New York Times* (September 20, 1995): p. A18.

Kahlenberg, Richard. "Equal Opportunity Critics." *New Republic* (July 17 & 24, 1995): pp. 20–25.

Kanter, Rosabeth M. "Some Effects of Proportions on Group Life: Skewed Sex Ratios and Responses to Token Women." *American Journal of Sociology*, vol. 82 (1977): pp. 965–991.

Katz Pinzler, Isabelle. "A Report on Presidential Reforms." Talk delivered at John W. McCormack Institute of Public Affairs. Boston, Massachusetts (December 8, 1995).

Kirby, Daria C. "Where Have We Been and Where Do We Go From Here?: A Historical Overview of Organizational Responses to Affirmative Action Mandates." Working draft, University of Pittsburgh (1995).

Kirschenman, Joleen and Kathryn M. Neckerman. "'We'd Love to Hire Them, But...': The Meaning of Race for Employers." In *The Urban Underclass* (1991): pp. 203–232.

Klein, Joe. "Affirmative Inaction?" *Newsweek* (June 26, 1995): p. 23.

Knox, R. E., and J. A. Inkster. "Postdecision Dissonance at Post Time." *Journal of Personality and Social Psychology*, vol. 8 (1968): pp. 319–323.

Kravitz, David A., and Judith Platania. "Attitudes and Beliefs about Affirmative Action: Effects of Target and of Respondent Sex and Ethnicity." *Journal of Applied Psychology* 78:6 (1993): pp. 928–938.

Kreiter, Nancy. March 10, 1994. Personal communication.

LaBonte, C. Joseph. "Jenny Craig Treats Her Men Just Fine." *Wall Street Journal*, Letter to the Editor (December 20, 1994): p. A15.

Landy, F. J., and D. A. Trumbo. *Psychology of Work Behavior*. Homewood, IL: Dorsey Press, 1980.

Leo, John. "Our Addiction to Bad News." *U.S.News & World Report* (June 5, 1995): p. 20.

Leonard, Jonathan. "The Impact of Affirmative Action on Employment." *Journal of Labor Economics*, vol. 2 (1984): pp. 439–463.

Montwieler, Nancy. "No 'Widespread Abuse' in Job Cases, Few Reverse Bias Claims, Study Says." *Daily Labor Record*, no. 56 (March 23, 1995).

Moore, David W. "Americans Today Are Dubious about Affirmative Action." *Gallup Poll Monthly* (March, 1995): pp. 36–38.

Morrison, Ann M. *The New Leaders: Guidelines on Leadership in America*. San Francisco, CA: Jossey-Bass Publishers, 1992.

Morrison, Ann M., and Mary Ann Von Glinow. "Women and Minorities in Management." *American Psychologist*, vol. 45, no. 2 (February, 1990): pp. 200–208.

Murphy, Kevin R. and Charles O. Davidshofer. *Psychological Testing Principles and Applications*. 3rd ed. Englewood Cliffs, NJ: Prentice-Hall, Inc., 1994.

Murray, Charles. "Affirmative Racism." In *Debating Affirmative Action: Race, Gender, Ethnicity, and the Politics of Inclusion*, edited by N. Mills, pp. 191–208. New York: Delta, 1994.

Murrell, Audrey J., Beth L. Dietz-Uhler, John F. Dovidio, Samuel L. Gaertner, and Cheryl Drout. "Aversive Racism and Resistance to Affirmative Action: Perceptions of Justice Are Not Necessarily Color Blind." *Basic and Applied Social Psychology* 15:1 & 2 (1994): pp. 71–86.

Nacoste, Rupert W. "Affirmative Action and Self-Evaluations." In *Affirmative Action in Perspective*, edited by F. A. Blanchard and F. J. Crosby, pp. 103–109. New York: Springer-Verlag, 1989.

Nacoste, Rupert W. "Sources of Stigma: Analyzing the Psychology of Affirmative Action." *Law and Policy*, vol. 5. (1990): pp. 223–238.

Nacoste, Rupert W. "The Truth about Affirmative Action." *Chronicle of Higher Education* (April 7, 1995): p. A48.

Nacoste, Rupert W., and Beth Hummels. "Affirmative Action and the Behavior of Decision Makers." *Journal of Applied Social Psychology*, vol. 24, no. 7 (1994): pp. 595–613.

Nettles, Michael T. "Black and White Students' Academic Performance in Majority White and Majority Black College Settings." In *Desegregating America's Colleges and Universi-*

ties: *Title VI Regulation of Higher Education*, edited by J.B. Williams, III, pp. 159–178. New York: Teachers College Press.

Neumark, David, Roy J. Bank and Kyle D. Van Nort. *Sex Discrimination in Restaurant Hiring: An Audit Study*. Working Paper No. 5024. Cambridge, MA: National Bureau of Economic Research, 1995.

Newkirk, Pamela. "Expert Unexpectedly." *New York Times* (November 15, 1995): C1: 2–5.

Newman, Jim D. "Affirmative Action and the Courts." In *Affirmative Action in Perspective*, edited by F.A. Blanchard and F.J. Crosby, pp. 31–49. Published under the auspices of the Society for the Psychological Study of Social Issues. New York: Springer Verlag, 1989.

Nisbett, Richard, and Lee Ross. *Human Inference: Strategies and Shortcomings of Social Judgement*. Englewood Cliffs, NJ: Prentice Hall, 1980.

Nisbett, Richard, and Lee Ross. *The Person and the Situation*. New York: McGraw Hill, 1991.

Olson, Craig A., and Brian E. Becker. "Sex Discrimination in the Promotion Process." *Industrial and Labor Relations Review*, vol. 36, no. 4 (1983): pp 624–641.

Olson, James M., and Carolyn L. Hafer. "Affect, Motivation, and Cognition in Relative Deprivation Research." In *Handbook of Motivation and Cognition: The Interpersonal Context*, vol. 3, edited by R. M. Sorrentino and E. T. Higgins. New York: Guilford (in press).

Owen, David. *None of the Above: Behind the Myth of Scholastic Aptitude*. Boston: Houghton Mifflin Company, 1985.

Parks, Gerald H. Personal communication. Fairfield, CT: General Electric Company, Dec. 1, 1995.

Pettigrew, Thomas F., and Joanne Martin. "Shaping the Organizational Context for Black American Inclusion." *Journal of Social Issues*, vol. 43, no. 1. (1987): pp. 41–78.

Rawls, John. *A Theory of Justice*. Cambridge, MA: Harvard University Press, 1971.

Reed, Jr., Adolph. "Assault on Affirmative Action." *The Progressive* (June, 1995): pp. 18–20.

Reich, Robert B. *Good for Business: Making Full Use of the Nation's Human Capital. A Fact-Finding Report of the Federal Glass Ceiling Commission*. Washington, D. C., March, 1995.

Richardson, Lynda. "Caterer Favors a Butler Look, Waitress Says in a Bias Suit." *New York Times* (October 13, 1995): pp. B1, B3.

Robertson, Peter C. "ORC Survey of CEOs Shows Support for Affirmative Action." Arlington, VA: Organization Resources Counselors, Inc., 1995.

Rosen, Benson, Mabel Miguel, and Ellen Peirce. "Stemming the Exodus of Women Managers." *Human Resource Management*, vol. 28, no. 4 (1989): pp. 475–491.

Rosen, Jeffrey. "The Color-Blind Court." *New Republic* (July 31, 1995): pp. 19–25.

Rosener, Judy B. "Ways Women Lead." *Harvard Buisiness Review* (Winter. Nov.–Dec., 1995): pp. 119–125.

Rosser, Phyllis. *The SAT Gender Gap*. Washington, D.C.: Publications, Center for Women Policy Studies, 1989.

Rutte, Crystal G., Katrin A. Diekmann, Jeffrey Polzer, Faye J. Crosby, and David M. Messick. "Organizing Information and the Detection of Gender Discrimination." *Psychological Science* 5 (1994): pp. 226–231.

Schlei, B., and P. Grossman. *Employment Discrimination Law*. 2nd ed. Chicago: American Bar Association Press, 1983.

Shipler, David. K. "My Equal Opportunity, Your Free Lunch." *New York Times* (March 5, 1995): pp. 1, 16.

Sniderman, Paul M., and Thomas Piazza. *The Scar of Race*. Cambridge, MA: The Belknap Press Of Harvard University Press, 1993.

South, Scott J., Charles M. Bonjean, William T. Markham, and Judy Corder. "Social Structure and Intergroup Interaction: Men and Women of the Federal Bureaucracy." *American Sociological Review*, vol. 47 (1982): pp. 587–589.

Spann, Jeri. *Retaining and Promoting Women and Minority Faculty Members: Problems and Possibilities*. Madison, WI: The University of Wisconsin System, 1990.

Speizer, Jeanne J. "Role Models, Mentors, and Sponsors: The Elusive Concepts." *Journal of Women in Culture and Society*, vol. 6, no. 4 (1981): pp. 692–712.

Stake, Jayne E., and Margaret Noonan. "The Influence of Teacher Models on the Career Confidence and Motivation of College Students." *Sex Roles*, vol. 12, nos. 9/10 (1985): pp. 1023–1031.

Staples, Brent. "The Presumption of Stupidity." *The New York Times* (March 5, 1995): p. 14.

Steele, Shelby. *The Content of Our Character: A New Vision of Race in America*. New York: St. Martin's Press, 1990.

Stephanopoulos, George, and Christopher Edley, Jr. "Affirmative Action Review." *Report to the President*. Washington, D. C.: Government Printing Office, July 19, 1995.

Summers, Russel J. "The Influence of Affirmative Action on Perceptions of a Beneficiary's Qualifications." *Journal of Applied Social Psychology* 21:15 (1991): pp. 1265–1276.

Swim, Janet, Eugene Borgida, Geoffrey Maruyama, and David G. Myers. "Joan McKay vs. John McKay: Do Gender Stereotypes Bias Evaluations?" *Psychological Bulletin*, vol. 105 (1989): pp. 409–429.

Tajfel, H. *Human Groups and Social Categories: Studies in Social Psychology*. Cambridge, England: Cambridge University Press, 1981.

Taylor, Marylee C. "Impact of Affirmative Action on Beneficiary Groups: Evidence from the 1990 General Social Survey." *Basic and Applied Social Psychology*, vol. 15 (1994): pp. 143–178.

Taylor, Shelley. *Positive Illusions: Creative Self-Deception and the Healthy Mind.* New York: Basic Books, 1989.

Thomas, Evan, and Bob Cohn. "Rethinking the Dream." *Newsweek* (June 26, 1995): pp. 18–21.

Thurgood, Delores H., and Joanne M. Weinman. *Summary Report 1990: Doctorate Recipients from United States Universities.* Washington, D. C.: National Academy Press, 1991.

Trinity College Bulletin. September, 1995.

Turner, Margery Austin, Michael Fix, and Raymond J. Struyk, with others. *Opportunities Denied, Opportunities Diminished: Racial Discrimination in Hiring.* Washington, D.C.: The Urban Institute Press, 1991.

Turner, Marlene E., and Anthony R. Pratkanis. "Affirmative Action as Help: A Review of Recipient Actions to Preferential Selection and Affirmative Action." *Basic and Applied Social Psychology* vol. 15, nos. 1 & 2 (1994): pp. 43–69.

Turner, Marlene E., and Anthony R. Pratkanis. "Affirmative Action: Insights from Social Psychological and Organizational Research." *Basic and Applied Social Psychology* 15:1 & 2 (1994): pp. 1–11.

Twiss, Catherine, Susan Tabb, and Faye Crosby. "Affirmative Action and Aggregate Data: The Importance of Patterns in the Perception of Discrimination." In *Affirmative Action in Perspective*, edited by F.A. Blanchard and F.J. Crosby, pp. 159–167. Published under the auspices of the Society for the Psychological Study of Social Issues. New York: Springer Verlag, 1989.

Uchitelle, Louis. "Union Goal of Equality Fails the Test of Time." *New York Times* (July 9, 1995): pp. 1, 18.

U.S. Bureau of the Census. *Statistical Abstract of the United States: 1994.* 114th ed. Washington, D.C.: U.S. Government Printing Office, 1994.

U.S. Department of Labor. *Program Highlights.* "Fact Sheet No. ESA 1995-17, Executive Order 11246." Washington, D. C.

Watson, Warren E., Kamalesh Kumar, and Larry K. Michaelsen. "Cultural Diversity's Impact on Interaction Process and Performance: Comparing Homogeneous and Diverse Task Groups." *Academy of Management Journal,* vol. 36, no. 3 (1993): pp. 590–602.

Watters, Ethan. "Claude Steele Has Scores to Settle." *New York Times Magazine* (September 17, 1995): pp. 45–49.

Wharton, Amy S., and James N. Baron. "So Happy Together? The Impact of Gender Segregation on Men at Work." *American Sociological Review,* vol. 52 (1987): pp. 574–587.

Wilkerson, Isabel. "Discordant Notes in Detroit." *New York Times* (March 5, 1989): p. 30.

Wilson, William J. *The Truly Disadvantaged: The Inner City, the Underclass, and Public Policy.* Chicago: University of Chicago Press, 1987.

Wilson, William J. "The New Urban Poverty and the Retreat from Public Policy." Keynote Address to "Race, Poverty, and America's Cities: A Forum Sponsored by Trinity College" (October 16, 1995).

Winkelman, Christine, and Faye Crosby. "Affirmative Action: Setting the Record Straight." *Social Justice Research* 7 (1994): pp. 309–344.

Woody, Bette. *Corporate Policy and Women at the Top.* Working Paper, no. 211. Wellesley, MA: Center for Research on Women, 1990.

Wycliff, Don. "Affirmative on Affirmative Action." *Commonweal* (May 19, 1995): pp. 11–12.

Zimbardo, Philip G., and Michael R. Leippe. *The Psychology of Attitude Change and Social Influence.* New York: McGraw-Hill, 1991.

Part Two

Against Affirmative Action

I dedicate my part of *Affirmative Action* to the National Association of Scholars, an organization whose members are in the forefront of the struggle for an American system of higher education free of race, ethnic, and gender discrimination and preferences.

Acknowledgments

Tamara Holzapfel read the first draft of my part of this book and advised me to deal at a more general level with my subject and to refrain from being so involved with my own university. I accepted her judgments. Richard Barrett read a second draft and urged me to delete parts and revise other parts. Again, I complied. James Lorie read a near-final draft and pronounced it a sound piece of work. I agreed. I thank them all.

Section One

Affirmative Action: An Idea Whose Time Has Passed (And Perhaps Never Was)

Prologue

All persons, without regard to race or religion or national origin, are equal before the law. The equal protection of the laws, expressly guaranteed by the U.S. Constitution, seems the plainest and most comprehensive requirement for justice. No sophistication is needed to appreciate its force; the common conviction that categories like race have no bearing upon the just application of law is dramatized by the blindfold that the Goddess of Justice wears while balancing her scales....

Some would have the law be color-conscious now so that it may become color-blind in the future. That cannot be. One is reminded of political leaders who "suspend" constitutions to "build a firmer base for democracy." Once established as constitutionally acceptable grounds for discriminatory distribution, racial categories will wax, not wane in importance. No prescription for racial disharmony could be surer of success.

Official favoritism by race or national origin is poison in society. In American society, built of manifold racial and ethnic layers, it is deadly poison.

—Carl Cohen¹

A ffirmative action transformed the goals and values of the civil rights movement of the 1950s and 1960s into a state of mind and of law where race again took center stage, a place it has held throughout nearly all of American history and one the civil rights

movement was dedicated to eliminating. The change was from a prohibition of racial discrimination to claims for race-specific results. School desegregation became racial balancing. "No discrimination" in employment
became a demand for proportional representation and no "disparate impact." "Equal voting rights" became an insistence on proportional representation by race of elected officials. Ethnicity and gender later gained
parity with race in the demand for equity. This transformation, how it
came about, and the reaction to it, is the subject of Part One.

The Republican congressional victory of 8 November 1994 brought affirmative action out of the closet. Before, hardly any national politician,
except Jesse Helms, dared publicly to condemn it. It had no place in
Newt Gingrich's 1994 Contract with America. After this critical election,
most of the many Republican presidential candidates called for its elimination. After the *Adarand* decision in June 1995, the Clinton Administration issued strict guidelines for evaluating affirmative action plans, which
made some of them more difficult to justify. Yet a month later the president gave a ringing reaffirmation of the goals and purposes of affirmative
action. California's Governor Pete Wilson, with great fanfare, cut back all
affirmative-action programs under his jurisdiction and led the regents of
the University of California in phasing it out in the university's admissions
and hiring.

Civil rights leaders and their supporters in Congress equated the end of
affirmative action with the end of civil rights progress for women and
minorities. Boycotts and demonstrations in support of affirmative action
sprang up around the nation. The press was filled as never before with
Op-Ed pieces, pro and con, on the subject.

The Democrats, the party of unbending allegiance to affirmative action,
had lost control of the Congress that it had held for forty years. The
Republicans as the minority party for a quarter of a century had gone
along with the Democrats on affirmative action, or at least kept quiet on
the subject. By 1995, however, everything had changed. It now became
possible to speak out critically on the subject with some impunity. Supporters of affirmative action went on the defensive. For the first time in
decades, and very quickly, affirmative action became a subject of national
debate. The editorial page of the *New York Times* defended it; that of the
Wall Street Journal lambasted it. It became the great wedge issue of the
Republicans, as abortion has been for the Democrats. The Republicans

became the anti-affirmative action party, the party advocating a color-blind Constitution and legal system, and would capture Democratic support because of it. The Democrats, the party of choice on the abortion issue, would capture Republican support because of it.

In the spring of 1995 there was much concern about just where President Clinton really stood on affirmative action. He seemed to be equivocating. In June Representative Kweisi Mfume, past head of the Congressional Black Caucus and now president of the beleaguered NAACP, challenged the President:

> By not being clear and firm on the issue of equal opportunity, equal access and inclusion [i.e., affirmative action], the president runs the risk of permanently losing large segments of his base.... If you think racial minorities in this country, and in particular African Americans, are going to sit silently by and let 30 years of progress be taken away without a fight, you are in for a very rude awakening.[2]

The President responded to his critics, left and right, with a carefully tailored speech on 19 July 1995. It was a prototypically conventional defense of an inclusive, open-ended, affirmative action. He pleaded for a continuation of affirmative action for women and all "minorities" who can claim to have undergone "persistent discrimination."

"Mend it, but don't end it," was Clinton's slogan. America needs affirmative action, he claimed, "to bring our country together." The evidence "screams" that "the job of ending discrimination in this country is not over." Things that are wrong with it should be changed, and "it should be retired when its job is done.... The purpose of affirmative action," he continued,

> is to give our nation a way to finally address the systematic exclusion of individuals of talent, on the basis of their gender or race from opportunities to develop, perform, achieve and contribute. Affirmative action is an effort to develop a systematic approach to open the doors of education, employment, and business opportunities to qualified individuals who happen to be members of groups that have experienced long-standing and persistent discrimination.

He went on to oppose vigorously, and tautologically, what even the most adamant proponents of affirmative action oppose:

It does not mean, and I don't favor, the unjustified preference of the unqualified over the qualified of any race or gender. It doesn't mean, and I
don't favor, numerical quotas. It doesn't mean, and I don't favor, rejection or
selection of any employee or student solely on the basis of race or gender
without regard to merit.

Who favors preference for the unqualified over the qualified? Who, in
1995, would admit to favoring quotas? Who favors selection "solely" because of race or gender regardless of merit?

The leadership of women's and minority organizations praised the speech
and the president. He had returned to the fold after several months of
giving conflicting signals about what the administration should do about
the scores of federal affirmative action programs. They could hardly have
been more pleased. Even Jesse Jackson was pleased. He said the President had "set a good moral tone for the country." Republicans found
nothing to commend in the speech. They claimed he was just defending
the status quo. "End it, don't mend it," quipped then presidential candidate Pete Wilson. Clinton has not waffled on affirmative action since.

There is a momentum in the country supporting a return to a color-
blind, non-discriminatory Constitution and legal system. There is also
powerful opposition to it. It is a burning hot issue, like abortion and
welfare, that will be with us for a long time. But, unlike these other big
issues, there is no consensus on the terms of the debate. "Affirmative
action" itself is a very slippery concept. And there is always the question:
Affirmative action for whom?

From before the Civil War to the 1960s people who fought first slavery,
then racial segregation were dedicated to the idea of a color-blind Constitution which made no distinctions of race. As Justice John Marshall Harlan
put it in his famous dissenting opinion in *Plessy v. Ferguson* (1896):

> In respect of civil rights, common to all citizens, the Constitution of the
> United States does not, I think, permit any public authority to know the race
> of those entitled to be protected in the enjoyment of such rights.... There is
> no case here. Our Constitution is color-blind, and neither knows nor toler-
> ates classes among citizens.

By the 1950s and 1960s, specifically the decade between *Brown v. Board
of Education of Topeka* (1954) and the Voting Rights Act of 1965, the

color-blind view reached its high water mark. It was the bedrock belief of the civil rights movement. During that mostly buoyant and optimistic decade, liberal Americans thought we were moving irresistibly in the direction of a nonrace-conscious Constitution and legal system. But this was not the road taken.[3] Within a brief three-year period, 1965 to 1968, our major institutions, led by the federal government, got back on the race-conscious road. Before the color-blind decade, we had the age of segregation and after it the age of affirmative action. Both were equally race conscious; the former oppressively so, the latter benignly so.

This optimistic decade was a time when no photographs were allowed on college and job applications. No questions about a person's race could be asked when applying for college or a job. The American Civil Liberties Union was committed to eliminating the race question from the 1960 Census. Integration in all aspects of societal life was the great goal. It still remains the goal of those octogenarian black scholars, psychologist Kenneth Clark and historian John Hope Franklin, who were the intellectual leaders of the civil rights struggles of the '50s and '60s.[4] The failure of integration during the age of affirmative action is the source of the ubiquitous sadness about race relations in America.

The root cause of the post-1965 change was the realization that even with full civil rights, blacks remained a terribly disadvantaged and frustrated people in an affluent society. This was brought home to Americans most dramatically by the rioting in the cities in the summers of 1965, 1966, and 1967.

In early 1965, before the Watts riot in August, the often prophetic Daniel Patrick Moynihan wrote (not at the time intended for publication) that "a new crisis in race relations" was upon America. A new period had begun.

> In this new period the expectations of the Negro Americans will go beyond civil rights. Being Americans, they will now expect that in the near future equal opportunities for them as a group will produce roughly equal results, as compared with other groups. *This is not going to happen. Nor will it happen for generations to come unless a new and special effort is made.* [Emphasis added.]
>
> There are two reasons. First, the racist virus in the American blood stream still afflicts us: Negroes will encounter serious personal prejudice for at least another generation. Second, three centuries of sometimes unimaginable

mistreatment have taken their toll on the Negro people. The harsh fact is that as a group, at the present time, in terms of ability to win out in the competitions of American life, *they are not equal to most of those with which they will be competing* [emphasis added]....

The principal challenge of the next phase of the Negro revolution is *to make certain that equality of results will now follow* [emphasis added]. If we do not, there will be no peace in the United States for generations.[5]

The views of a number of social scientists, above all Moynihan, were responsible for Lyndon B. Johnson's 1965 Howard University commencement address in which he publicly proclaimed the policy of affirmative action for Negroes, but without the use of the term. By the late 1960s preferential affirmative action had become basic to the liberal view of race relations and was becoming entrenched in government, industry, and the universities. Even many conservatives, including Supreme Court justices, became convinced of the need and rightness of affirmative action. This was the road to take to bring Negroes to full integration in American society.

What has happened to the black population over these three decades has been a huge and healthy increase in its proportions in the professional, technical, and managerial occupations, in white-collar occupations, and in the skilled trades. At the same time the plight of inner city blacks has horribly worsened, reaching epic levels of illegitimacy, teen pregnancy, crime, mental retardation, obesity, drug addiction, AIDS, welfare dependence, and paranoid victimization. And their numbers, too, have greatly increased. Affirmative action has helped the former group to some unknowable extent, but has been irrelevant to the latter, as William Julius Wilson observes, and few social scientists can claim otherwise: "the race-specific policies emanating from the civil rights movement [i.e., affirmative action], although beneficial to more advantaged blacks...do little for those who are truly disadvantaged."[6] Still, the black underclass is the most proffered argument for race-based affirmative action. But it is no argument at all.

No other rich democracy in the world has spawned an underclass of such dimensions as the United States. And, numerically, most are not black. No other rich democracy compares with the United States in degree of economic inequality, the lack of universal health care (15 percent of the population without coverage), the extraordinary degree of racial and ethnic segregation in housing and public education (American *apartheid*), and being so far down the list on many measures of quality of life (life expectancies, infant mortality, book reading, newspaper circulation, percentage voting). The underclass is the most serious and intractable problem of American society. The mother of the underclass is runaway illegitimacy, most significantly among the young, and all that flows from this.

The great American problem is not racism, prejudice, and discrimination. These have reached something close to an irreducible minimum in present-day America, bigots aside. To believe, as we are continuously bombarded to believe, that "racism," group stereotypes, and differential evaluations of categories of people will disappear with a new multicultural consciousness, will ever disappear, is a hopelessly utopian view of the crooked timber of humanity. Finding the explanation of the condition of the underclass in *racism* acts to divert attention from what the real causes are. It takes our sights away from meaningful public policy dedicated to lessening the miseries of the underclass, to decrease their numbers.

Affirmative action is what Shelby Steele calls an iconographic public policy.[7] It exists "to solve a social problem but actually functions as an icon for the self-image people hope to gain by supporting the policy. From the beginning, affirmative action could be cited as evidence of white social virtue and of emerging black power—the precise qualities that America's long history of racism had denied to each side." Affirmative action is a feel-good policy that puts us on the side of the angels.

It is past time for a definition of affirmative action. A one-sentence definition of it and a one-sentence justification for it, which might temporarily satisfy both proponents and opponents, is this: Affirmative action is the protective or preferential treatment of persons in employment, the admission to selective schools and universities, and the granting of other social goods and resources (e.g., government contracts and licenses, set-asides) by giving positive consideration to specified races and ethnicities and to one gender or the other. (Race/ethnicity and gender, in a peculiar way, become proxies for merit.) The established justification for such practices is to compensate for past hurtful discrimination; a newer justification is to promote *diversity*, the idea that desirable and powerful positions in society, indeed, all areas of society, should reflect the ethnic and gender composition of the population. *Diversity* has become the euphemism for affirmative action.

Affirmative action, in most discourse on the subject, generally applies to education and work. The term is not usually used when talking about voting rights, or questions of political districting, housing, issues of public accommodation, or membership in organizations. These areas are covered by Title II of the Civil Rights Act of 1964, the Voting Rights Act of 1965, and other legislation.

There is agreement that affirmative action is mostly applicable to higher-status positions over lower-status ones, white-collar work over blue-collar work, skilled work over nonskilled work, managerial and supervisory positions over those which are not, appointive positions over nonappointive positions, and so forth. Yet there are exceptions. Sometimes the Justice or Labor Departments criticize the high percentages of minorities in unskilled or semiskilled manual and service work, but rarely does this lead to any affirmative action.

* * *

It is a tragic and ironic observation that during the age of affirmative action we have moved away from the idea and the reality of an integrated society. America has become a separatist society—one with a growing *sense* of apartness among blacks and Hispanics, but, above all, blacks. We are becoming a society where one's primary identification is to race, ethnicity, and, to a lesser extent, gender and sexual orientation.

How much preferential affirmative action is cause and how much result of this enhanced American apartheid is disputable. Most reasonable to conclude, I think, is that it is both cause and effect. What is less disputable is that the elimination of governmentally sanctioned preferences and its attendant mentality will result in a decline in race- and ethnic-consciousness. They will wane and not wax. Their diminution is a necessary condition for an integrated society.

The battle over preferential affirmative action will persist in America. There are few more indisputable generalizations about societal life than this one: People welcome special privileges, no matter the justification, and people will not give them up, no matter the justification, without a fight.

Chapter 8

The Origins of
Affirmative Action

"Affirmative action" began as an undefined, apparently innocuous, phrase, in an executive order with no direct reference to any duly passed law, and it just grew, with the eager cooperation and inventiveness of the courts. Even now [1984] it has no fixed meaning, and...its proponents find it convenient to avoid fixing one, adopting hard or soft meanings depending on whether affirmative action is on the attack or the defensive.

—Harvey C. Mansfield, Jr.[1]

The first use of the term "affirmative action" was probably in the National Labor Relations Act of 1935. The Wagner Act, as it is popularly called, prohibited private employers from discriminating against persons because of membership in labor unions. It was used to define the authority and obligation of the National Labor Relations Board (NLRB) to remedy an unfair labor practice by ordering the offending party "to cease and desist from such unfair labor practice, and to take such *affirmative action*, including reinstatement of employees with or without back pay, as will effectuate the policies of this Act" [emphasis added].[2]

Probably the first proposal for preferential affirmative action came from President Franklin D. Roosevelt via his wife, Eleanor, in the spring of 1941. Doris Kearns Goodwin reports:

Eleanor returned to Washington armed with stories about blacks with PhDs and law degrees finding it impossible to secure work in defense plants except as janitors and cleaners. The stories had an effect on the president. This was not how a democracy was supposed to work, and he knew it....

On a Sunday in late May, Roosevelt sent a handwritten note to William Knudsen and Sidney Hillman containing a radical suggestion that may well be the first official call for what later became known as affirmative action. "To order taking Negroes up to a certain percentage in factory order work. Judge them on *quality*--the 1st class Negroes are turned down for 3rd class white boys." Two days later Knudsen replied: "I have talked with Mr. Hillman and we will quietly get manufacturers to increase the number of Negroes for defense work. *If we set a percentage it will immediately be open to dispute*, quiet work with the contractors and the unions will bring better results [emphasis added].[3]

The realization that "quiet work" with defense contractors wouldn't work led A. Philip Randolph, president of the Brotherhood of Sleeping Car Porters, to call for a March on Washington by fifty thousand people. After repeated attempts to dissuade Randolph, Roosevelt issued Executive Order 8802 in June 1941, prohibiting discrimination by any defense contractors and establishing the Fair Employment Practices Commission (FEPC) to investigate charges of racial discrimination.

The Wagner Act and the NLRB, together with the FEPC, became the model for New York State's 1945 law against discrimination, which created the State Commission Against Discrimination (SCAD), the first of many state fair-employment practice laws passed before the Civil Rights Act of 1964. The Wagner Act was also the model for Section 706(g) of Title VII of that act, wherein the term "affirmative action" is used in the same sense.

Executive Order 10925 issued by President John F. Kennedy in 1961 used the term "affirmative action" once along with similar phrases such as "affirmative steps" and (twice) "positive measures."[4] It prohibited discrimination in government employment and contract programs, and it required federal contractors to "take *affirmative action* to ensure that applicants are employed and that employees are treated during employment *without regard* to their race, creed, color, or national origin" [emphases added]. From this beginning, the concept of affirmative action has been plagued by a fundamental ambiguity. It has meant *both* the achievement of "equality of opportunity" and "equality of results." Hugh Davis Graham has observed this conundrum:

> Its [affirmative action's] positive obligations were undefined, although they seemed to imply more aggressive recruiting and training of authorities to broaden the pool for subsequent merit selection. But these positive measures were also tightly linked to the negative commandments of nondiscrimination; affirmative action was required to insure that citizens were treated *without regard* to race, color, or creed [emphasis in original].[5]

The organ to enforce this ambiguous conception of affirmative action was the Equal Employment Opportunity Commission (EEOC), an independent government agency, established by Section 705 of Title VII of the Civil Rights Act of 1964. The function of the EEOC was to mediate disputes resulting from individual complaints of discrimination.

After President Kennedy's assassination on 22 November 1963, President Johnson gave the passage of civil rights legislation his highest priority. Five days later, he told a joint session of Congress that no eulogy "could more eloquently honor President Kennedy's memory" than the "earliest possible passage of the civil rights bill for which he fought so long."[6]

Still, most representatives from the states that made up the old Confederacy opposed such legislation. So did some midwestern Republicans. So did Senator Barry Goldwater. So did George Bush campaigning for the Republican nomination for the Senate in Texas. (He didn't make it.) Dozens of mischievous amendments were proposed in the House and Senate to the proposed Civil Rights Bill (H.R. 7152) to defeat it or to weaken it. Some passed. Amendments were introduced to permit employers to refuse to hire atheists (passed by the House, deleted by the Senate, not in final bill) and Communists (passed by both Houses, became Section 703(f) of Title VII).[7]

On 8 February 1964, Representative Howard W. Smith, a crusty conservative Virginia Democrat, dropped a bombshell amendment to add "sex" to the categories for which discrimination was originally prohibited: race, color, religion, and national origin.[8] There was much laughter rippling in the background during debate on the amendment. Remember, this was before the women's movement had taken off, just a year after the publication of Betty Friedan's *The Feminine Mystique*. The National Organization of women (NOW) did not come into being until 1966, two years later.

The "sex amendment" was opposed by many liberals who believed H.R. 7152 was mostly for "the Negro" and that discrimination was much greater against Negroes than against white women. In all the debate over H.R. 7152 there was virtually no specific mention of any other "minority" than Negroes. Representative Edith Green, Democrat of Oregon, spoke for many liberals, but for few of her House colleagues, when she said in debate:

> Today, I repeat, let us not add any amendment that would place in jeopardy in any way our primary objective of ending that discrimination that is most serious, most urgent, most tragic, and most widespread against the Negroes of our country.
>
> May I also say I am not in complete agreement with everything that has been said by my women colleagues. I think that I, as a white woman, have been discriminated against, yes—but for every discrimination that I have suffered, I firmly believe that the Negro woman has suffered ten times that amount of discrimination.... If I have to wait for a few years to end this discrimination against me and my women friends—then as far as I am concerned I am willing to do that if the rank discrimination against Negroes will be finally ended under the so-called protection of the law.

Mrs. Green went on to note that there was not "one word of testimony" regarding this sex amendment before the House Committee on the Judiciary or the House Committee on Education and Labor, "not one single bit of testimony." The American Association of University Women formally opposed the amendment as did the president's Commission on the Status of Women, a collection of vintage liberals appointed by President Kennedy in 1961. Sex was added to H.R. 7152 by a vote of 168–133, no big majority, with virtually all of the bill's opponents voting in favor.

An amendment in the House, by Democratic Representative John Dowdy of Texas, to add age to the list of protected categories was defeated as were eight other sabotaging amendments he made. One was to specifically prohibit discrimination "against Caucasian, white, Protestant citizens as well as other races, colors, religions, and national origins." Perhaps the most notable amendment introduced in the Senate was one by Senator Sam Ervin, Democrat of North Carolina, to eliminate entirely Title VII from H.R. 7152. It was defeated by a roll call vote of 33–64, something less than an overwhelming defeat.

On no issue were the sponsors of what was to be known as the Civil Rights Act of 1964 more unambiguous than their total opposition to preferential hiring, quotas, or the seeking of any sort of "balance." These liberals continually pointed out to their opponents that no part of Title VII could in any way support quotas. Senator Hubert H. Humphrey, liberal Democrat from Minnesota, in one of his defenses of Title VII said in the Senate in March 1964:

> Contrary to the allegations of some opponents of this title, there is nothing in it that will give any power to the Commission or to any court to require hiring, firing, or to achieve a certain racial balance.
>
> That bugaboo has been brought up a dozen times; but it is nonexistent. In fact, the very opposite is true. Title VII prohibits discrimination. In effect, it says that *race, religion and national origin are not to be used as the basis for hiring and firing* [emphasis added].

Two months later, on 25 May, he elaborated on how "affirmative action" would work under Title VII:

> The burden of proof that discrimination [under Title VII] has occurred rests with the complainant. The relief available is a court order enjoining the offender from engaging further in discriminatory practices and *directing the offender to take appropriate affirmative action* [emphasis added]; for example, reinstating or hiring employees, with or without back pay....

Senator Harrison Williams, Democrat from New Jersey, responded with as much vigor as Senator Humphrey to charges in the Senate on 23 April that Title VII would lead to quota hiring on a racial basis:

> For some reason, the fact that *there is nothing whatever in the bill* [H.R. 7152] *which provides for racial balance or quotas* in employment has not been understood by those opposed to civil rights legislation. They persist in opposing a provision which is not only not contained in the bill, *but is specifically excluded from it.* Those opposed to H.R. 7152 should realize that *to hire a Negro solely because he is Negro is racial discrimination,* just as much as a "white only" employment policy. Both forms of discrimination are prohibited by Title VII of this bill [emphases added].

On 19 June 1964 the Senate passed what has come to be known as the Civil Rights Act of 1964. The House passed it on 2 July by a roll call vote of 289–126, and President Lyndon B. Johnson signed it into law on the same day, saying that "its purpose is not to divide, but to end divisions."[9] No Senate debate in American history lasted as long, eighty-three days, as that over H.R. 7152.

The Civil Rights Act of 1964 and its offspring, the Voting Rights Act of 1965, are two of the most extraordinary legislative accomplishments in American history. The former outlawed segregated restaurants, hotels, theaters, and other public facilities, helped guarantee the right to vote, and made job discrimination illegal. It remains very much intact, if not in practice. A few changes were brought about by the Equal Employment Opportunity Act of 1972, which extended coverage to employers and unions with fifteen or more full-time employees, increased from the previous threshold of twenty-five; employees in state and local government were added, as were employees of educational institutions.

The Voting Rights Act of 1965, which we have defined as outside our concern here, successfully and with amazing speed righted a "clear and simple wrong" (President Johnson's words). It ensured the right to register and vote to blacks in the southern states and changed the face of American politics. The Voting Rights Act, like the Civil Rights Act, has undergone a transmogrification of values and goals.[10] It, too, has become a vehicle for demanding ethnic- and race-specific results. But this is not to be part of our account here.

Title VII of the Civil Rights Act of 1964 is most pertinent to affirmative action, and most central to this concern is Section 703(a). It states that:

It shall be an unlawful employment practice for an employer—

(1) to fail or refuse to hire or to discharge any individual, or otherwise to discriminate against any individual with respect to his [sic] compensation, terms, conditions or privileges of employment, because of such individual's race, color, religion, sex, or national origin;

or

(2) to limit, segregate, or classify his employees or applicants for employment in any way which would deprive or tend to deprive any individual of employ-

ment opportunities or otherwise adversely affect his status as an employee, because of such individual's race, color, religion, sex, or national origin.

Also, in Section 703, these same discriminatory prohibitions are applied to employment agencies [703b], labor organizations [703c], and training programs [703d].

On one occasion in Title VII the term "affirmative action" is used, but it has a quite different meaning from that which it has variously come to mean since the late 1960s. It covered nothing more specific than allowing recompense for back pay lost because an individual was found by a court to have been discriminated against on the basis of "race, color, religion, sex, or national origin." This is the "old" meaning of affirmative action, in effect from the mid-1930s to the second half of the 1960s. In Section 706(g) we read:

If the court finds that the respondent has intentionally engaged in...an unlawful employment practice charged in the complaint, the court may enjoin the respondent from engaging in such unlawful employment practice, and order such *affirmative action* as may be appropriate, which *may include* reinstatement or hiring of employees, with or without back pay.... Interim earnings or amounts earnable with reasonable diligence by the person or persons discriminated against *shall operate to reduce* the back pay otherwise allowable [emphases added].

The Equal Employment Opportunity Act of 1972 amended and strengthened Section 706(g), the affirmative action clause, to add that judicial relief may include "any other equitable judgment [in addition to reinstatement or hiring with or without back pay] as the court deems appropriate."

Title VII of the Civil Rights Act of 1964 remains the most misinterpreted of the eleven titles of the Act; and of the sixteen sections of Title VII, the most distorted is 703, specifically 703(a) and (d), prohibition of discrimination, and 703(j), prohibition of required preferential hiring, to which we now turn.

Opponents of Title VII in the Senate, obsessed with issues of "quotas" and "balance" and to whom Senators Humphrey and Williams directed their eloquence, led to the inclusion of a measure in the Dirksen-Mansfield substitute, the Senate's alternative to H.B. 7152, to prohibit any required preferential hiring. This is clearly prohibited by paragraph 703(j) of Title VII (taken without change from paragraph 703(a) of the Dirksen-Mansfield substitute). Here it is in its entirety:

> *Nothing contained in this title shall be interpreted to require* any employer, employment agency, labor organization, or joint labor-management committee subject to this title to grant preferential treatment to any individual or to any group *on account of an imbalance which may exist* with respect to the total number or percentage of persons of any race, color, religion, sex, or national origin employed by any employer, referred or classified for employment by any employment agency or labor organization, admitted to membership or classified by any labor organization, or admitted to, or employed in, any apprenticeship or other training program, in comparison with the total number or percentage of persons of such race, color, religion, sex, or national origin in any community, State, section, or other area, or *in the available work force in any community, State, section, or other area* [emphases added].

President Johnson's Executive Order 11246 of 1965 reaffirmed Kennedy's Executive Order 10925 of 1961. It was also responsible for the establishment of the Office of Federal Contract Compliance (OFCC) under the secretary of labor. The term "affirmative action" is used only one time in the entire text.[11] However, Johnson's conception of affirmative action, the "equality of results" meaning, is not found in this Executive Order but in his enormously influential 1965 Howard University commencement address in which he celebrated the imminent passage of the Voting Rights Act of 1965. This was, he said, only the most recent victory in a long struggle in which freedom was just the beginning:

> But freedom is not enough…. You do not take a person who for years has been hobbled by chains and liberate him, bring him up to the starting line of a race and then say, "You are free to compete with all the others," and still justly believe you have been completely fair.[12]

The president then proclaimed in this historic address "the next and more profound stage in the battle for civil rights. We seek not just freedom but opportunity—not just equity but human ability—not just equality as a right and a theory but *equality as a fact and as a result*" [emphasis added]. Here we have the first and only presidential articulation of the idea of *preferential* affirmative action. Here we have the first and only presidential articulation of the concept of equity, the idea of equality meaning equality of outcome. Johnson only had Negroes in mind when he talked of this "more profound stage" in the civil rights struggle.

For more than three decades two governmental agencies, the Office of Federal Contract Compliance (OFCC) and the Equal Employment Opportunity Commission (EEOC), have been the main organizations adjudicating affirmative action cases in the United States. The awesome bureaucratic power of the OFCC and a comparison of it with the EEOC, oriented toward cases of individual discrimination, is described by historian Herman Belz:

> Affirmative action in contract compliance was directed at collective social and institutional discrimination, rather than individual discriminatory acts defined as denial of equal treatment in a procedural sense [as with EEOC]. Implicitly resting on the theory of disparate impact discrimination, the executive order program constituted a simpler and more direct form of government coercion than Title VII enforcement because it was not concerned with the legal question of the meaning of unlawful discrimination. Whereas under Title VII judicial relief could not be ordered except on a finding of unlawful practices, the executive department agencies that awarded government contracts operated under no such limitation. They could require affirmative action as a condition of doing business with the government, and could define it to mean whatever they pleased. If employers wanted to retain or bid on federal contracts, they had to accept the government's view of affirmative action or be found in noncompliance.[13]

Both Title VII of the Civil Rights Act of 1964 and Executive Order 11246 of 1965 manifest a color-blind, nondiscriminatory public philosophy. Both established agencies to enforce their respective provisions, the EEOC and the OFCC. Both bureaucracies proceeded from the time of their establishment in the mid-1960s to subvert the goal of ensuring procedural equality and equal opportunity and replaced it with a race/ethnic/gender redistributionist ethic mandating result-oriented procedures, quotas, goals, and time tables.

So began the evisceration of the civil rights movement of the 1950s and '60s.

Chapter 9

The Varieties of
Affirmative Action

The academic hiring process presented here is not premised on the traditional notion of using peoples' talents regardless of their race, national origin, gender etc.... Of particular importance is the question of evaluating the special competencies that women and racial/ethnic minorities bring to their academic endeavors, such as, different perspectives, distinctive "voices" and intellectually challenging insights.

—Handbook for Academic Recruitment and Hiring[1]

There are a number of race-, ethnic-, and gender-conscious practices that are called affirmative action. Five "models" of it have been identified and distinguished by legal scholar David Oppenheimer, and he is sympathetic to all of them.[2] Still, they are worthy distinctions, and they are the basis of the typology adopted here.

It is useful to conceive of the varieties of affirmative action as lying on a continuum. At one extreme are those of an employer or educational institution which affirmatively—positively, actively—carries out a policy of non-discrimination on the basis of race, ethnicity, gender, or other characteristics not germane to the position of employee or student. At the other extreme is the deliberate seeking of a person because of that person's ascribed status, be it a black skin, an Hispanic surname, or yy chromosomes. This is called *targeted hiring* in the affirmative-action business. The most famous case of this variety, but without the term affirmative action even being whispered, was President Bill Clinton's determination to hire a woman as U.S. Attorney General. After two ill-fated attempts with Zoe Baird and Kimba Wood, he succeeded with Janet Reno, the first female Attorney General. Let's begin with this "Targeted Hiring Type."

Consider the following boxed advertisement which appeared in a Sunday *New York Times* under the heading "Visiting Distinguished Hispanic Scholar."[3] "Demonstrated outstanding achievement in some aspect of Hispanic Culture" was the first mentioned and most fundamental of the necessary qualifications. What is really asked for in this advertisement? It is for an Hispanic scholar and one who, almost certainly, is ethnically Hispanic and who Dean John O'Connor of the School of Humanities, Management, and Social Sciences at William Paterson College in Wayne, New Jersey can point to with pride as his hire.

Just consider how wide the net is cast. An Hispanic scholar of "some aspect of Hispanic Culture" would include persons from many specific ethnicities, from at least a dozen disciplines, a gross of specialties: a Spanish medievalist, a critic of contemporary Mexican theater, an author of a biography of Fidel Castro, an Argentine historian (but not a Brazilian one), a student of Puerto Rican culture in the South Bronx. Surely an Hispanic sociologist out of the *barrio* would be much preferred to an Argentine Jew who is an authority on Latin American theater.

Sometimes, commonly in the universities, the filling of a position is contingent on finding a person of the desired race, ethnicity, or gender. Among the faculty searches approved for the 1992–93 academic year by Mary Elizabeth Shutler, provost and vice president for academic affairs at California State University, Los Angeles was "One probationary position in Sociology, *to be filled only if a black or Hispanic colleague can be appointed*" [emphasis added].[4] Sometimes positions are created to be filled *only* by a person of a specified ascribed characteristic.

The "Quota Type" is what most people who oppose affirmative action mean by the term. These are all the programs that set specific numbers. The University of California at Davis before the *Bakke* (1978) decision of the Supreme Court set aside sixteen of 100 places in the entering class specifically for minority students. In *Weber (Kaiser Aluminum and Chemical Corporation v. Weber* [1979]), the Supreme Court sustained a quota plan whereby 50 percent of the positions in a training program were to be reserved for black employees, until such time as the proportion of craft workers was similar to the proportion of blacks in the local workforce. In 1988 Duke University announced a plan *requiring* every department and program in the university to hire at least one new black by 1993 or face penalties from the administration; in the same year the University of Wisconsin-Madison announced plans to hire seventy minority professors during the next three years. (Neither plan succeeded.) Many law schools— Berkeley, Georgetown, and Texas among the most well known—have had "Quota Type" admissions programs.

In *Fullilove (Fullilove v. Klutznick* [1980]), the Court upheld a federal law requiring that at least 10 percent of all federal funds for local public works go to minority businesses. The city of Richmond, Virginia had a plan, before it was overturned by the Supreme Court [*City of Richmond v. J. A. Croson Company* (1989)], to set aside a minimum of 30 percent of work on city contracts to be subcontracted out to minority-owned firms. The Supreme Court and the lower courts, since *Fullilove,* have shown themselves to be distinctly negative to "Quota Type" plans. It has now become casuistically fashionable to claim that the plan calls for "goals," not "quotas."

A third type are "Preference Programs." These are programs which do not have quotas, but give preference to certain categories of persons. "As part of its Affirmative Action Program, Marquette [University] gives preference in hiring to Jesuits," wrote the chairman of that university's sociology department to a job applicant.[5] Those university admission programs which give preference to persons of certain racial or ethnic background are more common. An example of these "Preference Programs" are those that give veterans bonus points on civil service examinations. A well-known example of a "Preference Program" is the consent decree entered into by the city of Memphis (1984) resulting from a claim of racial discrimination against the city's fire department. The agreement was that women and minority city employees not employed by the fire department could apply for openings there before white male city employees or any noncity employees. In *Johnson v. Transportation Department, Santa Clara County* (1987), discussed in detail in the next chapter, the Supreme Court rendered a judgment that a "Preference Program" involving gender was in accord with Title VII of the Civil Rights Act of 1964.

Here is how one typical university "Preference Program" worked. It was upheld by the U.S. Department of Education in 1994 after being challenged as discriminatory against white and Asian-American applicants. It is a variant of the program that has operated at all nine of the University of California campuses. At the University of California, San Diego the admission of 10,600 students in 1991 was done in three stages.[6] In the first stage 60 percent of the slots were filled wholly on the basis of objective criteria: grades, test scores, and courses taken. At this stage 3 percent of those accepted were black, Hispanic, or American Indian. The second stage filled 35 percent of the slots. At this stage points were added for various categories. Black, Hispanic, and American Indian students were awarded an additional three hundred points; in-state students got two hundred points; low-income applicants one hundred points; veterans one hundred points; and disabled applicants one hundred points. At the second stage 12 percent of the applicants accepted were black, Hispanic, or American Indian.

The Department of Education found this adding of points to be legal because, in the words of the judgment:

> UCSD tailored its criteria to award more supplemental points for underrepresented ethnicity than for other supplemental criteria because the faculty found the achievement of diversity with respect to race and ethnicity was the most difficult task UCSD faced.

The remaining 5 percent of the slots were filled in the third stage. These were to go to applicants who "demonstrated enough potential for success," according to the admissions policy, that they were worthy of admission. The department found that UCSD had used these slots "primarily for applicants from underrepresented ethnic groups" but that this "may not have been consistent" with the *Bakke* decision of the Supreme Court! (It certainly was not because according to *Bakke* race could be used only as a *plus* factor, not the *determining* factor.)

A telling appraisal of the implications of this UCSD "Preference Program" was made by Michael S. Greve, executive director of the Center for Individual Rights: "Any university can just intone the magic word 'diversity' and set the numbers to admit whoever it wants."[7] This plan is similar to those used in the Communist countries of Eastern Europe, but there the beneficiaries were applicants of proletarian and peasant background.

Success in hiring under "Preference Programs" is taken as success in one's job, something to boast about. Mary Sue Coleman, provost and vice president for academic affairs at the University of New Mexico and now president of the University of Iowa, claimed in 1994 that more than 50 percent of recent faculty hires were women.[8] But Jonathan Porter, chairman of history, could claim relatively greater success. In a letter to his dean, "Continuation as Chair," he listed his accomplishments as chairman. He wrote: "Successfully pursued *affirmative action* faculty recruitment, including the hiring of five women and one minority out of six hirings" [emphasis in original].[9]

The "Self-Examination Type," the fourth kind of program, is common in government, the universities, and large private industries. Typically, research is done to determine what the numerical situation is with respect to minorities and women. Then goals and timetables are set up for increasing their proportions in certain, generally upper-level, job categories. The attempt is to achieve representation of underrepresented categories corresponding to the proportions of persons qualified to fill the positions. Sometimes, particularly for many professional and scientific specialties, minorities are only a tiny or nonexistent proportion. At the other extreme, those considered qualified to fill a particular job category or training program are the same as the category's proportion in the local workforce.

Sometimes self-examination reveals that certain practices neutral on their face allegedly have an adverse impact on the employment or educational opportunities of women and minorities. Sometimes the courts decide that this is the case. Requirements such as high school graduation or the passing of certain standardized tests for, say, firefighters are suspect. Neither, it is argued, is germane to attributes needed by firefighters.

These kind of requirements were, in fact, outlawed in theory, if not in practice, in *Griggs v. Duke Power Company* (1971), the first Title VII case of the Civil Rights Act of 1964 to reach the Supreme Court. It was a class action suit in which black employees charged that hiring, transfer, and promotion policies that were racially neutral on their face were, in practice, racially discriminatory in their impact. Specifically in question were employment practices that required a high school diploma and a passing grade on an objective test. The Court unanimously agreed that such practices were indeed racially discriminatory. They had a *disparate impact* on the hiring and promotion of blacks.

Griggs marks the beginning of the concept of *disparate impact*, judging as racially (and, by extension, gender) discriminatory, practices which are neutral on their face, but allegedly result in a racial (gender) category to be statistically underrepresented. In 1989 the Supreme Court, in effect, reversed *Griggs* by its *Ward's Cove v. Antonio* decision. Here minority employees claimed that the racial stratification of the workforce in two Alaska canneries was the result of *disparate impact*. In a 5–4 decision the Court held that the statistical comparison between minorities in skilled and unskilled jobs in the canneries, which the lower court accepted, was not sufficient to make a *prima facie* case. The appropriate comparison, the Court held, was between the racial composition of the jobs in the canneries and the racial composition of the qualified population in the local labor market. Congress in the Civil Rights Act of 1991 overruled the Court and re-established the concept of *disparate impact* as a proper legal interpretation of the Civil Rights Act of 1964.

A fifth type of affirmative action is "Outreach." This subsumes a wide variety of programs that attempt to recruit minorities and women to positions in the workforce and to schools and programs where they are underrepresented.

A final type of affirmative action suggested by Oppenheimer is "nondiscrimination." There are two subtypes: active and passive nondiscrimination. The former may involve a wide variety of practices to avoid discrimination such as "sensitivity training" of employees and abandoning practices which are believed to have a discriminatory effect, such as tests and educational requirements, most usually for high school graduation.

Passive nondiscrimination would logically be outside of a discussion of affirmative action, but Oppenheimer argues that public perception of affirmative action and "nondiscrimination" are "intertwined." This is an important aspect of the intellectual confusion that surrounds affirmative action. Oppenheimer argues that:

> When a court's decision that an individual was the victim of unlawful discrimination results in the payment of damages and an order of employment, admission or reinstatement, the remedy is likely to be perceived as a form of affirmative action. When an employer-defendant, or potential defendant, agrees to a remedy to settle or avoid a discrimination action, it is even more likely to be seen as affirmative action, by observers if not by the participants. The failure to recognize that at least some of the participants in a public debate about affirmative action are likely to use the term to include nondiscrimination compounds the confusion which occurs when the subject is discussed.[10]

That the public does "intertwine" perceptions of nondiscrimination and affirmative action and that the above examples are intuitively reasonable is not sufficiently convincing to regard passive nondiscrimination as belonging under the rubric of affirmative action. It muddies the waters. It lends to affirmative action the moral high ground of nondiscrimination. Indeed, affirmative action *is* affirmative discrimination.

Chapter 10

Affirmative Action's High-Water Mark: *Johnson v. Santa Clara County* (1987)

Johnson was the first case in which the Court held that voluntary affirmative action is permissible under Title VII to overcome the effects of societal discrimination. *Johnson* also established that the legality of voluntary affirmative action as approved in *Weber* applied to sex discrimination and to Title VII claims in public sector employment.

—*Herbert Hill[1]*

It is in fact comforting to witness the reality that he who lives by the *ipse dixit* dies by the *ipse dixit*. But one must grieve for the Constitution.

—*Justice Antonin Scalia[2]*

On 25 March 1987 Paul E. Johnson's six-year struggle through the courts ended in defeat. On that day the Supreme Court affirmed in a 6–3 decision, a court of appeals decision overturning a district court finding that he had been a victim of sex discrimination under Title VII of the Civil Rights Act of 1964. In its decision,

143

the Court also judged the affirmative action plan of Johnson's employer, the Transportation Agency of Santa Clara County, to be legal under Title VII.

Johnson (1987) is the high-water mark in the Court's validation and expansion of preferential affirmative action. Eight years before, in 1979, in *United Steelworkers v. Weber*, the Court had decided that a private employer who had not discriminated in the past could adopt an affirmative action plan for underrepresented blacks under Title VII. The Court construed that the demonstration of a "manifest" statistical imbalance of blacks in a "traditionally segregated job categor[y]" was sufficient justification. In *Johnson*, the Court upheld this same interpretation, and expanded it, in a challenge to a public employer's voluntary affirmative action program. In *Johnson* the pertinent category was sex, not race, and the "manifest" statistical imbalance was among women. More than this, *Johnson* set no limits, defined no parameters, for affirmative action plans. The subtext of this decision is "anything goes" as long as it is called affirmative action.

The written opinions in this case, particularly those of Justices William Brennan and Antonin Scalia, are the most comprehensive and most vigorously expressed of any of the Supreme Court's decisions on affirmative action. The two justices hold diametrically opposed views as to the legality of preferential affirmative action, of the meaning of Title VII. It will not do to call one view liberal or populist or activist or sympathetic to the plight of women and minorities and the other elitist or conservative or nonactivist or unsympathetic to the plight of women and minorities. These justices hold bedrock irreconcilable positions on the role of the Court, its role in the interpretation of law, and the role of government. Their opinions show in the highest relief the legal arguments for preferential affirmative action and those in opposition to it. Both, however, in the words of Michel Rosenfeld, "loudly proclaim their allegiance to the ideal of equality."[3]

The case began 12 December 1979 when the Transportation Agency of Santa Clara County posted a vacancy for the job of road dispatcher in the agency's Roads Division.[4] The position involved assigning road crews, equipment, and materials for road work, together with maintaining the related records. A basic requirement for the job was at least four years of road maintenance or dispatch work experience for the county. The EEOC classifies a road dispatcher as a skilled craft worker.

Twelve county employees applied for the job. Two of them are of central concern in this case. One is Johnson, then a 54-year-old male employed by the county since 1967. He expected to be chosen for the job of road dispatcher, but was passed over in favor of Diane Joyce, a 42-year-old female employed by the county since 1970.

Johnson worked for the agency as a road yard clerk. Prior to being employed by the county, he had worked in private employment as a dispatcher and supervisor. In 1974 he unsuccessfully applied for the road dispatcher opening. In 1977 his road yard clerk position was downgraded, and he requested and received a position as road maintenance worker. At the same time he occasionally worked "out of class" as a road dispatcher.

Joyce was employed as an account clerk. In 1974 she applied, as did Johnson, for the road dispatcher position. However, she was declared ineligible for consideration because she did not have the minimum of four years' experience of dispatch or road maintenance work. In 1975 Joyce left her position as a senior account clerk for a position as a road maintenance worker, being the first woman to fill such a position in the county. During her four years in that position, like Johnson, she sometimes worked "out of class" as a road dispatcher.

Of the twelve applicants for the road dispatcher position, nine, including Johnson and Joyce, were deemed qualified for the position. Each of the nine was interviewed by a two-person team. Seven of the nine scored above seventy on this interview, making them eligible for selection by the appointing authority. Johnson tied for second place with a score of seventy-five; Joyce ranked next with a score of seventy-three.

The qualified candidates were next interviewed by a committee of three agency supervisors. It recommended that Johnson be given the job of road dispatcher.

Before the second interview, Joyce telephoned the county's affirmative action office, because she feared that her application would not be treated in an objective manner. She had earlier had disagreements with two of the agency supervisors, one of whom had described her as a "rebel-rousing [sic], skirt-wearing person."

The county's affirmative action office contacted the agency's affirmative action coordinator, Victor Morton, one of whose responsibilities was to keep the agency director informed of ways to promote the objectives of the agency's affirmative action plan. Later this affirmative action coordinator recommended to the director of the agency, James Graebner, that Joyce be given the job of road dispatcher. At this time *none* of the 238 skilled craft worker positions, of which the road dispatcher position was one, was held by a woman; and no woman in the agency had ever been classified as a road dispatcher.

The director had undisputed final authority to choose any of the seven persons deemed eligible to be road dispatcher. He chose Joyce.

On the certification form naming Joyce to the dispatcher position, her evaluation read: "Well qualified by virtue of 18 years of past clerical experience including 3 1/2 years at West Yard plus almost 5 years as a [road maintenance worker]." Johnson's evaluation was as follows: "Well qualified applicant; two years of [road maintenance worker] experience plus eleven years of road yard clerk. Has had previous outside Dispatch experience but was 13 years ago." (Never up to this point, and never afterward, was it deemed pertinent or, in any way, considered in any opinion that Johnson was a dozen years older than Joyce or that he had three years more seniority with the county. Could Johnson also have charged age discrimination?)

Johnson filed a complaint with the EEOC alleging that he had not got the job of road dispatcher because of sex discrimination in violation of Title VII of the Civil Rights Act of 1964. He made no appeal then, or later, to the Equal Protection Clause of the Fourteenth Amendment. He obtained a right-to-sue letter from the EEOC on 10 March 1981. Ten days later he filed suit in the United States District Court for the Northern District of California. Johnson and his attorney believed they had an "open and shut" case. Santa Clara County, represented by Steven Woodside, was confident that it had acted in a fully lawful manner.

The district court found for Johnson. The court determined that "plaintiff was more qualified for the position of Road Dispatcher than Diane Joyce," and that Joyce's sex was the "*determining factor* in her selection" [emphasis in original]. The court also found the agency's plan invalid because it did not satisfy the criterion put forth in *Weber*, and upon which the agency justified its decision, that the plan be temporary.

The Board of Supervisors of Santa Clara County eventually decided to fight back. Pressure from Local 715 of the State Employees' International Union, which supported the agency's plan, and to which Diane Joyce belonged, was probably decisive here.[5] The United States Court of Appeals for the Ninth Circuit informed both sides that their case would be heard on 14 February 1984. This was one month less than three years after Johnson filed suit in district court. The court of appeals decision was not handed down until 4 December, almost ten months later. The wheels of justice turn slowly.

The court of appeals decided for Joyce. It reversed the district court in all particulars. It held that considering Joyce's sex in choosing her for the road dispatcher position was lawful. It also found that the absence of a termination date in the plan was not "dispositive," because the plan consistently maintained its objective as the attainment of, rather than the maintenance of, a workforce mirroring the workforce in the county. Further, the plan established no fixed percentages of positions for women and minorities, making it less critical that the plan contain a deadline. The plan, said the Court, was adopted because of the "manifest imbalance" in the workforce of the agency, and neither unnecessarily trampled on the rights of other employees, nor created any insuperable bar to their advancement.

Justice Brennan wrote the decision of the Supreme Court. He was supported by Justices Blackmun, Marshall, and Powell; Justice Stevens wrote a concurring opinion, and Justice O'Connor wrote an opinion concurring in the judgment. Chief Justice Rehnquist and Justices Scalia and White dissented.

The majority opinion began by noting "that petitioner bears the burden of establishing the invalidity of the agency's plan." This was justified by a decision of the previous year, *Wygant v. Jackson Board of Education* (1986), in which the Court held that "the ultimate burden remains with the employees to demonstrate the unconstitutionality of an affirmative action program." No different rule, claimed the Court, is needed for an alleged Title VII violation. Thus, it rested with Johnson to demonstrate the invalidity of the agency plan. The Court claimed Johnson failed to do this.

The Court further claimed the agency plan legal on the basis of the decision in *United Steel Workers of America v. Weber* (1979). In this historic decision, the first of its kind, the Court approved a voluntary affirmative action plan by a private employer under Title VII designed "to eliminate manifest racial imbalances in traditionally segregated job categories." Plaintiff Brian Weber challenged the affirmative action plan of the Kaiser Aluminum and Chemical Company, a part of a collective bargaining agreement with the United Steelworkers. He had been denied a position in the company's newly established craft training program, even though blacks with less seniority than he were selected for the program. He claimed the Kaiser plan "impermissibly" considered the race of the applicants.

Brian Weber instituted a class action suit in federal district court claiming he and other white employees had been discriminated against in violation of paragraphs 703(a) and (d) of the Civil Rights Act of 1964. The district court held that the Kaiser plan did indeed violate Title VII. The court of appeals subsequently affirmed this decision. The United Steelworkers then appealed to the Supreme Court.

The Kaiser plan provided that 50 percent of the new trainees in the program were to be black until the percentage of black skilled workers at Kaiser came to approximate the percentage of blacks in the local labor force. The rationale for the Kaiser plan was a situation where only five of 273, or 1.8 percent, of skilled craft workers were black, when about 39 percent of the workforce in the local area was black. The former practice of Kaiser had been to hire trained workers from outside the plant. The aim of the plan was to redress the racial imbalance in the company's workforce.

The Court upheld Kaiser's decision to choose less senior black applicants over more senior white applicants. In *Weber* the Court for the first time found that taking race into account was consistent with Title VII's aim of "breaking down old patterns of racial segregation and hierarchy" [Justice Brennan's wording; no such language is to be found in Title VII]. *Bakke* (1978), it should be noted here, was prior to *Weber*, but it was a Title VI case. In this context Justice Brennan quoted from *Weber*:

> It would be ironic indeed if a law triggered by a Nation's concern over centuries of racial injustice and intended to improve the lot of those who had "been excluded from the American dream for so long" (words of Senator Humphrey) constituted the first legislative prohibition of all voluntary, private, race-conscious efforts to abolish traditional patterns of racial segregation and hierarchy.

In summarizing *Weber* in his *Johnson* opinion, Justice Brennan made three observations about the Kaiser plan. First, it did not "unnecessarily trammel the interests of the white employees," as it did not require "the discharge of white workers and their replacement with new black hires." Second, the plan did not create "an absolute bar to the advancement of white employees," as whites made up half of those admitted to the new program. And, third, the plan was only temporary. Its aim was to "eliminate a manifest racial imbalance," not to *maintain* a racial balance. He further referred to Justice Blackmun's concurrence in *Weber*, which held that an employer seeking to defend a plan does not need to claim prior discriminatory practice, or even to show an "arguable violation" on its part. It need only demonstrate a "conspicuous... imbalance in traditionally segregated job categories." Justice Brennan concluded his summary justification of *Weber* with these words:

> Our decision was grounded in the recognition that voluntary employer action can play a crucial role in furthering Title VII's purpose of eliminating *the effects* of discrimination in the workplace, and that Title VII should not be read to thwart such efforts [emphasis added].

The previous two paragraphs summarize what might be called the *Weber* doctrine, a most contested interpretation of Title VII, and to which Justice Scalia directs all his ire in his dissent in *Johnson*. A summary of what Melvin Urofsky calls "the *Weber* criteria" is this:

- The interest of whites would, to some extent, be restricted, but not to an unnecessary degree, and no white worker could be fired to make room for a black.
- The plan would have to be temporary, with either a fixed end date or a specific goal that would terminate the program.
- The plan could not be used to maintain a fixed percentage of minority workers, but only to eliminate obvious disparities.[6]

Next, Justice Brennan turned to whether the court of appeals decision in *Johnson* was in accord with the *Weber* doctrine. In all respects he found it to be so.

First was the question of whether consideration of the sex of the applicants for skilled craft worker jobs was justified by the presence of "manifest imbalance" in the proportion of women in "traditionally segregated job categories." The Justice observed that this was indeed the case and noted that the plan intended to remedy this imbalance through the "hiring, training and promotion of...women throughout the agency in all major classifications where they are underrepresented." Indeed, "*none* of the 238 [skilled craft] positions was occupied by a woman" [emphasis in text]. He approved of "the long-term goal of a workforce that mirrored in its major job classifications the percentage of women [and minorities] in the area labor market." However, he does offer a caveat: "Where a job requires special training...the comparison should be with those in the labor force who possess the relevant qualifications."

Second was the question of whether the agency plan "unnecessarily trammeled the rights of male employees or created an absolute bar to their advancement." Not at all. Johnson had no "absolute entitlement" to the road dispatcher position. No "legitimate" deeply rooted expectation on the part of Johnson was "unsettled." And, in addition, he kept his job with the agency under the same conditions as before, and he continued eligible for other promotions.

Finally, was the plan intended to maintain a balanced workforce, as disallowed by the *Weber* doctrine? Again, not at all. Justice Brennan noted that there were ten references in the plan to the agency's goal of *attaining* "a balance," but not a single reference to a goal of *maintaining* it. There was no end date in the plan, because it was expected to take a long time to accomplish its goals. Only gradual increases were anticipated.

Justice Brennan went on to observe that in most cases there is no "best qualified" person for a position. He noted that the case at hand is an example of this point. He concluded the discussion of "precisely this point" with this sentence: "The selection of Joyce thus belies the dissent's contention that the beneficiaries of affirmative action programs will be those employees who are merely not 'utterly unqualified.'" [This point is a response to Justice Scalia's charge in his dissent that *Johnson* "will let loose a flood of 'less qualified' minorities and women upon the work force."]

In his conclusion—the decision—to the majority opinion in *Johnson*, he recapitulates the often repeated arguments from the body of the discussion:

> We therefore hold that the Agency appropriately took into account as one factor the sex of Diane Joyce in determining that she should be promoted to the road dispatcher position. The decision to do so was made pursuant to an affirmative action plan that represents a moderate, flexible, case-by-case

approach to effecting a gradual improvement in the representation of minorities and women in the Agency's work force. *Such a plan is fully consistent with Title VII*, for it embodies the contribution that voluntary employer action can make in eliminating the vestiges of discrimination in the workplace [emphasis added]. Accordingly, the judgment of the Court of Appeals is affirmed.

Justice Stevens wrote a concurring opinion to express his views of "our evolving antidiscrimination law" and his concern that the majority opinion does not specify "the permissible outer limits of voluntary [affirmative action] programs." He clearly understood that "*petitioner*[Johnson] *would unquestionably prevail*" [emphasis added] if the "color-blind" intention of Title VII of the Civil Rights Act of 1964 prevailed. With unusual candor, he forthrightly accepts the totally different interpretation given to Title VII by a number of Court decisions beginning with *Weber* as determinative, rather than his own common sense interpretation of what Title VII says. This is what he means by "evolving antidiscrimination law." This is an extraordinary manifestation of the conservative legal doctrine of *stare decisis*, meaning to stand by decisions and not disturb settled matters.

Justice O'Connor concurred in the judgment, but decided to write separately, because the Court had followed "an expansive and ill-defined approach to voluntary affirmative action" which failed to give sufficient guidance to courts and litigants. Justice O'Connor wrote that employers should not have to prove that they discriminated before they adopted affirmative action plans. She maintained that the standard should be one between "societal discrimination" and evidence of a statistical imbalance in a workforce sufficient for "a prima facie Title VII pattern or practice claim" against an employer. *Johnson* was such a case. She was most impressed by the fact that there was not a single woman in a skilled craft position in the agency, "the inexorable zero."

Justice Scalia's dissent in *Johnson* was made, in the words of Justice O'Connor, with "excruciating clarity." It was also seething with passion, unlike the cool majority opinion of Justice Brennan. At the outset of his opinion Justice Scalia cited Section 703(a) of the Civil Rights Act of 1964, calling it "a model of statutory draftsmanship." [Justice Brennan relegated this disputatious section to a footnote, as he did with all criticism of the decision.] He continued:

The Court today completes the process of converting this [Section 703(a)] from a guarantee that race or sex will *not* be the basis of employment discrimination, to a guarantee that it often *will* [emphasis in text]. Ever so subtly, without even alluding to the last obstacles preserved by earlier opinions that we now push out of our path, we effectively replace the goal of a discrimination-free society with the quite incompatible goal of proportionate representation by race and sex in the workplace.

The dissent, joined by Chief Justice Rehnquist and in part by Justice White, had three components: the first described the agency plan and its effects on Johnson; the second, prior decisions the Court "tacitly overruled," and previous distinctions it had ignored; and the third, "the engine of discrimination" the Court had "completed." It was also a plea for overturning *Weber.*

Justice Scalia noted several "salient features" of the agency plan absent from the majority opinion. Most important was that the purpose of the plan was "assuredly not to remedy prior sex discrimination by the Agency. It could not have been, because there was no prior sex discrimination to remedy." He pointed out that the majority opinion failed to mention the observation of the district court—which found *for* Johnson—that the agency "has not discriminated in the past, and does not discriminate in the present against women in regard to employment opportunities in general and promotions in particular." The court of appeals did not disturb this finding.

The agency plan did not seek to bring about a state of affairs that would exist if there were a total absence of discrimination. What the plan did was impose racial and sexual "tailoring" that would, "in defiance of normal expectations and laws of probability," create, albeit gradually, an agency workforce that in every case would reflect the racial and sexual composition of the county workforce, not just the agency workforce. In a world without discrimination any such outcome would be "a statistical oddity," "utterly miraculous."

The "one message" that the plan communicated was that "concrete results were expected" of supervisory personnel. And they would be judged on the basis of "the affirmative action numbers they produce." Several sentences from the plan were quoted to support this "one message." Two of them were these:

- [Implementation of the plan is expected to] result in statistically measurable yearly improvement in the hiring, training and promotion of minorities, women, and handicapped persons in the major job classifications utilized by the Agency where these groups are underrepresented.
- The degree to which each Division *attains the Agency Affirmative Action employment goals* will provide a measure of the Director's commitment and effectiveness in carrying out the Division's EEO Affirmative Action requirements [emphasis in opinion].

Supervisors, in the agency plan, were directed to give "special consideration" to affirmative action "in every individual hiring action" and to explain any failure to hire a woman or minority person.

Justice Scalia showed a special concern for the qualifications of Johnson, indeed, a sympathy for him, quite missing from the majority opinion. He pointed out that Johnson had been a road dispatcher for a private company for seventeen years before becoming an employee of the agency in 1967. He noted that Johnson came in second when he applied for the job of road dispatcher with the agency in 1974, and that a few years later Johnson asked for and received a demotion from road yard clerk to road maintenance worker to gain greater experience and thus enhance the possibilities for future promotion. (Admittedly, the Justice did not mention that Diane Joyce did the same thing. Feminist legal scholar Martha Minow charged that Justice Scalia "demonstrated no comparable understanding of Joyce."[7]) When the road dispatcher job became vacant in 1979, Johnson "was the leading candidate." He based this judgment on the observation that Johnson was assigned to full-time work "out of class" as road dispatcher for nine months, from September 1979 until June 1980.

"There is no question why he [Johnson] did not get the job." He was discriminated against. And it was "much clearer, and its degree more shocking, than the majority and Justice O'Connor's concurring opinion would suggest." This, Justice Scalia maintains, was because neither opinion cited any of the district court's proceedings which the district court "implicitly rejected." He observed that if the agency's affirmative action coordinator had not intervened, "the decision as to whom to promote...would have been made by [the road operations division director]," and he had recommended that Johnson be given the appointment.

Even more extraordinary to the Justice were the findings in the transcript of the trial that the agency director who made the appointment "did not inspect the applications and related examination records of either [Paul Johnson] or Diane Joyce before making his decision" and "did little or nothing to inquire into the results of the interview process and conclusions which [were] described as of critical importance to the selection process." He implied that the agency director simply accepted the recommendation, not based on a careful review of the evidence, of the affirmative action coordinator.

The district court after a two-day trial found that Diane Joyce's sex was "*the determining factor*" in her selection as road dispatcher [emphasis in text]. It found that "[b]ased upon the examination results and the departmental interview, [Mr. Johnson] was more qualified for the position of road dispatcher than Diane Joyce; that "[b]ut for [Mr. Johnson's] sex, male, he would have been promoted to the position of road dispatcher"; and "[b]ut for Diane Joyce's sex, female, she would not have been appointed to the position.... [The Court of Appeals of] [t]he Ninth Circuit did not reject these findings as clearly erroneous," concluded the Justice, "nor could it have done so on the basis of the record before us."

The "most significant proposition of law" established by *Johnson*, according to Justice Scalia, was that racial and sexual discrimination was allowable under Title VII when it was intended to overcome the effects of "societal attitudes that have limited the entry of certain races, or of a particular sex, into certain jobs." *Johnson* was thus "squarely inconsistent" with *Wygant v. Jackson Board of Education* (1986) which held "the objective of remedying social discrimination cannot prevent remedial affirmative action from violating the Equal Protection Clause" [Justice Scalia's words]. While Johnson did not make a constitutional claim, "it is most unlikely that Title VII was intended to place a *lesser* restraint on discrimination by public actors than is established by the Constitution" [emphasis in text].

The dissent observed how the majority opinion "so readily (and so silently)" disregarded the limitations set forth in *Sheet Metal Workers v. EEOC* (1986). The decision in this case held that the remedial provision of Title VII empowers courts to order race-conscious remedies for persons who are not identifiable victims of discrimination *only* in cases "involving particularly egregious conduct" [Justice Powell's wording]. The agency plan was not directed to remedying discrimination, much less "egregious" discrimination. Thus, "(t)here is no sensible basis for construing Title VII to permit employers to engage in race-or-sex-conscious employment practices that courts would be forbidden from ordering them to engage in following a judicial finding of discrimination."

The phrase "traditionally segregated job category" meant very different things in *Weber* and in *Johnson*. In the former it referred to skilled jobs that "systematically and intentionally" excluded black workers; in the latter it referred to a job category that "has not been regarded *by women themselves* as desirable work" [emphasis in text]. These were two distinct phenomena. "And it is the alteration of social attitudes, rather than the elimination of discrimination, which today's decision approves as justification for state-enforced discrimination. This is an enormous expansion, undertaken without the slightest justification or analysis."

The arguments of the dissenting opinion in Part III were less clear and more convoluted than the earlier parts of the opinion. Perhaps this is why Justice White did not here join Justice Scalia and Chief Justice Rehnquist.

The *Johnson* decision, opined Justice Scalia, removed any distinction between public and private employers, a distinction made in *Weber,* in which it was emphasized over and over again that it was private affirmative action that was being dealt with and that the Court did not want to intervene too much here. (Public employees were brought under Title VII by the Equal Opportunity Act of 1972.) Actually, Justice Scalia claimed to see no difference between private and public employers regarding Title VII, and then went on to say that "the only good reason for creating such a distinction [between private and public employers] would be to limit the damage of *Weber....* It is well to keep in mind just how thoroughly *Weber* rewrote the statute it purported to construe." What *Weber* really did, "in effect," was to hold the legality of discrimination against "disfavored groups and individuals," in other words, nonminority persons and men, and that was to be judged by a vague "judicially crafted code of conduct" rather than by what Title VII said.

The majority's (Justice Brennan's) response to the dissent's (Justice Scalia's) criticism of its "dramatic departure" from the Court's earlier Title VII precedents was that, since "Congress has not amended the statute to reject our construction...we...may assume that our interpretation was correct." Justice Scalia called this a "patently false premise" because it wrongly based the correctness of a statutory construction on "what the current Congress desires rather than by what the law as enacted meant." More than that, it took the particular provision in isolation, disregarding the "total legislative package containing many *quids pro quo.*"

Justice Scalia called this "vindication by congressional inaction" a "canard." The complex checks on legislation constructed by our Constitution [citing *The Federalist No. 62*] create

> an inertia that makes it impossible to assert with any degree of assurance that congressional failure to act represents (1) approval of the status quo, as opposed to (2) inability to agree upon how to alter the status quo, (3) unawareness of the status quo, (4) indifference to the status quo, or even (5) political cowardice.

What Justice Scalia and his fellow conservative justices wanted, above all, in the affirmative action area, was an opportunity to overturn *Weber.* To do so would have "the desirable side-effect of eliminating the requirement of willing suspension of disbelief that is currently a credential for reading our opinions in the affirmative action field."

The closing paragraphs of the dissenting opinion told of the dire consequences of *Johnson.* It would encourage employers, public and private, to discriminate intentionally on the basis of race and sex. Indeed, failure to engage in "reverse discrimination" might even be an abdication of responsibility to shareholders or taxpayers because of the cost of litigating Title VII cases. The decision would please corporate and government employers, many of whom filed briefs as friends of the Court, all on the side of Santa Clara County. For them life would be easier. The costs of hiring less qualified workers might be less for them than litigating Title VII cases. And it would certainly be more predictable. And they would not have to try to convince federal agencies that no discrimination existed by nonnumerical means.

> In fact, the only losers in the process are the Johnsons of the country, for whom Title VII has not been merely repealed but actually inverted. The irony is that these individuals—predominantly unknown, unaffluent, unorganized—suffer this injustice at the hands of a Court fond of thinking itself the champion of the politically impotent. I dissent.

Chapter 11

The Lowering of the Tide: Affirmative Action after *Johnson*

If liberalism is to revive, it will only do so on the ashes of affirmative action. It will revive by articulating the principles that liberalism was founded on: equality before the law, equal treatment by the state, and freedom as the guiding principle of the society. It is a liberalism that provides a space for individuals to achieve the success that has to be won, not provided—fought for, not fought over.

The paradox is that if there was ever a time for this liberalism, it is now. It is the only creed that can recognize and repulse, the ethnic, collective urges that are darkening the old world, and the only creed that can guide the dazzling racial and cultural complexity of the new. History's joke is that it has taken conservatives to rediscover it.

—*Andrew Sullivan* [1]

The trend of court decisions after *Johnson*—the peak in the Supreme Court's opinions sanctioning preferential affirmative action—has reversed itself. Only one major decision by the Supreme Court since *Johnson* has supported an expanded preferential affirmative action, *Metro Broadcasting v. Federal Communications Com-*

mission(1990), and that was overturned five years later by *Adarand Constructors v. Pena*.

In M*etro*, a 5–4 decision, with Justice Brennan again writing for the Court, two federal affirmative action programs were upheld. Both programs were intended to increase minority ownership of broadcast licenses, "minority" being defined as those of "black, Hispanic surnamed, American Eskimo, Aleut, American Indian, and Asiatic [*sic*] American extraction." The decision did not subject federal affirmative action programs to the "strict scrutiny" which Justice O'Connor's dissenting opinion called for. The opinion of the Court was not to remedy any sort of discrimination, past or present, but to promote *diversity.* The assumption underlying the opinion was that minority station owners would structure programming differently than majority station owners.

Metro was the most wrong-headed, groupthink, and sloppy of all the Court's affirmative action decisions. It might be defined as a "no scrutiny" decision. It uncritically accepted the FCC's list of certain ethnic groups as subject to preferential treatment in the granting of broadcast licenses. These preferences might well be defended, as Carl Cohen pointed out, by the following statement which appeared in an official government publication: "The policy is not based on the concept of superiority or inferiority [of any race] but merely on the fact that people differ, particularly in their group associations, loyalties, cultures, outlook, modes of life."[2] The government that made this defense of preference was South Africa defending apartheid in 1960!

In *Adarand* (1995), the Court decided, again in a 5–4 decision, with Justice Sandra Day O'Connor writing the majority opinion, that federal affirmative action programs must meet the same strict scrutiny standard as state and local programs. It reaffirmed *Richmond v. J.A. Croson* (1989) which for the first time got a majority of the Court to support strict scrutiny in determining the constitutionality of affirmative action programs based on race, and overturned the intervening *Metro* decision. Immediately afterward the Federal Communications Commission announced that it would scrap its program of preferences for women and minorities in its sale of wireless telephone licenses. Other government agencies began to examine their programs more critically.

Adarand Constructors, a Colorado Springs concern, went to court to challenge a federal highway construction affirmative action program of the Department of Transportation which gave contractors a 1.5 percent bonus for using subcontractors controlled by "socially and economically disadvantaged individuals," i.e., women and minorities. Adarand contended that the program was reverse discrimination, that it violated the equal protection component of the Fifth Amendment's Due Process Clause. The court of appeals had previously rejected Adarand's claim.

The Supreme Court did not strike down the program, nor did it render an opinion on Adarand's Fifth Amendment claim, but sent the case back to a lower court for reconsideration in light of the new strict scrutiny standard.

The strict scrutiny doctrine was established by *Croson* with three general propositions regarding governmental racial classifications. O'Conner quoted them from *Croson.* The first was *skepticism:* "Any preference based on racial or ethnic criteria must necessarily receive a most searching examination." The second was *consistency:* "The standard of review under the Equal Protection Clause is not dependent on the race of those burdened or benefited by a particular classification," i.e., all reviewable racial classifications must be strictly scrutinized. And, third, *congruence,* "Equal protection analysis in the Fifth Amendment area is the same as that under the Fourteenth Amendment." These three propositions led to the conclusion that "any person, of whatever race, has the right to demand that any governmental program subject to the Constitution justify any racial classification subjecting that person to unequal treatment under the strictest judicial scrutiny." (Nothing was said in any of the written opinions in this case about gender! Is that, too, subject to strict scrutiny?)

The Court is now divided into two camps on federal affirmative action. There is the thinnest majority of five favoring strict scrutiny (O'Connor, Rehnquist, Scalia, Kennedy, and Thomas) and a minority of four favoring a lesser scrutiny, the overturned precedent of *Metro,* (Stevens, Souter, Ginsburg, and Breyer).

In fact *Adarand* is not an important affirmative action decision in the league with *Griggs, Bakke, Weber,* and *Johnson,* because all that it did was to compel government affirmative action programs to "satisf[y] the 'narrow tailoring' test this Court has set out in previous cases." And Justice O'Connor clearly left the door open for governmental affirmative action programs. Close to the end of her opinion she wrote: "The unhappy persistence of both the practice and the lingering effects of racial discrimination against minority groups in this country is an unfortunate reality, and government is not disqualified from acting in response to it...."

An important precedent was set by the Supreme Court in May 1995 when it let stand a lower court ruling that the Benjamin Banneker Scholarship program at the University of Maryland in College Park was unconstitutional.

Banneker scholarships were awarded to about thirty high-achieving blacks each year. The program was adopted in 1978 after a Justice Department complaint that Maryland was running a racially segregated system of higher education.

In 1989 a Maryland Hispanic with the unlikely name of Daniel J. Podberesky sued the State of Maryland after he was denied a Banneker scholarship for which he would have been eligible had he been black. The U.S. Court of Appeals for the Fourth Circuit unanimously agreed that the university's program "more resembles outright racial balancing than a tailored remedy." This is the highest federal court so far to rule on the legality of race-based scholarships. The Supreme Court's refusal to review the appeal's court finding means that there were fewer than four justices who might have voted for review.

Because the Supreme Court refused to hear the circuit court's decision, it is applicable only to the five states in the circuit: Maryland, North Carolina, South Carolina, Virginia, and West Virginia, but it certainly establishes a powerful precedent.

The U.S. Justice Department, many universities, many education associations, the American Civil Liberties Union, and virtually all the national civil rights and women's organizations, not excluding Hispanic ones, supported the University of Maryland's appeal to the Supreme Court.[3] That the Mexican-American Legal Defense and Educational Fund (MALDEF) and the Puerto Rican Legal Defense and Education Fund supported the university revealed their support for the principle of specific-race-based scholarships outweighed their support for an Hispanic plaintiff.

In August 1994 Judge Sam Sparks of the U.S. District Court for the Western District of Texas handed down his decision in *Cheryl Hopwood, et al. v. State of Texas*. This is the first time since *Bakke* (1978) that a federal court declared quotas in student admissions unconstitutional. In this case, dealing with law school admissions, the court declared that separate admission committees for minorities was unconstitutional. Judge Sparks wrote:

> The issue before the Court is whether the affirmative action program employed in 1992 by the [University of Texas Law School] in its admissions procedure met the legal standard required for such programs to pass constitutional muster. The Court having carefully considered the evidence presented at trial, the arguments of counsel, and the briefing provided by the parties, finds that it did not.

Because the court did not go so far as to order the University of Texas to admit the four plaintiffs to the law school, they appealed portions of Judge Sparks' decision.

On 18 March 1996 the most important legal setback yet for race- and ethnic-based affirmative action was handed down by the United States Court of Appeals for the Fifth Circuit.

In a unanimous decision, a three-judge panel struck down the lower court's ruling supporting the affirmative action program of the University of Texas law school. "It [the university] has presented no compelling justification," wrote Judge Jerry E. Smith, "that allows it to continue to elevate some races over others.... [T]he use of race in admissions for diversity in higher education contradicts, rather than furthers, the aims of equal protection. Diversity fosters, rather than minimizes, the use of race. It treats minorities as a group, rather than as individuals. It may further remedial purposes but, just as likely, may promote improper racial stereotypes, thus fueling racial hostility."

As of now it appears that race- and ethnic-based affirmative actions programs will need to be put on hold in the public institutions of the states under the jurisdiction of the Fifth Circuit court: Texas, Louisiana, and Mississippi. The ruling is being appealed to the Supreme Court.

A most extraordinary affirmative action case in the post-*Johnson* decade is that of Sharon Taxman, white, who was laid off as a business school teacher by the Piscataway, New Jersey, Board of Education, in order to retain Debra Williams, black, for the sole reason of promoting diversity.

The case is extraordinary for three reasons. First, the Justice Department changed sides. During the Bush administration, the department sided with Taxman and won its case in federal district court. In July 1994, President Clinton's Assistant Attorney General for Civil Rights, Deval L. Patrick, claimed the government had changed its mind and disagreed with the Taxman ruling. There is no precedent for the government changing from plaintiff to appellant in a case after a judgment has been handed down by a district court. Second, there are no differences between the two sides on what the facts of the case are. It is a singularly crystal-clear case of two opposing views on the limits of affirmative action. And, third, it represents an attempt to make new law in the face of *Wygant* (1986), in which the Supreme Court rejected diversity as an allowable reason for the Jackson, Michigan, school board to lay off white teachers with greater seniority than black teachers with lesser seniority in order to maintain a racial balance.

The case began in 1989 when the Piscataway school board had to decide which of two equally qualified teachers, Taxman or Williams, it needed to let go. Both were hired on the same day in 1980, both were deemed by the board to be equally qualified, and the Piscataway high-school faculty was an integrated faculty. Citing a need to maintain racial diversity, the board laid off Taxman and retained Williams. It did not make the decision by a toss of a coin, as it might (and should) have done.

Taxman then took her case to the Equal Employment Opportunity Commission office in Newark, which informed the Civil Rights Division of the Justice Department. In September 1991, the government filed suit as the principal plaintiff, joined by Taxman. Justice Department lawyers argued that diversity was not sufficient reason for the laying-off of Taxman without evidence of discrimination, and both sides agreed there was none, under Title VII of the Civil Rights Act of 1964. Two years later, in September 1993, Judge Maryanne Trump Barry of federal district court in Newark ruled in favor of the Government's case. She maintained that race can be considered in a voluntary affirmative action program *only* if it is used to remedy past discrimination or if there is "manifest" underrepresentation of minorities. She found neither of these conditions to exist in this case.

On 17 November 1995 the U.S. Court of Appeals for the Third District refused to allow the Clinton Justice Department from participating in this case. Deval Patrick has been rebuffed by the Court! We can guess what the verdict will be.

It is the Supreme Court which has in the past and will continue in the future to decide what affirmative action is, what kinds of plans are acceptable, for whom, and what the limits of these plans are. The Court could declare all preferential affirmative action to be in violation of the Civil Rights Act of 1964 or the Equal Protection Clause of the Fourteenth Amendment. Justices Scalia and Thomas would love to do just that, and maybe Justices Rehnquist and Kennedy would join them. But there is no case on the horizon which might give them the opportunity.

Ideology and Practice

[T]he affirmative action debate is not between persons who are "pro-equality" and others who are "anti-equality." Both the most ardent advocates of affirmative action and its most vehement foes loudly proclaim their allegiance to the ideal of equality.

—*Michel Rosenfeld*[4]

In the words of the title of Herman Belz's critical history of affirmative action, America has seen *Equality Transformed* (1991) since the late 1960s from an ideology stressing individual rights and equality of opportunity to one stressing group rights and equality of outcome. Compare the civil rights ideology of liberal Senators Hubert H. Humphrey and Harrison Williams in the 1960s with that of liberal Supreme Court Justice Brennan in the 1980s. Sometimes the shift can be observed in a single individual. Thurgood Marshall is the best example. Before he became a Supreme Court justice, when he was the leading NAACP lawyer, he was critical of any racial/ethnic groups' claim to preferential treatment:

- What we want is the striking down of race.... They give tests to grade children so what do we think is the solution? Simple. Put the dumb colored children in with the dumb white children, and put the smart colored children with the smart white children—that is no problem.
- There are geniuses in both groups and there are lower ones in both groups, and it has no bearing. No right of an individual can be conditioned as to any average of other people in his racial group or any other group.[5]

For opponents of affirmative action, like this writer, this sea change is seen as the decadent phase of the civil rights movement; for its proponents, a movement toward a more equal and inclusive and just society. In typical American fashion, the new equality has an almost total lack of class consciousness about it. A black is a black. A Latino is a Latino. A woman is a woman. The trinity of ethnicity, class, and gender is ritually cited, but then class ignored. It is a movement less idealistic and altruistic than the civil rights movement of the color-blind 1950s and 1960s. It is more separatist and characterized by more group self-interest and more individual self-interest than the old equality.

In addition to the ideology of retribution—the justification of affirmative action to correct for past injustices—several overlapping ideologies came to the fore in the 1980s which lend ideological support to the theory and practice of affirmative action: diversity, ethnic entitlement, and multiculturalism.

Diversity, along with its cousin concept inclusiveness, is the undergirding and most general of the ideologies. The ideology of diversity maintains that institutions should reflect the racial, ethnic, and gender (almost never class) composition of a heterogeneous population, that each has different perspectives to contribute to the whole, that it is *just* for the different elements to be represented to something like a proportionate degree, and that it is impermissible to single out any cultural tradition as more worthy than others, most notably that of Western civilization, the "Eurocentric tradition." All is relative, except that women and minorities have been oppressed, have been victims, and that race- and gender-consciousness in hiring and promoting and in admissions to selective colleges and universities is necessary not only to compensate for past oppression, but to promote diversity. A core idea of the ideology of diversity is that race, ethnicity, gender, and, sometimes, sexual orientation, are *the* fundamental determinants of a person's being, that this being cannot, should not, wrest itself from its biological or sociological origins. Yet it is mostly blacks who have race, mostly Hispanics who have ethnicity, mostly women who have gender, and mostly gays who have a sexual orientation.

Pluralism is an older ideology than diversity, one which recognizes cultural differences as important, maybe sometimes more important than similarities. It is a gentler, vaguer, less comprehensive, more open version of difference than the ideology of diversity. It differs from the latter in that it emphasizes integration of the group into a larger whole, which diversity does not. It has an implicit commitment to *e pluribus unum,* one from many.

Ethnic entitlement is the ideology of diversity in the political and economic realms. It is certainly not a new idea in American society, but the pervasiveness and officiality of it is. Multiculturalism is the ideology of diversity in the realm of education and the workplace. A basic component of multiculturalism, in addition to diversity, is the promotion of racial, ethnic, and gender (again, rarely class) "sensitivity." (A more appropriate word for what is meant by the multiculturalists is sensibility.) This latter component of multiculturalism acts to inhibit open criticism of affirmative action. Promiscuous multiculturalists assume all cultures are equal and have a disbelief in language standardization, that Spanish and "black English" should have equal standing with "standard" American English.

The preferential affirmative action plans that have been blessed by the courts and politicians, in spite of the "extraordinary clarity" of Title VII and the old American values of individualism and individual responsibility, are enormously at odds. The explanation is the rise of the new equality with its emphasis on numerical equality, the concern with group rights, enhanced by collective guilt about our oppressive past, the emergence of the ideology of diversity, plus a goodly dose of awakened pragmatic self-interest. This has been a consequence of the organization of minorities and quasi-minorities—women, gay people, the disabled—whose ideological shapers have collectively defined each category as historically victimized. When we add up the proportions of women, minorities, the disabled, and gay people, three-quarters of the population can be defined as victims of an oppressive past. Even white men are now defining themselves as victims.

In the ideological debate over affirmative action, its proponents have a slippery linguistic advantage over their opponents. Just the term itself has a positive ring to it. It means *positive* action as opposed to negative action. It sounded...well, so positive! In older opinion surveys people responded favorably to it, negatively to what it usually meant: preferential treatment, quotas, goals, government intervention and bureaucracy. By the '90s, if not before, the term had become stigmatized. People became aware of just what it meant. It has been replaced, above all, by diversity; but other terms are used as a surrogates for affirmative action: "equal opportunity," "inclusion," and "true" or "real" "equality. "

A positive connotation adheres to a number of other words related to affirmative action. "Civil rights organizations" sounds more idealistic than "women's and minority organizations." "Diversity" and "pluralism" are more appealing than their implied opposite "uniformity," just as "multiculturalism" is more attractive than its implied opposite, "monocultural." "Inclusiveness" suggests a feeling for humanity that "exclusiveness" and "elitism" certainly do not. "Non-traditional"programs, plans, and practices sound more progressive than their "traditional" counterparts.

Terms that refer to what proponents of affirmative action hate, to make matters worse, all have sinister connotations. Who can be sympathetic to "disparate impact," "manifest imbalance," "underrepresentation," "underutilization," "inequities," or "glass ceilings," or any kind of ceilings; and those words bandied about by radical feminists, "patriarchy," "hegemony," and "sexism." Even to suggest the presence of "institutional racism" or "structured inequality" raises a specter of silent oppression and makes any institution so accused suspect.

On the other hand, the anti-affirmative action forces have a few loaded terms in their lexicon to help them: "fairness," "equal treatment," and "nondiscrimination"; most powerful is "reverse discrimination."

Affirmative action was supposed to be temporary, but it hasn't turned out that way. For many years it has been part and parcel of the institutionalized landscape of business, industry, government, and education, particularly higher education, where it is practiced in its most free-wheeling form. By the mid-1980s affirmative action had become so firmly established in the corporate world that, according to a survey of the Fortune 500, "88 percent of 197 corporations responding said they would maintain quotas even if not required to do so."[6] American companies don't want to get rid of affirmative action. Many just want to be rid of an intrusive EEOC and OFCC. American companies want a "diverse" work force because it is good business. It helps them to appeal to all categories of people and compete better in a global market.[7] The passing of governmentally mandated affirmative action would cause hardly a ripple in the business and corporate world.

Before 1995 there was little public, as opposed to private, criticism of affirmative action. The exceptions were a few columnists, a handful of conservative organizations and think tanks, Senator Jesse Helms, and the editorial page of *The Wall Street Journal.* To oppose affirmative action publicly before 1995 often put one in the racist company of David Duke.

Still, no president since Kennedy, including Bill Clinton before 1995, uttered the words "affirmative action" in public except for George Bush who claimed, probably with tongue in cheek, that he supported it after signing the Civil Rights Act of 1991. Presidents Ronald Reagan and George Bush expressed their opposition to quotas. Bill Clinton called them "bean counting." Yet as Nathan Glazer has observed, affirmative action has become so entrenched in government that even the few agencies that opposed quotas and goals "report[ed] to the Equal Employment Opportunity Commission on their progress toward meeting affirmative action numerical goals."[8]

Bill Clinton wanted his administration to "reflect the face of America," and his administration has been more attuned to race, ethnicity, and gender than any that preceded it. More than any of his predecessors he deserves the title of *the* affirmative action president. A majority of his original cabinet were minorities and women (four blacks, two Hispanics, and two women) as were many of his other top appointments. In a number of cases his administration has taken extreme positions on affirmative action. Most notorious was the Justice Department's switching sides in the Piscataway case. In April 1995, provoking intense resentment among some of his supporters, Clinton decided to bypass a highly qualified and experienced white lawyer to appoint a much less experienced and younger lawyer as the first black U.S. attorney in the history of Mississippi.[9]

Nearly 60 percent of Clinton's federal court appointments have been minority group members or women. This is an epic increase over those of Presidents George Bush with 28 percent women and minorities, Ronald Reagan, 14 percent, and Jimmy Carter, 38 percent. "Unfortunately," Jeffrey Rosen, legal affairs writer for *The New Republic,* has written, "his single-minded pursuit of diversity [e.g., affirmative action], combined with an eagerness to avoid controversy, has kept him from appointing the best available legal minds to the courts."[10] He concludes his *New York Times* Op-Ed piece, "Mediocrity on the Bench," by warning that if Clinton doesn't stop playing affirmative action with the courts and fill the remaining seats with candidates like his "superb" nominees, Ruth Bader Ginsburg and Stephen Breyer, "he will leave office with a bench that appears superficially to be more diverse but whose intellectual leadership remains firmly under Republican control."

Dealing with Dissonance

[B]y a *tour de force* reminiscent not of jurists such as Hale, Holmes, and Hughes, but of escape artists such as Houdini, the Court eludes clear statutory language, "uncontradicted" legislative history, and uniform precedent in concluding that employers are, after all, permitted to consider race in making employment decisions.

—Justice Warren H. Rehnquist, dissenting in Weber

To favor the majority opinion in *Johnson* and in *Weber,* on which it is based, requires a belief that the Court should use its authority to create a better society in a way it favors; that it should follow some "evolving antidiscrimination law" (Justice Stevens's phrase) rather than what the law says; that it should generously reinterpret legislation; and to make that cutting charge, should *legislate from the bench.* The most celebrated, but flawed, statement by a justice of this position is that of Justice Blackmun in his partial dissent in *Bakke* (1978):

> I suspect that it would be impossible to arrange an affirmative action program in a racially neutral way and have it successful. To ask that this be so is to demand the impossible. In order to get beyond racism, we must first take account of race. There is no other way. And *in order to treat some persons equally, we must treat them differently* [emphasis added]. We cannot—we dare not—let the Equal Protection Clause perpetuate racial supremacy.

The famous, praised, and much quoted italicized sentence above is, in fact, vacuous, unclear, and derivative. All it says is that "some persons" to be treated equally must be treated unequally ("differently"). This could be used to cover an infinite variety of persons in disadvantaged situations. It is empty of empirical meaning. Justice Felix Frankfurter said the same thing in *Dennis v. United States* (1950): "It was a wise man who said that there is no greater inequality than the equal treatment of unequals." The paragraph gives the impression that Justice Blackmun is thinking about blacks, but *Bakke* dealt with minority categories, not specifically blacks.

To favor the opposing view of Justices Rehnquist, Scalia, and White, and almost certainly Justice Thomas, that *Weber,* and then necessarily *Johnson,* should be overruled would certainly follow from one who believes the Court's function is to interpret the law as written and as intended.

One can, in the cases of *Weber* and *Johnson*, be sympathetic to the affirmative action plans that gave rise to these cases, but still oppose them. This is because the interpretation given Title VII by the majority of the justices has no basis in a common sense reading of the law, nor in the legislative history of the law, nor in any congressional legislation. Chief Justice Warren Burger's dissent in *Weber* shows these sympathies:

> The Court reaches a result I would be inclined to vote for were I a Member of Congress considering a proposed amendment of Title VII. I cannot join the Court's judgment, however, because it is contrary to the explicit language of the statute and arrived at by means wholly incompatible with long-established principles of separation of powers. Under the guise of statutory "construction," the Court effectively rewrites Title VII to achieve what it regards as a desirable result. It "amends" the statute to do precisely what both its sponsors and its opponents agreed the statute was *not* intended to do [emphasis in text].

There are at least three reactions to this turnabout, perhaps the most extraordinary in American constitutional history, in the interpretation of Title VII on the part of scholars of the subject. They manifest the same differences as the jurists themselves. They deplore it, accept it, or are in denial that there has been a transformation of meaning.

Historian Herman Belz deplores it. His 1991 book *Equality Transformed* documents in painstaking detail how a law based on individual rights and equality of opportunity has been transformed into a justification of group rights and equality of results.

Sociologist Nathan Glazer, writing in 1988, rather nonchalantly, accepts it:

> The critic of quotas or goals and timetables is regularly attacked for opposing affirmative action, even though he may well support the clear intention of the "affirmative action" of Title VII as understood in 1964.... But there is no point arguing with changes in the meaning of words: whatever the term meant in the 1960s, since the 1970s affirmative action has come to mean quotas and goals and timetables.[11]

However, the mercurial but sensitive Glazer seems to have changed his views after reading Belz's *Equality Transformed* some three years later. On the back page of the paperback edition of the book is a laudatory endorsement by Glazer of this searing critique of affirmative action. He writes: "[It] is by far the most thorough account of the tortured history of affirmative action in employment that has ever been written. It describes...transforming a national commitment to developing what was color-blind nondiscrimination into a set of legal requirements that have made race and sex crucial elements in employment and promotion decisions."

Constitutional historian Melvin Urofsky is in denial about it. He does not even acknowledge that "the meaning of words" has changed. He writes:

> [W]hile some sections of the bill [Title VII] did seem to have been written with remarkable directness, other sections *left a great deal to the imagination*. Moreover, *evidence—strong evidence* existed that the Court's interpretation [in *Johnson*] of the "spirit" of Title VII, so derided by Scalia, had been right on target, that the Court had in fact gotten it right. [Emphases added.][12]

There is not a sentence in Title VII, as I hope I have demonstrated, that leaves "a great deal to the imagination." Urofsky makes no citation of the "evidence" that the Court's interpretation of the "spirit" of Title VII was "right." This is because none exists.

The tens of thousands of race- and gender-conscious affirmative action plans that currently exist in America are legal because the Supreme Court in a number of decisions from *Bakke* in 1978 and *Weber* in 1979 to *Johnson* in 1987, say they are. If and when *Weber* and *Johnson* are overruled, the clear language of Title VII will once again be the law of the land.

Section Two

The Insuperable Problems
of Affirmative Action

The rest of the world, much of the rest of the world, can in turn offer warnings [about affirmative action]...[C]areful, factual analyses of "preferential policies" in various societies [show] [t]hey are,...with the rarest exception, the surest formula for "interethnic" conflict.

—Daniel Patrick Moynihan[1]

Caste, it seems, makes an irresistible case for government action to help the lower orders, for the social barriers to individual advancement are impossibly high. Yet India's system of affirmative action, designed to achieve this through the reservation of caste quotas for government jobs and university places, seems to be doing just the opposite...[I]t has strengthened, not weakened, the hold of the caste system over Indian society.... India's central and state governments need to face up to the horrible political problem of unraveling the reservation system. They also need to ask themselves what, if affirmative action does more harm than good, can be done to undermine caste.

—The Economist[2]

Introduction

In Part One we looked at the rise of the new equality and the convoluted and changing legal underpinnings of affirmative action in America. In Part Two we look at the insuperable practical problems of affirmative action. They are many. Who should be the clients of affirmative action? Some believe that affirmative action will wither away, but how can this be with persisting group differences? Should persons of "mixed" background be treated differently from those who are of "full-blooded" background? After a quarter of a century of worsening race relations, isn't it time to give up affirmative action? Hasn't it contributed to the balkanization of our society? Isn't affirmative action quite beside the point when we look at the black underclass? How can we continue to defend the use of race-conscious admission programs in our selective colleges and universities when they result in high dropout rates of minorities and their defensive self-segregation? Hispanics have piggybacked on the affirmative action entitlement of blacks as "people of color"; is there any justification for this? Is there any case at all for women being clients of affirmative action in the 1990s? Should class or economic situation, being "disadvantaged," be a revised basis for affirmative action? Has the idea of affirmative action spread to the criminal justice system resulting in the differential treatment of minorities? Does the public support affirmative action? Historically, isn't the whole notion of preferences based on race, ethnicity, and gender an atavistic movement, a throwback to a pre-democratic time when inherited characteristics (lineage, birth order, etc.) out-

173

weighed achieved characteristics? Doesn't affirmative action subvert our American liberal tradition of equality before the law? Doesn't it imply an inferiority on the part of the clients of it? Doesn't it breed resentment in those who are excluded from it? Hasn't it reached ridiculous proportions when three-quarters of the population are covered by it? Don't people have a predilection to "choose" whatever ethnic category is most beneficial to them? Isn't it an incentive to fraud?

These are questions that suggest the insuperable problems of affirmative action.

Chapter 12

Affirmative Action for Whom?

We have thus far been spared the historically laden nightmare of having legislatures and courts decide what constitutes membership in [racial and ethnic groups]. Our luck, however, may not hold out. In an economy in which good jobs and scholarships are ever scarcer, someone will finally have to decide: What constitutes being black? Will one grandparent do?

—Martin Peretz[1]

Washington in the millennial years is a city of warring racial and ethnic groups fighting for recognition, protection, and entitlements.

—Lawrence Wright[2]

In Title VII of the Civil Rights Act of 1964 discrimination was prohibited on the basis of race, color, religion, sex, and national origin. Nowhere in this Act, nor in the Equal Opportunity Act of 1972, nor in any legislation or court decision is there any mention of the specifics of these categories. It is *individual* discrimination that is prohibited.

With the onset of affirmative action programs it became necessary to specify who were to be its beneficiaries. First targeted were women and

175

"minorities." Other "protected" categories were to come later. Women is a pretty straightforward category; sex is almost as immutable a demographic category as age. (The word is *sex* in official affirmative action language, rarely *gender.*) Minorities, by contrast, are categories whose definitions in America are variously arbitrary, ad hoc, vague, fickle, confused, racialist, racist, controversial, relative, self-defined, regional, cultural, political, utilitarian, a proxy for "disadvantaged," and historically conditioned.

The most authoritative definition, though not very much so, of minorities subject to affirmative action is that used by the federal government. Since the mid-1970s racial and ethnic categories have been defined by Statistical Directive 15 of the Office of Management and Budget (OMB).[3] The four minorities defined are these:

American Indian or Alaskan Native—Persons having origins in any of the original people of North America, and who maintain identification through tribal affiliation or community recognition.

Asian or Pacific Islander—Persons having origins in any of the original peoples of the Far East, Southeast Asia, the Indian Subcontinent, or the Pacific Islands. This area includes, for example, China, Japan, Korea, the Philippine Islands, and Samoa.

Black, not of Hispanic Origin—Persons having origins in any of the black groups of Africa.

Hispanic—Persons of Mexican, Puerto Rican, Cuban, Central or South American or other Spanish culture or origin, regardless of race.

Whites, it should be noted, are defined in the same manner as are the protected minorities:

White, not of Hispanic Origin—Persons having origins in any of the original peoples of Europe, North Africa, or the Middle East.

These are the five race or race-like "communities" defined by the OMB during the Carter Administration. Their influence has been extraordinary. They have become the most official candidates for affirmative action in business and industry, education and government. They have become America's five communities. Implicit in the definition is that four of them are "disadvantaged" and have been oppressed by the fifth, whites.

Scores of observations, criticisms, and queries can be made of this racial/geographic classification, about the assumptions underlying it, about whom it includes, about whom it doesn't.

(1) This definition of minorities has many omissions, assuming it is concerned with "disadvantaged" people as opposed to those with "origins" in "Europe, North Africa, or the Middle East"—supposedly "advantaged" peoples. Native Australian blacks would find no place here, their origin is not Africa; nor would the indigenous people (usually disadvantaged) of any geographical area outside of North America, Africa, and Asia and the Pacific Islands; nor would any of the "white" ethnic groups of North America, North Africa, or the Middle East; nor would Central and South American Indians; nor would the French Canadians of New England and the northern Midwest. What about the poor Finns in northern Michigan? And what about the gypsies? Maybe they could be included as having their "origins" in "the Indian sub-continent."

(2) The racial/geographic categorization is qualified in two of the categories. In order to be classified as "American Indian and Alaskan Native," one needs to "maintain cultural identification through tribal affiliation or community recognition." In practice this qualification is generally ignored. The potential advantage of status in a "protected minority" is not lost on people. The 1960 census enumerated a mere half million American Indians; the 1990 census almost two million, a 259 percent increase.[4] In one case, admittedly epic, a California contractor who was one sixty-fourth American Indian got $19 million in set-aside contracts for minority-owned businesses on the rapid transit system in Los Angeles by claiming American Indian status.[5]

A second exception to the racial/geographic conceptualization of minorities is for Hispanics. Here "Persons of Mexican [etc.]... or other Spanish culture or origin" are included. This can only mean that those of non-Hispanic origin (e.g., non-Spanish Europeans) who come from "Spanish culture" countries are to be included, though often in practice they are not. Sephardic Jews would be included. Regardless of where they have lived in recent centuries, their "origins" are in Spain. Filipinos have a double eligibility for affirmative action; they can define themselves as protected because of coming from "Spanish culture" or as being "Asian or Pacific Islander."

(3) In practice, slight attention is paid to any literal interpretation of these official definitions. A colleague of mine, Miguel Korzeniewicz, was born in Argentina of Polish and Russian "origins." Even though he is a third generation Argentine and his first language is Spanish, he tells me that sometimes he is regarded as Hispanic and sometimes not, as when he was eliminated from consideration for a Rockefeller Foundation minority grant.

How arbitrary these affirmative action categories are is demonstrated by a statement from the dean for faculty affairs at the University of Michigan. When this dean was queried by a chairman as to who precisely were the designated candidates for Target of Opportunity appointments, a University of Michigan affirmative action program, he responded:

> The definition of a "Target of Opportunity" candidate is not always clear. It can even be influenced by the current composition of a department. As things stand, an American citizen of African or (recent) Hispanic ancestry would certainly qualify. Recent immigrants of Caribbean or Latin American origin generally qualify. Immigrants from South America whose recent ancestors emigrated from Western Europe do not qualify. Native Africans who have immigrated [sic] to the U.S. have qualified in the past, and probably will continue to do so for a while. Native Americans always qualify.[6]

Note that the dean didn't even mention women. But this communication dates from 1990, just before the period when women replaced minorities as the most eagerly sought category in the universities.

(4) According to the official definition, persons from Spain or who are of Spanish descent, "origin," are included as affirmative action candidates, but not persons of Balkan, Italian (though they are in New York City), Greek, or Portuguese (though they are in California and Massachusetts) "origins." Why should those of Portuguese "origin," in particular, be generally excluded, while those of Spanish "origin" are included? More numerically important, those of Brazilian "origin" are excluded. Brazil, the most populous country in Latin America, is not of "Spanish culture or origin."

In practice, persons of Brazilian "origin" are sometimes included as affirmative action candidates. A Brazilian professor of Portuguese, a friend of mine, was not regarded as being in a protected category at the University of New Mexico, but later discovered he was a Target of Opportunity hire when he moved to the University of Michigan. This professor's daughter with a telling Iberian surname—and a well-to-do "Anglo" mother—got a minority scholarship to an elite American college!

Better for affirmative action purposes than "Hispanic" would be "Hispanic-American" or "Latino/a." Both these terms are more precise and would exclude persons of Spanish "origins," usually not regarded as affirmative action candidates, but whose surnames are sometimes used for body-count purposes. Better than Hispanic-American or Latino/a would be "Indo-Hispanic." Still better would be "Indo-Iberian," because it is more inclusive. It would correctly designate the miscegenated descendants of both Spain and Portugal with the indigenous people of the New World. An additional category might be "Indo-Iberian black" to designate the many Brazilians and persons of Caribbean "origins."

(5) These minority categories give no consideration to persons of mixed "origins." The great majority of Americans are mixed. This is true of the black population as well as the white population. It is commonly asserted that 30 percent of the genetic makeup of American blacks is of white origin (Cavalli-Sforza's estimate). And the proportions "mixed" are increasing. There are lots of estimates around. A majority of both Japanese-Americans and American Indians marry outside their groups. A third of Hispanics marry outside their specific ethnic group. Four-fifths of Italian-Americans born after 1950 have married non-Italian-Americans. Blacks are less likely to do so than other groups, but their numbers, too, are increasing. Six percent of all black householders had nonblack spouses according to the 1990 census.

An unresolved issue is how affirmative action programs should treat persons of mixed background. Are those of "mixed" background to be treated differently from those of "full" background, whatever that may be? Perhaps people can "choose" whatever categorization is most advantageous to them. That in fact is what many people of mixed background do.[7]

A thoughtful categorizing of people's "culture and origin" was developed by the Germans in the mid-1930s. Persons were classified as being of German "origin," Jewish "origin," and *Mischlinge* (literally, hybrid), mixed "origin." Consider the precision of this mixed category as described by Raul Hilberg. It delineates:

(1) any person who descended from two Jewish grandparents (half-Jewish), but who (a) did not adhere (or adhered no longer) to the Jewish religion on September 15, 1935, and who did not join it at any subsequent time *and* (b) was not married (or was married no longer) to a Jewish person on September 15, 1935, and who did not marry such a person at any subsequent time (such half-Jews were called *Mischlinge* of the first degree), and (2) any person descended from one Jewish grandparent (*Mischlinge* of the second degree). The designations "Mischlinge of the first degree" and "Mischlinge of the second degree" were not contained in the decree of November 14, 1935, but were added in a later ruling by the Ministry of Interior.[8]

The opposite way of responding to the issue of "mixed" people is to do what to us Americans at present is unthinkable, what Canada began *not* doing in 1951. It dropped "the race question" from that census and has not reinstated it since. The American Civil Liberties Union, commendably, tried to get the race question dropped from the 1960 census. And, as we know, without success. Asking about race is an improper governmental query in a liberal democratic society, one devoted to a color-blind legality and mentality. Here is a proposal: *Let the 2000 U.S. census be the first in our history not to ask about race.* There is also a practical reason for not asking "the race question": the data from such questions are very bad. More about this when we get to Hispanics and affirmative action.

(6) The conception of ethnic minorities in the United States is similar to the historical conception of Negro: any known Negro ancestry defined one as Negro. It is the "one drop of blood" conception of race, unique to American history. Homer Plessy, who brought his case to the Supreme Court in 1896, was an *octoroon*, one eighth Negro. Walter White, a past president of the National Association for the Advancement of Colored People, was one sixty-fourth Negro. Hazel O'Leary, secretary of energy in President Clinton's Cabinet, is categorized as black, but is phenotypically "white." A few years ago two Boston policemen, brothers, changed their racial classification from white to black, for affirmative action advantages, because they could claim a black great-grandmother. Is Lani Guinier, whose mother is white and Jewish, a dark-skinned Jew or a light-skinned black?

For affirmative action consideration, not only any known black ancestor qualifies one, but so does any claim to an American Indian, Asian, or Latino ancestor. That American folk hero, Will Rogers, celebrated his (slight)

Cherokee heritage. Larry EchoHawk, when campaigning for governor of Idaho in 1994, made much of his Indian heritage, but he has a mother of German background, is a Mormon, graduated from Brigham Young University, and looks like his mother. No court decision in American history has ever called into question the "one drop of blood" definition of who is a black or who is of any other racial/ethnic group.

(7) Sometimes all one needs to qualify for the special advantages of affirmative action is an appropriate surname: Li or Rodriquez, Sirjamaki (Finnish, but sounds Japanese) or Garcia, Chin or Park, Jojola or Begay. Blacks do not have this name advantage, though sometimes given names provide a clue. Some nonminority women get a double qualification by marrying an appropriately named husband. Sometimes they keep the advantageous surname after divorce. Sometimes women take their maiden names back after divorce, because to do so is ethnically advantageous. Who would dare question anyone who bears an Hispanic surname about what proportion of that person's background is Hispanic?

An American friend of mine with a Spanish surname got a minority scholarship to a graduate school of social work solely by virtue of her name. Her "origins" are in fact partly Hungarian, partly Jewish, partly some other things, but in the distant California past there was a paternal ancestor who was Mexican or Spanish (she doesn't know which).

(8) American English is anemic in describing racial characteristics. Rarely in the press and never in public discourse is there mention of racial characteristics, and there are few words in the language to describe different configurations of features. This is another manifestation of the "one drop of blood" conception of race in America, of blacks being "invisible people" to whites. The opposite situation prevails in Brazil, no interracial paradise, but at least Brazilians don't deny what they see. In one Brazilian community with a highly intermixed population eight descriptive categories and several sub-categories were in everyday use:

(1) *preto*, Negro or dark; (2) *cabra* (female *cabrocha*), lighter in skin color than *preto*, hair less kinky, and facial features less Negroid; (3) *cabo verde*, dark skin color but straight hair, thin lips, and narrow nose; (4) *escuro*, literally a "dark man" but meaning dark skin with some Caucasoid features—generally used for an individual who does not quite fit the three above categories; (5) *mulato*, yellow skin color, kinky to curly hair, thin to

thick lips, narrow to wide nose—subtypes are "light" and "dark" mulatto; (6) *pardo*, "brown," a classification most often used officially for census and the like, but sometimes applied in common parlance for individuals who "are closer to the white than a light mulatto"; (7) *sarara*, light skin, reddish-blond but kinky hair, and Negroid facial features; and (8) *moreno*, literally brunette—"excellent" fair skin, dark curly hair, features—much more Caucasoid than Negroid.[9]

A rich *preto* can be considered "white" in Brazil. "Money whitens" is a national aphorism. Charles Wagley calls this "social race."

(9) It would seem reasonable for color to be an operative affirmative action variable. But it hardly ever is. It is one of the five variables against which discrimination is prohibited in the Civil Rights Act of 1964, but only rarely is it a factor in discrimination cases and never in affirmative action plans. Yet dark-skinned blacks, Hispanics, and Asians are at a disadvantage in America compared to their lighter-skinned co-ethnics. Itabari Njeri, a *Los Angeles Times* journalist who writes about ethnic relations, claims that the social and economic differences between light-skinned blacks and dark-skinned blacks are as great as those between whites and blacks in America.[10] A recent labor force study found marked differences in the employment situation of light-skinned blacks compared with their dark-skinned counterparts:

> We found that only 10.3 percent of light-skinned African-American men with thirteen or more years of schooling were unemployed, compared with 19.4 percent of their dark-skinned counterparts with similar education....
>
> Among men who had participated in job-training programs, light-skinned blacks actually had a lower jobless rate than their white counterparts—11.1 percent, compared with 14.5 percent. Yet the rate for dark-skinned African-American men with job training was 26.8 percent.[11]

Blacks are more sensitive to color differences among them than are whites. Or, are they? In an account of Savannah, Georgia, John Berendt reports on a wonderful character and keen social observer who called herself Chablis, a black transvestite dancer who liked "white boys." Here she reveals "truths" to author Berendt about the significance of color among blacks at the most fashionable black debutante ball in that ancient southern city which *she* had "crashed":

"Whenever I'm around high yellas, I get jumpy. Know what I mean? And this place is loaded with 'em. Just look around." Chablis leaned on an elbow and scanned the crowd, panning slowly from one end of the hall to the other. "What you are lookin' at is 'black society,'" she said. "And now you know the big secret of black society: The whiter you are, the higher you get to rise in it."

"But the debutantes don't all have light skin," I [author John Berendt] said. "They represent a pretty broad mix if you ask me."

"They can make debutantes in any color they want," said Chablis, "but it won't make any difference. The ones with the light skin are the ones the successful black men are gonna marry. It gives them status. Black may be beautiful, honey, but white is still right when it comes to gettin' ahead in the world, in case you didn't know. I ain't got nothin' against high yellas. Their color ain't their fault, but they do tend to clan together. You oughta see 'em at Saint Matthew's Episcopal Church on West Broad Street. That's the black status church here in Savannah. People say they got a comb over the front door, and they won't let you in unless you can run the comb through your hair without breakin' it. Inside the church the real light-skinned people sit in the pews up front, and the darker ones sit in the back. That's right, honey. Just like it used to be on the buses. Y'see, when it comes to prejudice, black folks are right up there with white folks. Believe me. It's no big deal, but when I see black folks start actin' white, honey, it brings out the nigger bitch in me." A sly smile crept across Chablis's face. She peered seductively over her shoulder at me.

"Behave yourself," I said.[12]

Bessie Delany, the younger, darker, and now deceased, of those famous centenarian sisters, agrees with Chablis. Bessie claimed she always had a more difficult time making her way in life than her lighter sister, Sadie: "It's been a little harder for me, partly because I'm darker than she is, and the darker you are, honey, the harder it is."[13]

(10) It is striking how race and ethnicity are defined in the United States compared with Latin America. Americans are race conscious while Latin Americans are color conscious, and there is even a little of this in Mexico and other Latin American countries with predominantly intermixed populations. One might say that in Brazil race is defined in terms of physical appearance as we've already noted, in Mexico it is mainly a sociocultural

concept, while in the United States it is based on ancestry, on "origins." Affirmative action would be far from the ken of Mexicans, at least in Mexico.

Mexico is the polar opposite of the United States in its conception of racial differences. Mexico is a country which, while recognizing phenotypic differences, which we *gringos* don't, minimizes concern with race just as the old civil rights movement did. As a student of Mexico once told me, an Indian in Mexico becomes a Mexican as soon as he puts on shoes and learns to speak Spanish.

Two processes have dominated Mexican history for centuries: hispanization and mestizoization, that is, the genetic mixture of three human stocks—the European, the Indian, and, slightly, the African. The Mexican population is extraordinarily mixed both culturally and racially. Particularly since the revolution of 1910 the dominant ideology has been strongly antiracist. Pierre van den Berghe argues, perhaps with some exaggeration, in *Race and Racism* that Mexico has progressed much further than her northern neighbor in abolishing race as a basic variable in the life of the society. America since the 1960s has proceeded in the opposite direction, to emphasize race:

> Racial characteristics have so little social relevance in modern Mexico and the complex interplay of race and culture through that process of miscegenation and hispanization have so homogenized the Mexican population that race and ethnic relations in that country have received scant attention from social scientists.... The concept of race has become almost totally alien to modern Mexican culture.... Although there probably is some slight residual tendency toward racial homogamy, physical appearance is not an appreciable factor in social mobility, or, more generally, in social behavior.[14]

(11) The official minority categories say nothing about socio-economic status. Should persons in "protected" categories from professional or upper managerial backgrounds be given special consideration when applying to law or medical school? Should they be eligible for any special financial aid reserved for "minorities"? Should Clarence Thomas's son be given any special consideration when he applies to Cornell? Should his race be regarded as a plus? By the same token, should not poor nonminority persons who are also "culturally disadvantaged," say, rural Appalachians, be equally eligible for all the considerations of affirmative action? Socio-

economic and class factors are, most of the time, ignored in the practice of affirmative action. A black is a black. A Latino is a Latino. A woman is a woman.

(12) "Asian or Pacific Islander" is the most incongruous of the four protected minorities. Japanese and Chinese, trailed closely by Indians, Koreans, and Vietnamese, do well educationally, from grade to graduate school, and have earnings above American averages. The category also includes Filipinos and Pacific Islanders who do less well in school and on the job market and are more burdened down with social problems. Should the mainland Asians—sometimes called the Confucian Asians or East Asians—be eligible for affirmative action? Are they not, in an affirmative action sense, *more white* than whites?

(13) The same problem of incongruity arises with the second largest American "minority," Hispanics. They are, though to a lesser degree than Asians, many different ethnic groups, but their leaders try to present a united front and emphasize their unity as Latino, the term used more than Hispanic from Texas to California to New York, but not among the long-term indigenous inhabitants of the Southwest. Indeed, before the age of affirmative action there were no Hispanics or Latinos, only discrete ethnic groups like Mexican-Americans (or Chicanos or *Hispanos* or Spanish), Puerto Ricans, Cubans, Dominicans.

The Cubans, at one pole, are more middle class, more educated, more Republican, with higher incomes and lower fertility, and fewer social problems than other Hispanic minorities. They are hardly "disadvantaged" as American ethnic groups go. At the other pole are the Puerto Ricans, who fall below blacks on some measures of economic and social well-being. Other Hispanic groups fall between the Cubans and the Puerto Ricans.

Should all Hispanic populations be protected populations? Should the Cubans? What about the indigenous Hispanics of the American Southwest? What about persons of recent European "origins" who emigrate to the United States from Mexico? What about the Mexicans who arrived last year? Last week? Should a distinction be made between those who are American citizens and those who are not? What about illegals?

(14) Many categories beyond minorities and women have come, willy nilly, to be defined as "protected" on an ad hoc basis. Affirmative action statements have come to read like shopping lists. At hand is the Univer-

sity of New Mexico *Faculty Handbook*. Its typical statement reads: "We have an ongoing obligation to seek out, hire, and develop the best persons we can, regardless of their sex, marital or parental status, race, color, religion, age, national origin, ethnicity, physical handicap, sexual preference or military involvement (Vietnam Era Veteran or handicapped Veterans)." In other university documents "mental handicap" [?], "ancestry," and "medical condition" are noted as attributes not to be discriminated against. The University of Arizona's "Diversity Action Plan" adds "individual style" to the list. When *U.S.News & World Report* columnist John Leo inquired as to what was meant by "individual style" he was informed by "diversity specialist" Connie Gajewski that this "would include nerds and people who dress differently. 'We didn't want to leave anyone out,' she said."[15] But she did leave out pedophiles (i.e., persons who have sex with children) regarded by some as a "protected minority" at the University of Massachusetts-Amherst.[16]

The Population Council of New York in its "Affirmative Action Statement of Policy" printed on the inside back cover of its *1994 Annual Report* adds to the *UNM Faculty Handbook* list above "creed" and "political opinion," and "veterans [*sic*] status," not just "Vietnam Era Veteran or handicapped Veterans." But the council's statement does omit "marital or parental status." Both omit "ex-convict status," sometimes a protected category.

These affirmative action statements include extraordinarily comprehensive lists of all the aspects of employment, about which there is to be no discrimination. The *UNM Faculty Handbook* statement reads: "We intend that all matters related to recruiting, hiring, training, compensation, benefits, promotions, transfers, layoffs, institutionally sponsored education, social and recreational programs, and all treatment of the workforce be free of discriminatory practices." The Population Council says the same, also with eleven aspects, but with slightly different wording. At the bottom of a quarter-page advertisement in *The Chronicle of Higher Education* for a vice president for extended university affairs at Washington State University, it says in italics:

WSU is an Equal Opportunity/Affirmative Action educator and employer. Members of ethnic minorities, women, Vietnam-era or disabled veterans, or persons of disability, and/or persons age 40 and over are encouraged to apply.

Presumably persons who do not fall in these categories are not "encouraged" to apply. Among the listed qualifications for the position is "proven commitment to affirmative action, equal opportunity and diversity."[17]

Affirmative action statements have become so all-inclusive of particularistic categories as to cover the large majority of people in virtually all aspects of employment. The only persons excluded are nonminority, nonhandicapped, heterosexual, younger (as opposed to *older*) males who are not Vietnam Era veterans. The subtext of these patronizing, virtue-claiming, and ridiculous statements is that it is negative discrimination that is to be prohibited, not positive, affirmative discrimination toward persons with certain desired ascribed characteristics.

A comprehensive statement in opposition to all manner of discrimination, negative or positive, is an easy one to write, but it would not be acceptable to devotees of affirmative action:

> The Widget Manufacturing Company [the Democratic Party, the University of Vermont, whatever] will not tolerate any individual to be discriminated against, or given preferential treatment, or deprived of any rights, or given additional rights, because of any characteristics irrelevant to ability.

But as soon as we have done this, we have abolished affirmative action.

Chapter 13

Affirmative Action in Education

Diversity benefits us all, because it brings to campus a diversity of opinions, which are largely shaped by race and gender and income.

—Charles E. Young, Chancellor, UCLA[1]

I challenge anyone who supports affirmative action yet opposes all stereotypes to provide a coherent set of answers to the following questions: If there are significant differences among races, what are they (be specific), how do they contribute to the Harvard community, and why do you accuse of bigotry anyone who points them out? If there are no such differences, what is the value of racial diversity, and how can it possibly outweigh the losses of accepting less qualified minorities over more qualified non-minorities?

These questions leave...a paradox as inescapable as anything Joseph Heller could ever imagine.

—Matt Selove[2]

We are committed to a program of affirmative action, and we want to make the university representative of the population of the state as a whole.... We take more in the groups with weaker credentials and make it harder for those with stronger credentials.

—Dean of Admissions, University of Virginia[3]

189

A ffirmative action for designated race and ethnic categories in higher education is, at worst, patronizing, cor-
rupting, and eventually demoralizing to its intended beneficiaries; at best,
quite unnecessary in a country oversupplied with colleges and universities.

Actually, preferential undergraduate admissions has relevance for only
a tiny, but very significant, proportion of colleges and universities, those
that are able to be selective. Fewer than 5 percent of freshmen are en-
rolled in the twenty-five "top" universities and the twenty-five "top" small
colleges.[4] The great majority enroll in institutions that require little more
than graduating from high school along with some mild provisions regarding grades or test scores. Some state schools have no admission requirements at all beyond high school graduation; in a few states, law
mandates admission to any graduate of a high school in the state. Community colleges admit anyone.

But to elite colleges and universities affirmative action is an obsessive
concern. The most touted public reason is to achieve a diverse student
body. The old reason, to compensate for past hurtful discrimination, has
faded away as the clients of affirmative action have expanded beyond
blacks to include other groups for whom the claim of past discrimination
is less compelling, or not compelling at all. (Interestingly and revealingly,
there is a virtual absence of gender-based affirmative action in higher
education.)

There is another sort of preference, much less publicly celebrated by
universities than that of achieving ethnic diversity. It is an affirmative
action for the privileged. And it is used to justify race and ethnic preferences. If a college gives special treatment to the offspring of alumni, so
goes the argument, is it not equally just to give similar treatment to minority applicants? Can one accept the former sort of preference and not the
latter? Isn't there a *quid pro quid* here? If being an alumnus offspring is
treated as a plus when applying to Dartmouth, fairness would seem to
insist that being a minority person should also be treated as a plus. Justice
Lewis Powell argued just this in his famous *Bakke* opinion of 1978, but, as
John Jeffries, Jr., has written in his biography of the justice, he intended it
to be only a temporary measure, maybe to last a decade. What the justice
feared was that special admissions programs like those at Davis "would
become entrenched bureaucracies, and minorities would come to regard

them as perpetual entitlements. What Powell feared most was permanence. For him, racial preferences were a short-term response to a pressing need."[5]

At Harvard College in 1968 almost "half of alumni sons were being admitted"; this has declined in recent years to "approximately 40 percent of alumni children...against 14 percent of nonalumni applicants."[6] This preference is justified by the claim that alumni are one of the "constituencies important to the college." It really exists to encourage alumni to be generous with their pocketbooks.

Preferential treatment of "legacies" in elite colleges and universities has received little criticism.[7] It is a deplorable practice, more so than any preferential treatment of minorities and for which it provides perverse justification. Favoring legacies is a worse sin than favoring minorities because it lacks the altruistic, if misguided, intentions of affirmative action. It most directly discriminates against Asians, few of whom are legacies, and from whom it takes away places. Both forms of preference are violations of the universalistic and meritocratic standards that should be of bedrock importance to universities.

Presidents of major universities are among the most vocal Cassandras when contemplating the passing on of affirmative action. The president of the University of California, Chang-Lin Tien, has claimed that without affirmative action only about 2 percent of Berkeley undergraduates would be black. The president of the University of Texas at Austin, Robert A. Bergdahl, has lamented that without affirmative action only some 3 percent of those accepted to the university's law school would be black. Even if these estimates are on target, and they probably are, they should not be cause for alarm, nor a last-ditch argument for affirmative action in university admissions.

In a world without affirmative action, maybe only 2 percent of Berkeley undergraduates would be black, but maybe 15 percent of the undergraduates at nearby San Francisco State and San Jose State would be black. If only 3 percent of the entering students at the University of Texas Law School were black, maybe 10 percent of those at the state's somewhat less selective law school in Houston would be black. The most thoughtful reaction to such an unbalanced but discrimination-free system is, *So what!* The student—and faculty—composition of universities in our multi-ethnic country will always be unbalanced and in flux. Jews and Asians are more overrepresented in selective colleges than blacks and Hispanics are underrepresented. About a quarter of Ivy League undergraduates are Jews; over 40 percent of recent freshman classes at Berkeley and UCLA have been Asian. It took Italian-Americans six or seven decades after their heaviest immigration to this country in the first decade of this century to achieve parity with the general population in higher education.[8]

Only in America do we find the practice of admitting students to upper tier schools by using, in addition to academic criteria—grades and test scores—such dubious, presumptive, and downright irrelevant criteria as potential for leadership, character, personality, unusual life experiences, extracurricular activities, charitable activities, athletic, musical and other talents, special qualities allegedly revealed by written essays, plus letters of recommendation and interviews. If all this subjectivism and departure from objectively measurable academic merit is allowable in the name of achieving the elusive diversity and a balanced entering class, why not race and ethnicity too?

No fewer than twenty-three diverse people make up the admissions staff at Harvard.[9] "We obviously want to get talented students from all backgrounds," says William R. Fitzsimmons, dean of admissions and financial aid at Harvard. He continues with a non sequitur, often unavoidable when attempting to defend what admissions people do: "One of the roles we've always played is to educate future leaders. Increasingly, African Americans are becoming more involved in the leadership of cities, states, and in Congress, and in that context we would be remiss if we weren't going out and getting talented people from every background." "To say that one person is more qualified for admission than another is tough to do," claims Karl M. Furstenberg, dean of admissions at Dartmouth.

There are no data anywhere to suggest that university admissions committees in highly selective institutions have any greater success in choosing successful entering classes, using all their subjective criteria, than if they went strictly by the numbers. Quite the contrary, since the publication more than four decades ago of Paul Meehl's *Clinical vs. Statistical Prediction*, the evidence is compellingly the other way: statistical prediction is better than clinical prediction in determining successful educational outcomes and successful job performance.[10]

Elite American colleges and universities would do well to admit students at all levels and in all programs solely on the basis of objective academic measures, just as is done in all western European universities except the colleges of Oxford and Cambridge. Universities, of all our institutions, should abhor discretionary and informal methods of selection when selection must be made. This includes law schools and medical schools. Law and medicine are both wide and varied fields in which there is scope for many different types of personality, many sorts of talent. Race and ethnicity—like being a so-called legacy or having had unusual life experiences or coming from Wyoming—should be irrelevant considerations.

Many people will argue that in such a coldly objective system narrow grade grubbers and successful test takers will beat out the erratic geniuses with wide interests, but less than stunning grades and test scores. But, again, *So what!* They can go to the University of Wisconsin instead of Yale.

This would be a great reform for American higher education. It would abolish the rampant subjectivism that now prevails in deciding who gains admittance to America's elite colleges, those that bestow extraneous status and career advantages.

The fairest, most efficient, and simplest system of admissions to our extraordinarily competitive colleges and universities would be a lottery system. Here is how it might work: A portion of an entering freshman class, say, a third, would be offered early admission only on the basis of grades and test scores. This means doing away even with interviews and letters of recommendation. These are the superbly qualified. The remaining two-thirds would be chosen by lottery from *all* those deemed qualified on the basis of the same measures used to choose the superbly qualified. These are the well qualified.

Not only would such a system remove the gratuitous discretion presently used in admissions to elite schools, it would make them a bit less elite, a move in the right direction for the world's most stratified system of higher education. It would produce a natural diversity instead of a contrived diversity.

A lottery system would not overcome the current over-representation of whites, most notably Jews and Asians, and the under-representation of blacks and Hispanics. *But it would lessen the over- and under-representation of the various groups because the net has been cast more widely.* More applicants are in the pool. Chance would be a factor as it is in life. No more would there be stigmatized "affirmative action babies," and no more would there be the excessive dropout rate of black and Hispanic students along with the sad consequences.

Below the super-selective institutions there is a tier of more modestly selective institutions for those who don't quite make it to the major leagues. And let it be put up in neon lights that most American colleges and universities are hardly selective at all. There is more than enough room for everybody.

If elite law schools adopted an analogous mode of admissions there would be no more insulting affirmative action mix-ups such as experienced by affirmative action baby Stephen L. Carter:

> As a senior at Stanford back in the mid-1970s, I applied to about half a dozen law schools. Yale, where I would ultimately enroll, came through fairly early with an acceptance. So did all but one of the others. The last school, Harvard, dawdled and dawdled. Finally, toward the end of the admission season, I received a letter of rejection. Then, within days, two different Harvard officials and a professor contacted me by telephone to apologize. They were quite frank in their explanation for the "error." I was told by one official that the school had initially rejected me because "we assumed from your record that you were white." (The words have always stuck in my mind, a tantalizing reminder of what is expected of me.) Suddenly coy, he went on to say that the school had obtained "additional information that should have been counted in your favor"—that is, Harvard had discovered the color of my skin. And if I had already made a deposit to confirm my decision to go elsewhere, well, that, I was told, would "not be allowed" to stand in my way should I enroll at Harvard.[11]

It is a subversive and dangerous practice to manipulate entrance requirements by race to achieve some allegedly desirable balance. Who is to decide what that balance should be? It is subversive because it is an assault on a merit-based ethic and on fairness to discrete individuals as opposed to a racial or ethnic category. This ethic is one of the fundamental values of modern democratic society, and it is being squeezed out by the new equality of group representation. Such social engineering is also socially dangerous because of its unintended consequences. Lowering entrance standards for blacks and Hispanics requires raising standards for whites and Asians. Within the selective institution this widens the gap between, on the one hand, whites and Asians, and blacks and Hispanics, on the other. In recent years the gap in SAT scores between whites and blacks has been an enormous 235 points at UCLA, 218 at Dartmouth, 206 at the University of Virginia, 171 at Stanford. Harvard has the lowest average difference in SAT scores among elite colleges, 95 points.[12] The 1994 national gap in scores was 198 points, 217 for males and 181 for females. The implications of the gap between white and black undergraduates at Berkeley has been distressingly described by Vincent Sarich, who teaches anthropology there:

> [T]he gap between the two means [in SAT scores] has increased by more than 100 points in the past decade [1988 compared with 1978] (from 149 to 270), leading to a situation of minimal overlap (15 percent or less) between the two distributions. This current difference is equivalent to a four-year gap in academic preparation/achievement; in other words, the difference between a college junior and a high school junior.
>
> The enormous, and growing, disparity tells us that, *on the average*, "minority" group students are not going to be competitive with "Asians" and "whites" at Berkeley. And whatever the faults of the SAT, or any standardized achievement test, we are being told the truth here. That truth is seen crudely in dropout figures, but is much more apparent to those of us who spend much of our time teaching undergraduates—in relative performance in the same classes, and in the lack of "minority" representation in our more demanding courses and majors. All this is depressing and most unfortunate, but nonetheless true—and, as you get more and more selective among "Asians" and "whites," the competitive gap necessarily increases. This is [*sic*] simple statistics, and nothing anyone here at Berkeley can do, short of admitting only those "Asians" and "whites" who score *below*, say, 1100, could change it.[13]

An affirmative-action-induced division such as Sarich describes at Berkeley has become institutionalized in much of American higher education. But this will change for the better at the University of California if the regents' 1995 elimination of race- and gender-based affirmative action in admissions is actually carried out in practice.

In no institutional sector is the balkanization of our society seen more clearly than in the universities.[14] In no sector will it be more difficult to phase out preferential affirmative action than in the universities. University of California Regent Ward Connerly made a shrewd assessment of why it will be so difficult to eliminate affirmative action in America's universities:

> With each passing day it should be clear to us that our system of preferences [at UC and elsewhere] is becoming entrenched as it builds its own constituency to defend and sustain it as a permanent feature of public decision-making.... Our excessive preoccupation with race contributes to the racial divide, and nowhere is the art of race-consciousness practiced more fervently than on our university campuses.[15]

Chapter 14

Group Differences
Won't Go Away

"To ignore race and sex is racist and sexist."

—Jesse Jackson, speaking before the Regents of the University of California immediately before they voted to phase out race- and gender-based affirmative action[1]

[T]he most common and pervasive of all forms of discrimination [is] the bias against short men.... Perhaps heightism is just a western cultural prejudice? Sadly not.... [T]he prejudice appears to be universal. Is there, then, no good news for short men? No: there is none.

—The Economist[2]

Even the most aggressive proponents of preferential treatment agree that a truly color-blind society is preferable to one where affirmative action is "needed." Yet the call for affirmative action will not go away as long as group differences exist and charges of discrimination can be made.

The reason affirmative action will not just wither away is that group differences will not just wither away. Affirmative action feeds on group differences. As long as there are visible group differences, by race and gender, in positions of prestige, power and authority, particularly when supported with statistics, the case for affirmative action will continue to be insistent. But group differences will persist forever. They will change their form, they will be in flux, but they will always be there. Only through an ideological change in the direction of individual rights over group rights together with a decline in race- and gender-consciousness, buttressed by the courts and legislation, can affirmative action be phased out. Maybe that is now happening. The opposite scenario is that America will continue being a race- and gender-based affirmative action society with persistent and broad-based demands for proportional representation in higher status positions and in admission to selective colleges and universities.

There are great differences in culture patterns among groups in this racially and ethnically heterogeneous society of ours. Some groups place a great value on education, have relatively stable family structures, controlled and delayed fertility, a commercial ethic, a value system which emphasizes deferred gratification, an instrumentalist orientation toward the world, and value hard work and worldly success—all those values and structures associated with upward mobility. In a phrase, middle-class values. Groups vary in their cultural capital for success in modern society. Groups, like individuals, all have the same claim to equality in a moral and democratic sense, but this does not mean that some do not have greater cultural endowments for achievement and success than others. And that necessarily means that some groups have less.

Consider any discussion, analysis, or complaint about the ethnic and gender distribution of talent and higher status in American society. They are all about upward mobility and that is what affirmative action is all about. Let's look at the Jews as an example of a particularly successful group at upward mobility, a category that has pretty much lost salient identifiability in America.

Jews in America, between 2 and 3 percent of the population, are vastly over-represented in the professions, science, intellectual life, the upper reaches of business, finance, government and the media, and as students in selective colleges and universities. Nathan Glazer once estimated that some 18 percent of the American professoriate was Jewish and that the proportion reached a quarter in major universities. About a quarter of the undergraduates at Ivy League universities are Jews, and so are five of their eight presidents.[3] Thirty percent of the law faculty at Berkeley is Jewish. In some fields of academic and scientific endeavor Jews are a majority. The prominence and ubiquity of Jews in physics, economics, and, until the recent past, sociology, is startling.[4] Even in the traditional disciplines of history and English, which so discriminated against Jews until the second half of this century, their prominence is remarkable. The assertion that Jews own and control the media in America is not made of whole cloth. In the 1920s and 1930s Jews were prominent in many sports and organized crime, just as they were among those convicted of insider trading in the 1980s. Something like 15 percent of doctors and lawyers in America are Jews. Twelve percent of those who gave a religious affiliation in the *1992–93 Who's Who* are Jews.[5] In the 1990s Jews were elected to Congress more than three times their proportion of the population.[6] Four of the sixteen justices appointed to the Supreme Court since 1962 were Jews. Note the frequency of Jewish (and Asian) names among the winners of the annual Westinghouse Science Talent Search competition for high school students whose names and projects appear each year in the *New York Times*. The financial status of Jews in contemporary America has no counterpart among any other group. Seymour Martin Lipset and Earl Raab write that "per capita Jewish income is almost double that of non-Jews. More than twice as many Jews as non-Jewish whites report household incomes in excess of $50,000, whereas almost twice as many non-Jews as Jews indicate incomes of less than $20,000."[7]

It may be relevant to some readers, but it is not relevant to the argument made here, that the late Richard Herrnstein and Charles Murray, in their epically controversial book, *The Bell Curve: Intelligence and Class Structure in American Life,* observe that:

Jews—specifically Ashkenazi Jews of European origins [the great majority of Jews in the United States] test higher than any other ethnic group [on tests of

'cognitive ability']. A fair estimate seems to be that Jews in America and
Britain have an overall IQ mean somewhere between a half and a full standard deviation above the mean, with the source of the difference concentrated in the verbal component [the opposite of East Asians where the source
of the difference is in the mathematical component]. [My emendations.][8]

Lipset and Rabb in *Jews and the New American Scene* (1995) attribute
their success to "characteristics and values, including their achievement
drive, [which] have been especially congruent with the larger culture.
These traits strongly resemble the modal national pattern set by the New
England Protestant sectarians."[9] Similar statements can be made about
other successful ethnic groups: East Asians, Greeks, Lebanese, and other
Middle Eastern groups. The Irish, Italians, and Poles who came to these
shores, by contrast, did not have these "congruent" values and were much
slower historically in their upward mobility.[10]

Chinese- and Japanese-Americans have demonstrated a dazzling level
of success in science and engineering, the professions, and admissions to
selective colleges and universities. At several of the University of California campuses, the percentage of Asians now exceeds that of whites; yet
the 1990 census enumerated only 9.5 percent of the California population
as Asian.

The gap between Asians and Hispanics in educational achievement in
California is now greater than that between Asians and blacks. A survey of
all nine University of California campuses during the 1993–94 year found
that Asians accounted for 36 percent of all new students, while Hispanics
accounted for 13 percent. Yet Hispanics make up more than a quarter of
the population of California. Asians as new students were over-represented, in proportion to population, *between seven and eight times* that of
Hispanics. This is an epic differential, particularly when one realizes that
the University of California system has been a vigorous practitioner of
affirmative action. *The Economist* observed: "The discrepancy starts in
high school. In 1992, 52% of Asian students in California's high schools
were taking the relatively demanding courses that prepare a student for
college. Among white students, only 34% were taking these courses; among
blacks, 27%; and among Latinos, last again, 21%."[11]

Marked ethnic variation is evident in the SAT (Scholastic Assessment Test) and in the ACT (American College Testing Program). Here are the 1995 scores for both tests for Asians, whites, American Indians, Mexican-Americans, and blacks. In spite of the criticism of these tests as being culturally biased, they reflect the ethnic distribution in the professions and upper level positions in American society:

	SAT Mathematical section	SAT Verbal section	ACT
Asian	538	418	21.6
White	498	448	21.5
American Indian	447	403	18.6
Mexican-American	426	376	18.6
Black	388	356	17.1

The ethnic distribution of doctorate recipients shows much bigger differentials. In 1993 Asians received, in proportion to population, *six to seven* times as many doctorates as did blacks, and there are enormous differentials by field. In education there is almost parity between Asians and blacks: Asians were about 2.9 percent of the population and received 2.4 of the doctorates in education, blacks were about 12.1 percent of the population and received 9.3 percent of the doctorates in education. At the other extreme are the physical sciences and engineering. In the physical sciences 11.2 percent of doctorates went to Asians and 1.5 percent to blacks. Proportionately, Asians were about *thirty-two* times as likely to earn a doctorate in the physical sciences as were blacks; they were between *three and four* times as likely as were whites. In engineering, 19.5 percent of doctorates went to Asians and 1.9 percent to blacks. Proportionately, Asians compared with blacks were about *forty-two times* as likely to get a doctorate in engineering; they were more than *seven* times as likely as were whites. These are extraordinary differentials. They are all areas which, unlike law and medicine, have not been much affected by affirmative action. Below are the percentages of doctorates awarded to Asians, whites, Hispanics, and blacks in engineering, physical sciences, social sciences, and education. The percentages awarded to women in 1993 are also included.

	Engineering	Physical Sciences	Social Sciences	Education
Asians	19.5	11.2	4.0	2.4
	(2.9 percent of U.S. population)			
Whites	75.1	82.7	86.1	83.2
	(80.3 percent of U.S. population)			
Hispanics	2.4	2.8	3.0	3.7
	(9.0 percent of U.S. population)			
Blacks	1.9	1.5	4.6	9.3
	(12.1 percent of U.S. population)			
Women	9.1	20.7	49.3	58.7
	(51.0 percent of U.S. population)			

Huge ethnic differences in rates of upward mobility exist in American society, and they will persist into the future. But this doesn't mean that upward mobility patterns won't change. The reason the California Hispanics do so poorly educationally is that they are predominantly peasant immigrants from Mexico. Expectations for the future upward mobility of Hispanics, however, are rosier than for blacks, a population in which two-thirds of births are to single mothers (80 percent in the inner cities) and a high percent are of low birth weight (related to development problems in children). The incarceration rate of blacks is seven times that of whites. Black children are 2.6 times as likely as white children to be "mildly retarded."[12] All the measures of social disorganization—crime, drug addiction, mental problems—so negatively associated with upward mobility are very high for blacks. Indeed the prognosis for their future upward mobility, *as a statistical category,* is bleak. Perhaps a quarter of the black population under age thirty is already out of commission for even minimal success in our country.

Similar, if less extreme, comparisons might be made between the white and East Asian populations of the United States.

The social problem of American society is the underclass with its attendant pathologies. And it is quite unrelated to affirmative action, conventionally and unjustifiably an argument for its existence. In Stephen Carter's phrase, it is "stunningly irrelevant."

Yet the only publicly acceptable explanation for the low estate of the black population, *as a statistical category*, is racism. The late William Henry observed that no other explanation is acceptable in mainstream discussion:

> The leadership sector of American society often asks in private why blacks and Hispanics cannot perform as Asians do. It is politically unacceptable— it would surely eliminate one from any job requiring legislative confirmation—to ask the same question out loud. This is because the question has only four possible answers: the Asians are inherently, i.e., genetically, superior; the Asian communities teach their people better values; the Asians are individually more ready to work hard, make sacrifices, and defer gratification; or that the Asians are just not victims, in the way blacks are, of the entrenched, all-explaining racism of American society. The only one of these answers that it is permissible to voice in mainstream debate is the last.[13]

Here is a permissible answer, from the highest level, citing "bias," i.e., racism and "discrimination" in defense of race-based affirmative action:

> Those effects [the "lingering effects" of discrimination], reflective of a system of racial caste only recently ended, are evident in our workplaces, markets and neighborhoods. Job applicants with identical resumes, qualifications and interview styles still experience different receptions, depending on their race. White and African-American consumers still encounter different deals. People of color looking for housing still face discriminatory treatment by landlords, real estate agents, and mortgage lenders. Minority entrepreneurs sometimes fail to gain contracts though they are the low bidders, and they are sometimes refused work even after winning contracts. Bias, both conscious and unconscious, reflecting traditional and unexamined habits of thought, keeps up barricades that must come down if equal opportunity and nondiscrimination are ever genuinely to become this country's law and practice.

This statement is from Justice Ruth Bader Ginsburg's dissent in *Adarand v. Pena* (1995), in which she opposed the "strict scrutiny" opinion of the majority. (Interestingly, *Adarand* involved an Hispanic defendant, but Justice Ginsburg had blacks on her mind.)

Chapter 15

Affirmative Action for Blacks? Hispanics? Women? the Disadvantaged?

A mong advocates of affirmative action, there is no agreement on who should be covered by it. Views vary from those who claim that it should apply only to blacks. At the other extreme are those who favor an open-ended conception of it, that it should apply to any category which can claim to have undergone "longstanding and persistent discrimination," in Bill Clinton's words. Others support an affirmative action that is not based on race, ethnicity, or gender, but rather on class or economic background, being disadvantaged. In this chapter, I make the case against the claims of blacks, Hispanics, women, and "the disadvantaged" to being entitled to preferential affirmative action.

Blacks Hold Center Stage

Question: You've seen the evolution from Negro to black to African-American? What is the best thing for blacks to call themselves?
Answer: White.

—Interview with Kenneth B. Clark[1]

Many blacks react to their history of oppression at the hands of white Americans by emphasizing the virtues of separation. And many whites, though favoring equal educational and economic opportunity, are led by the ideology of some militant African-Americans and by the news media's relentless focus on the pathologies of the ghetto to believe that the majority of blacks live wretched existences which produce high rates of crime and drug addiction, low commitment to education and other middle class values, and intense hatred of whites. Hence, a negative cycle of mutual suspicion and fear is perpetuated which keeps blacks further from the mainstream than most tribal groups.

—Seymour Martin Lipset[2]

When the Civil Rights Act of 1964 and the Voting Rights Act of 1965 were passed, the concern, virtually the only concern, was "the Negro." And this central concern continued into the 1970s. As late as *Weber* (1979) this was the case. Indeed, no Hispanic or women's group opposed Brian Weber's side, and the American G.I. Forum, a major national Hispanic organization, and the Women's Equal Rights Legal Defense and Education Fund, filed friend of the court briefs on Brian Weber's behalf.

Nearly all of the important Court decisions on affirmative action have involved "minorities" with blacks holding center stage. The big exception to this was *Johnson* (1987) which involved a white man against a white woman. Even when a case involved a Hispanic such as did *Adarand v. Pena* (1995), the written opinions of the justices read as though the parties were black. The same is true with the editorials in the *New York Times* (pro-affirmative action) and the *Wall Street Journal* (anti-affirmative action).

The central place of blacks in affirmative action concerns is fully justified. No other component of the population has a history of slavery, repression, denial of the most basic civil rights, and enforced segregation. Most critical in the history of blacks in America is that up until the 1950s the government and public policy sanctioned, supported, and participated in the repression of the black population of America.

A vigorous and clear-headed, though, I think, wrong-headed, defender of affirmative action, Gertrude Ezorsky, says just this very simply on the first page of her book *Racism and Justice: The Case for Affirmative Action* (1991):

This book focuses on black persons as beneficiaries of affirmative action in employment. In adopting that focus I do not mean to deny the entitlement of other minorities, women, or groups such as the handicapped to such benefits. Blacks, however, as descendants of slaves brought to this country against their will and as victims of the post-Reconstruction century of murderous racism, which was encouraged, practiced, and given legal sanction by our government, have a unique entitlement to special efforts to ensure their fair share of employment benefits.[3]

Blacks *should* hold center stage in any defense of affirmative action. Hispanics have no claim of repressive treatment comparable to blacks. Only to the most radical feminists can the patriarchal repression of women be compared to the historical oppression of blacks. American Indians have the best claim, after blacks, to repressive treatment by government and public policy, but still they were allowed some cultural and geographic autonomy, were never slaves, have a long tradition of being wards of the government, sometimes motivated by good intentions, and are numerically only a tiny proportion of the population.

Japanese-Americans underwent a repression and forced evacuation from the West Coast after Pearl Harbor and the beginning of war with Japan. This was a short-term hysterical reaction and one of the most deplorable chapters in America's history of the Second World War. But it was *sui generis*, a one-time event, and does not put Japanese-Americans anywhere close to blacks or even American Indians in the competition of the historically oppressed.

To make the case successfully against affirmative action for blacks is the most powerful way to make the case against affirmative action in general. This is because most opinion on the subject, pro or con, explicit or implicit, agrees that blacks are of central importance, both historically and contemporaneously, in any evaluation of this social policy. To demolish the case for affirmative action for blacks is to demolish the case for affirmative action in general.

There are at least five arguments that can be called up in support of black affirmative action: retribution, diversity, social contract theory, the sociological, and the pragmatic.

First to be done away with is the ideology of retribution. This has been the most powerful justification for affirmative action for blacks. A most eloquent statement of it was made by Justice Thurgood Marshall in *Bakke* (1978):

It is unnecessary in 20th century America to have individual Negroes demonstrate that they have been victims of racial discrimination.... The experience of Negroes in America has been different in kind, not just in degree, from that of other ethnic groups. It is not merely the history of slavery alone but also that a whole people were marked as inferior by law. And that mark has endured. The dream of America as the great melting pot has not been realized for the Negro; because of his skin color he never even made it into the pot....

It is because of a legacy of unequal treatment that we now must permit the institutions of this society to give consideration to race in making decisions about who will hold the positions of influence, affluence and prestige in America. For far too long the doors to those positions have been shut to Negroes. If we are ever to become a fully integrated society, one in which the color of a person's skin will not determine the opportunities available to him or her, we must be willing to take steps to open these doors. *I do not believe that anyone can truly look into America's past and still find that a remedy for the effects of that past is impermissible* [emphasis added].

Justice Marshall is expressing the same sentiment in the last sentence above as did Justice Blackmun in his most famous utterance, also from *Bakke:* "In order to get beyond racism, we must first take account of race."

The extreme version of the ideology of retribution is the call for monetary reparations for the sufferings of the race. Advocates of reparation point to payments made by our government to surviving Japanese-Americans who were interned during the Second World War and to payments made to survivors of the Holocaust by the Germans. But in both these cases, reparations were paid directly to the *actual* victims.

The arguments qualifying the ideology of retribution are that no black American alive today ever suffered slavery and no white American alive today was a slaveowner. These claims do little to assuage our *pro forma* expressions of guilt over our racist past. Yet to dwell on the injustices of the past is the worst prescription for achieving an harmonious society. To attempt to correct these past injustices by preferential treatment of blacks is only to undermine and upset our values of fairness, equality, and universality in our lives *now*. We can still be aware of our racist past—and we hear it all the time—without being committed to the societally danger-ous ideology of retribution. Shelby Steele has stated it better than anyone:

> [I]t is impossible to pay blacks living today for the historic suffering of the race. If all blacks were given a million dollars tomorrow morning it would not amount to a dime on the dollar of three centuries of oppression, nor would it obviate the residues of that oppression that we still carry today. The concept of historic reparations grows out of man's need to impose a degree of justice on the world that simply does not exist. Suffering can be endured and overcome, it cannot be repaid. Blacks cannot be repaid for the injustice done to the race, but we can be corrupted by society's guilty ges-tures of repayment.[4]

Justice Scalia has expressed the same antirestitution view from a consti-tutional vantage point when he wrote in his concurring opinion in *Adarand* (1995): "In my view, government can never have a 'compelling interest' in discriminating on the basis of race in order to 'make up' for past racial discrimination in the opposite direction. Individuals who have been wronged by unlawful racial discrimination should be made whole, but under our Constitution there can be no such thing as either a creditor or a debtor race."

What Steele says about historic reparation, in this case preferential treat-ment, approaches a universal historical generalization: the past suffering of oppressed racial and ethnic groups cannot be repaid, it can only be "endured and overcome." Consider the many peoples subject to murder-ous injustice throughout history: Jews, Armenians, Tutsi, Russian serfs, Indian untouchables, gypsies, Moslems in India and Bosnia, Koreans by the Japanese, Irish by the English, to name a few. Is there any case in history where governmentally institutionalized preferential treatment for people of some specified race or ethnicity has ameliorated inter-group relations? Where it has not led to resentment and inter-ethnic conflict? Donald Horowitz and Thomas Sowell, two social scientists who have studied preferential treatment of ethnic groups around the world, haven't been able to find any such cases.[5]

A second support of affirmative action for blacks has been the ideology of diversity. It was given prominence, if not invented, by Justice Powell and first stated in his enormously influential and misinterpreted opinion in *Bakke* (1978). In admiring the admission plan of Harvard College he wrote:

> A farm boy from Idaho can bring something to Harvard College that a Bostonian cannot offer. Similarly, a black student can usually bring something that a white person cannot offer. The quality of the educational experience of all the students in Harvard College depends in part on these differences in the background and outlook these students bring with them.

Since 1978 the influence of the ideology of diversity derived from Justice Powell has come to dominate the rationales for affirmative action for blacks, largely at the expense of the ideology of retribution. It has along the way become grossly misinterpreted. The Powell doctrine of diversity stipulated *only* that race could be a "plus" in college admissions, not that it could be a determining factor, much less *the* determining factor; that the need for racial preference would exist for only a short time (ten years, maybe); and that only institutions that discriminated in the past were entitled to use racial preferences. This enormously popular doctrine has been totally bent out of shape and used as a doctrine to justify race-conscious admissions across the land and practiced beyond its implied statute of limitations.[6]

The components of the ideology of diversity have been expanded to include Hispanics, other minorities, women, the disabled, and, sometimes, groups with other defining characteristics like sex orientation, age, and veteran status. All these victimized statuses have become proxies for merit in the collectivity, because they allegedly bring something positive to it. Significantly, the ideology of diversity is used mostly by those who practice affirmative action, while the ideology of retribution is used mostly by the beneficiaries of affirmative action.

What the ideology of diversity has become in practice is an ideology of proportionality, the idea that a college, a company, a legislature, whatever, should morally, democratically, ideally, or just properly, reflect demographically the population of which it is a part. Deviation from proportionality is ipso facto evidence of unfairness. At least three additional criticisms can be made of this ideology. First, it places an unhealthy, divisive, and mindless emphasis on the ascribed characteristics of race, ethnicity, gender, and other politicized ascriptive categories. Second, it ignores what are real group differences in cultural capital, traditions, experience and the self-selection that derives from these. And, third, it perversely treats specified races, ethnicities, and one of the genders as a proxy for merit. In practice the ideology of diversity supports a contrived and engineered diversity rather than a natural diversity continually in flux.

The liberal tradition of social contract theory can be used to defend affirmative action, and the liberal tradition of individualism (libertarianism in its radical form) can be used to oppose it. Both are inadequate and not very useful in the affirmative action debate. Consider the position put forth in John Rawls's *A Theory of Justice* which might appear to be sympathetic to affirmative action:

> [S]ocial and economic inequalities, for example, inequalities of wealth and authority, are just only if they result in compensating benefits for everyone, and in particular for the least advantaged members of society.[7]

However, opponents of affirmative action would want to define "least advantaged members of society" in socio-economic, not racial, terms. One can build a case for affirmative action based on Rawlsian thought, but when the object of concern is defined as "the disadvantaged" rather than blacks, the case for race-consciousness evaporates. Still, one can simply define blacks as disadvantaged, which is often the operative interpretation in legislation given to the term disadvantaged. But to automatically do this reflects a very *racialist* way of thinking.

On the other side, we have the Lockean tradition of liberal individualism which begins with discrete individuals. Persons are defined as making up groups, not the other way around. This has in the past been the major tradition in America and the ultimate reason why there is so little popular bedrock support for affirmative action, defined as preferential treatment, in this country. The major critique of affirmative action from this orientation is Richard A. Epstein's monumental *Forbidden Grounds: The Case against Employment Discrimination Laws*. The problem with this treatise and other libertarian critiques of affirmative action (like Dinesh D'Souza's *The End of Racism)* is that they leave out most of the sociological and psychological parts of human behavior: irrationality, stereotyping, sympathy, ignorance, hostility, and human inertia. The free market does not solve all social problems.

A fourth kind of approach to affirmative action questions might be termed the sociological. This too is not very useful in making a cogent case in favor of or against affirmative action. Sociological discussions of affirmative action are singularly shaped by one's orientation, by one's assumptions, by one's definition of the situation. Here are six sets of contradictory propositions which are used to defend and oppose affirmative action for blacks that will *not* be discussed here:

- America is very much a racist society and still needs affirmative action. **Or,** America has become a society with little tolerance for racism, outside of a small percentage of bigots, so affirmative action is no longer needed.
- The relatively small percentage of blacks in positions of power and authority in American society is indicative of discrimination and structural impediments to advancement. **Or,** The proportion of blacks in positions of power and authority in America has increased remarkably in recent decades.
- Black preference when extended to the "basically qualified" does not enhance white racism. **Or,** Any kind of race preference in employment will tend to generate hostility from nonbeneficiaries of the preferences.
- Affirmative action has helped all blacks, at the very least by providing role models. **Or,** Affirmative action has helped mostly advantaged blacks, and certainly not the underclass.
- Affirmative action is not harmful to the self-esteem of those who have been its recipients. **Or,** Affirmative action is harmful to the self-esteem of its black recipients.
- Blacks cannot fairly be compared with immigrant groups in America. **Or,** Now that blacks have achieved full civil rights, they will follow a path of advancement similar to that of American immigrant groups.

In all of the above pairs, the supporters of affirmative action for blacks choose the first alternative, the opponents the second alternative.

A fifth, and not much publicly proclaimed, defense of black affirmative action is the pragmatic reason: to prevent urban rioting. If "equality of results [is not attained for blacks, i.e., affirmative action]…there will be no peace in the United States for generations," wrote the prescient Daniel Patrick Moynihan in early 1965, before the urban rioting of the hot summers of the second half of the '60s. This was a major part of the impetus for affirmative action for blacks. No one, overtly, uses the pragmatic defense of affirmative action anymore.

It remains an unanswerable question as to whether the situation of blacks and the condition of race relations in America would have proceeded in a more successful manner than has occurred had the path taken been the color-blind legality and mentality of the late '50s and '60s, with discrimination in employment and education aggressively eliminated.

Affirmative action for blacks is patronizing. It assumes that they are a creditor race facing a debtor race, to use Justice Scalia's apt designations again. It also assumes that they need special treatment solely because of the color of their skin, and even that is not always necessary. Self identification as black will do.

Hispanics and Affirmative Action

When someone emigrates, he does not simply change countries; he also changes history.

—*Claude Barreau, French Office of Immigrant Affairs*[8]

These [Hispanic] newcomers have come to America to make a better life for themselves and their families, to enjoy the fruits of their labor, or to escape tyranny—all without the slightest notion that they deserved special privileges. And yet, they are eligible for affirmative action benefits immediately upon their arrival, despite the fact that they have no conceivable claim upon our nation's conscience.

—*Mark Krikorian*[9]

The extension of affirmative action to Hispanics, with their proliferation, has stretched any defense of preferential policies beyond the breaking point. Yet Hispanic leadership in America speaks as one in its defense. To the leaders, much less than to the rank and file, affirmative action has become an inalienable right of being Hispanic.

The Bureau of the Census estimated that the Hispanic population of the United States reached 10 percent in 1994, some twenty-seven million people. In the 1990 census 9.0 percent of the population claimed Hispanic origin; in 1980 6.4 percent did, and in 1960 4 percent are estimated to have been what is now called Hispanic. The projections are that early in the next century Hispanics will be the largest American minority, surpassing blacks. They are now conventionally paired with blacks, as "blacks and Hispanics," implying a similarity of disadvantage. (Some 3 or 4 percent also claim to be black.) Frequently blacks and Hispanics are collapsed into "minorities," sometimes with other groups included. Radical Hispanics cement their solidarity with blacks under the oppositional category "people of color."

Hispanics grew to be a mighty force in the age of affirmative action. Their leadership melded diverse Spanish language ethnic groups into a separate minority group officially called Hispanic and proclaimed it disadvantaged. Unlike the situation with earlier immigrant groups, assimilation gave way to seeking group entitlements: affirmative action, government set-asides, special education programs, and many others. Linda Chavez, vigorous advocate of assimilation and antagonist of much of the Hispanic leadership, has described the effects of being an ethnic group in the age of affirmative action:

> The effect of this change (gaining ethnic entitlements) was twofold: it strengthened Hispanic identity since entitlement was based on membership in an officially designated minority group; and it placed a premium on disadvantaged status. Hispanic leaders developed a vested interest in showing that Hispanic were, as head of one Hispanic organization described it, "the poorest of the poor, the most segregated minority in schools, the lowest paid group in America and the least educated minority in this nation." Such descriptions justified Hispanics' entitlement to affirmative action, but they also created a perverse standard of success. To succeed at the affirmative action game, Hispanics had to establish their failure in other areas. The point of this game was for Hispanics to show that they were making less social and economic progress than other groups and therefore deserved greater assistance. Hispanic leaders, ignoring tangible evidence to the contrary, complained as Representative Edward Roybal (D-Calif.) did [in 1972]: "...we are no better

off today than we were in 1949." Others invoked the specter of "a perma-
nent Hispanic underclass," as if to ensure no end to Hispanic entitlement.[10]

Two unique factors work to inhibit the assimilation of Hispanics into
the American mainstream. First, unlike all earlier immigrant groups in
America, Hispanics maintain much contact with their origins. Mexicans in
America are in continuous contact with their family and friends in Mexico,
by car, by plane, and by phone, just as the Puerto Ricans are by plane and
phone. Second, the controversial bilingual educational establishment in
America is overwhelmingly in the hands of Hispanics.

"Hispanic" is a bureaucratically defined pseudo-race. Individual Hispanics think of themselves as Cubans, Puerto Ricans, or Mexican-Americans, not as generic Hispanics. The tremendous consequence of the
invention of this category is suggested by an interesting hypothesis made
by Michael Lind, author of *The Next American Nation*:

> Suppose that the federal government created a category of citizens of east-
> ern European descent called Slavics, and made them eligible for affirmative
> action benefits. Soon, one can confidently predict, many Americans of par-
> tial Polish, Russian, Czech or Romanian descent would discover their com-
> mon Slavic identity and apply for favorable treatment in college admissions,
> minority set-asides, and so on. Before long, no doubt, there would be "Slavic
> Studies Departments" at major colleges and universities, where intellectuals
> would debate the exact elements of the "Slavic" culture common to Catholic
> Poles, Orthodox Russians and Protestant Hungarians. There might even be a
> Slavic Caucus in the House of Representatives, many of whose members
> were chiefly Irish or German and only slightly Slavic in descent. As night
> follows day, so would a renaissance of Slavic ethnicity follow the disbursal
> of government favors to Slavs.[11]

No other ethnic group on these shores has ever seriously proposed
making their language an official language of the country, which a few
Hispanic leaders have, yet making Spanish a de facto official language
has been realized in Miami. Spanish has always been an official language
in New Mexico, but it is not a result of recent immigration and is really of
little consequence. An outrageous accommodation to Spanish was made

in Arizona in June 1993 when Federal District Judge Aldredo Marquez held a swearing-in ceremony for citizenship primarily in Spanish.

Complete abolition of ethnicity-based affirmative action and other preferential programs would have as one of its unintended but beneficent consequences, an acceleration of Hispanics into mainstream America. Most of them want to be there.

Some Hispanic leaders would like to transform the meta-category "Hispanic" into a racial category for census—and affirmative action—purposes. They want a box in the racial question in the U.S. Census for *la raza*, a term that means more than race; it also means lineage and heritage, a cultural conception of race. They, and others, have criticized the race question as asked in the 1980 and 1990 censuses. The criticisms are well taken, if not their proposals for change.

In the 1990 census 3.9 percent of the population responded with "other" to the race question; the overwhelming majority were Hispanic. In California, with by far the largest Hispanic population of all the states, 13.9 percent of the population answered "other" to the race question.[12] This translates to 3.9 million people, *more than half the total of the "Hispanic origin" population of California.* If the race question is asked the same way in the 2000 census as in 1990, the numbers answering "other" will further increase. The Hispanic population will be larger and so will the proportions of "mixed" racial background, and they will choose the "other" alternative.

One response to the quagmire of racial and ethnic groups fighting for recognition would be to develop a series of specific race-conscious questions to be asked of the entire U.S. population. More economical would be to query only a sample of the census population. This is feasible. The color-blind response to this messy complexity, however, is to delete the race question altogether from the 2000 census. There is no "compelling governmental interest" to continue asking it in our increasingly mongrel nation.

In an effort to get a sophisticated defense of preferences for Hispanics, I wrote to David Featherman, president of the Social Science Research Council (SSRC). I asked him, in effect, how SSRC defended limiting certain awards to "Hispanic faculty" and "untenured Latina faculty."[13] He told me that the awards were sponsored by a "major grant" from the Ford Foundation, the leading foundation in the nation for supporting Hispanic causes and a vigorous practitioner of preferential policies. The main portions of this correspondence follow:

Tomasson to Featherman:

August 24, 1994

In the June-September issue of *Items* [the SSRC newsletter] there are three awards listed under the heading "Public Policy Research on Contemporary Hispanic Issues".... The ethnic and gender stipulations here beg many questions....

1) Is it a correct reading of these announcements that Award 1 is for an academic who is ethnically Hispanic of either gender, Award 2 is for a doctoral student of any ethnicity and either gender with a dissertation topic related to Latinos in the U.S., and that Award 3 is only for an Hispanic female? (I assume the terms *Hispanic* and *Latino* are synonymous here.)

2) Would a third generation Argentine Jew, with four grandparents born in Eastern Europe, be classified as an Hispanic by an SSRC committee making an award designated for an Hispanic?

3) Would an African-American of Puerto Rican background be given preference over a white of Cuban background, if the two candidates were judged to be "roughly equal"? Would the former be given preference over a white of Puerto Rican background if the two were judged "roughly equal"?

4) Would a person of European Spanish origins be considered an Hispanic (or Latina/o) for consideration of Awards 1 and 3? What about a second generation person from the 1930s immigration to Mexico?

5) Could a person of Brazilian background be defined as an Hispanic for the purpose of consideration by an SSRC committee?

6) Would a person with the same ethnic background as my congressperson, Bill Richardson, with a Mexican-American mother and an "Anglo" father, be given less preference than a person with two Mexican-American parents and an Hispanic surname?

7) Would a non-citizen Hispanic receive less preference than an Hispanic who is a U.S. citizen?

I know these questions pose a number of conundrums, but I think the SSRC (and other awarding agencies) that practice positive ethnic and gender selection have an obligation to answer questions like those posed here....

Featherman to Tomasson:

October 18, 1994

... I shared it [my letter] promptly with several staff, one of whom recently joined us to assume staff responsibility for the Council's program on Public Policy Research on Contemporary Hispanic issues. I asked staff to consider and help reply to your questions concerning eligibility requirements for the various competitions offered by the Program.

Supported by a major grant from the Ford Foundation, the Public Policy Research on Contemporary Hispanic Issues Program aims: to provide venture capital support for research on Hispanic issues that has the potential for challenging the social and behavioral sciences; to invest in a critical mass of creative scholars committed to the advancement of Latino/a scholarship; to stimulate new lines of research, new synthesis of emerging areas, and new networks of scientific collaboration through scientific conferences and workshops; and to inform social policy.

From our review of the Program, we developed a firm understanding of key ways in which resources can facilitate the growth of this sub-field and be used to nurture scientific work. The Program's payoffs are both direct and tangible. It includes substantive and methodological breakthroughs, the dissemination of scientific knowledge through publications, leverage for acquisition of additional research funds, and the diversification of the scientific research base.

Application for support includes a formal application and a proposal. While some of the Program's competitions target Hispanic scholars, all proposals are reviewed for scientific merit, with consideration given to the nature of the proposed research. Within this context, specific evaluation criteria include the appropriateness of the following elements: the potential of the study as a building block in the development of future research and social policy; appropriateness and significance of the research hypothesis; overall feasibility and adequacy of the project design; plans for analysis and evaluation of data; plans for dissemination of results; appropriateness of the requested budget.

Proposals are reviewed by members of the Program's committee. The structure of the committee assures that a panel of distinguished scholars reviews, evaluates, and awards the grants.

Regarding specific ethnic eligibility, the Program abides by the Council's affirmative action guidelines which seek to foster the development of research and training activities that are inclusive, both in scope and complexity. In addition, the Program follows the Ford Foundation's policies regarding pluralism and equal opportunity. The Ford Foundation is in the forefront of sponsoring programs designed to promote pluralistic and just societies, and to increase opportunities to historically disadvantaged groups in the United States and abroad.

As you know, efforts to achieve pluralism and equal opportunity require vigorous and sustained attention. The Council has pursued, and will continue to pursue programs to promote equal opportunities. This effort is shaped by the conviction that diversity is not merely compatible with excellence but actually promotes it. We are committed to working with others in achieving this goal and to ensure its success. Thank you for your interest in the Public Policy Research on Contemporary Hispanic Issues Program.

Your letter raises many probing issues—"conundrums" as you call them—which cannot be pursued to any depth in a short reply....

Wisely, Featherman, a sociologist, makes no attempt to deal with the "conundrums" of ethnic-based awards, nor to answer my rhetorical questions. In my continuing quest to find out how foundations define Hispanic for purposes of making ethnic-based awards I wrote to June Zeitlin, director of governance and public policy program at Ford. She sent me a brief response, but did not touch on a direct question I asked her: "Am I correct that Ford's (and, by extension, that of the SSRC) definition of 'Hispanic' is simply a self-classification, that is, one who defines him- or herself as Hispanic is so regarded?"[14] Yes, I am correct. And my guess is that, like everywhere else, they don't consider degree of "Hispanicness." All that matters is the self-identification.

In the Featherman letter we see the conventional justifications for affirmative action: diversity, equal opportunity, and the dubious contention that diversity "promotes" excellence. What is particularly noteworthy in the letter is the following sentence: "The Ford Foundation is in the forefront of sponsoring programs designed to promote pluralistic and just societies, and to increase opportunities to historically disadvantaged groups in the United States *and abroad.*" Here is an extension of affirmative action to members of disadvantaged groups around the world. Unlike gender and unlike race, ethnicity is very fluid. Many people have a choice in whether to be ethnic. And most people most of the time will choose that identification which is most to their advantage.

I once asked my congressman, Bill Richardson, Democratic whip of the House of Representatives, how he identified himself: as a white male, an Hispanic, or both? He immediately answered "Hispanic." I asked about the ethnic background of his wife. He also immediately answered "Irish."

Born in the well-to-do community of Pasadena, California, to an "Anglo" father and a Mexican mother in 1947, he lived for a while in Mexico City with his mother, became bilingual, went to Tufts University in Massachusetts, where he got a B.A. and an M.A. (in diplomacy), went to work for several years on Capitol Hill, moved to heavily Hispanic northern New Mexico in 1978 (ostensibly to enter elective politics), got elected to Congress four years later, and shortly after became chairman of the House Hispanic Caucus. Bill Richardson "chose" his identity as a New Mexico Hispanic, and he is everywhere recognized as such. Had he gone to Oregon to get into politics, he might have just been another white male. (To his credit, I have never read that he has said anything about affirmative action.)

I have an eleven-year-old nephew born in Paraguay in 1984. He was legally adopted by his professional parents when he was two weeks old. He lives with his parents in a big house in Greenwich, Connecticut, where he goes to school and plays ice hockey, chess, and the cello. I asked his father how he would identify himself when he applied to college. "Hispanic, of course," he answered.

Women and Affirmative Action

Women across all continents, all political systems (including socialism and communism), all racial groups, all religious groups, and all systems of mating (from intense polygyny to presumptive monogamy) place more value than men on good financial prospects.

—*David M. Buss*[15]

Gender feminism…interprets *all* data as confirming the theory of patriarchal oppression…. [It] is *nonfalsifiable*, making it more like a religious undertaking than an intellectual one. If, for example, some women point out that *they* are not oppressed, they only confirm the existence of a system of oppression, for they "show" how the system dupes women by socializing them to *believe* they are free, thereby keeping them docile and cooperative.

—Christina Hoff Sommers[16]

One of the most transforming revolutions in the developed nations in the second half of this century has been the women's movement. It took off later in America than in Western Europe, particularly Scandinavia, but has been spectacularly successful in improving the social and economic situation of some categories of women, mainly the young and the white.[17] It has also been successful ideologically. It has been able to equate the situation of women with disadvantaged racial and ethnic minorities and to portray it as deserving of the same special entitlements, among them candidacy for affirmative action. Like Hispanics, women have piggybacked onto a program originally intended only for blacks. We even give them first billing. We speak of "women and minorities," rather than the reverse.

Ideological feminists, the most vocal of whom are to be found in the universities, legislatures, and organizations devoted to women's causes, have become vigorous opponents of "racism," along with the minorities, with whom they so identify. They see women as a kind of historically oppressed race. They stand shoulder to shoulder with minority civil rights advocates. At least nine of the major national women's organizations went on record in support of the appeal by the University of Maryland to the Supreme Court of a lower court decision striking down a race-specific scholarship program, the hardest sort of affirmative action.[18] Minority causes have become feminist causes, and, feminists hope, vice versa. They know racism has more resonance than sexism. All victim causes have become feminist causes. "Feminists will not be satisfied until every abortion is performed by a gay black doctor under an endangered tree on a reservation for handicapped Indians," quipped Florence King.[19] The gap between the feminist leadership and the great mass of women is greater than that between minority leadership and minorities. A majority of women in fact oppose gender- and race-based affirmative action in some polls.[20]

'[T]he core concept of [radical or gender] feminism," as simply put by one of them, Jill Johnston, in a critique of *malist* John Bly's *Iron John*, "is that the attributes of masculinity and femininity are cultural fabrications, rooted in a caste system in which one sex serves the other."[21] Women have been and are being oppressed just like blacks. That women earn less than men, work in more sex-segregated occupations, are less represented in upper-level jobs, are given less attention in history books and in the media, and are paid less attention to in school is a consequence of a patriarchal and oppressive society.

To rectify this situation the radical feminist answer is affirmative action. It is needed to compensate for "continuing systematic uncorrected discrimination."[22] It should "include women workers in all occupations." Barbara Bergmann, economist and long-time affirmative action advocate, goes on to summarize why gender affirmative action is "necessary":

> Without affirmative action, the period in which sex segregation is the rule on the job is likely to be prolonged indefinitely. A continued failure to press affirmative action would rob young women of a chance to choose from a full range of occupations the one most congenial to their talents. Continued segregation would make the efforts to close the pay gap between women and men a continual uphill struggle. And only when women have a share in the roles that men occupy will men and women be comfortable interacting as equals.[23]

Every statement of Bergmann here is wrong or ideological or both, a charge that can be leveled against most general statements in defense of gender affirmative action. To wit:

- Evidence for "continuing systematic uncorrected discrimination" in the workforce is just inferred from the evidence of sex segregation there. She puts forth no measure of discrimination—admittedly, a concept difficult to define.
- Affirmative action should "include women workers in all occupations." Such a statement flows simply out of an ideology that all occupations *should* be gender-balanced. There is no recognition of the different occupational proclivities of the sexes.
- Without affirmative action "sex segregation…is likely to be prolonged indefinitely." Even a fervent opponent of gender affirmative action

like this writer can find no evidence that it can have more than a marginal effect on occupational sex segregation. The great change in the proportion of women in the professions and upper-level positions is mostly a consequence of the women's movement, not of affirmative action. There is virtually nothing that can be construed as *affirmative action* in the admissions policies of selective colleges, universities and professional schools, the first step in gaining entrance into the professions and upper-level occupations. It is only in matters of hiring, promotion, and compensation where affirmative action can become operative.

- Without affirmative action young women will be "robbed" of their opportunity "to choose from a full range of occupations the one most congenial to their talents." There is no evidence that young women *now* have any less occupational *choice* than do young men, assuming similar resources. They just *choose* differently.

- "Continued segregation" will make it more difficult to "close the pay gap" between men and women. It has already become closed within most occupations, if not between so-called "comparable" occupations. But, as we shall see, women, more than men, are likely to "choose" to enter lower-paying occupational fields, rather than the reverse.

- "Only" when women share in men's roles will the sexes be "comfortable interacting as equals." This is a tautology and a nonfalsifiable assertion.

Radical feminists oppose or ignore the differences between men and women wrought by nature and nurture. If they don't ignore the nurture part, they want to change it. The nature part they ignore or deny. Conflict between *difference* feminism and *equality* feminism there is, but the former is not so useful in social action. Equality feminists view difference feminists as defenders of the status quo.

A voluminous and virtually uncited older scientific literature has documented many fundamental differences between the sexes that are as valid now as they were before the coming of proportional feminism. Anne Anastasi's monumental *Differential Psychology*, written almost four decades ago, appends 150 scientific references to her objective, non-advocating, and nonideological chapter on sex differences. Here are some sentences from the summary statement on sex differences from Anastasi:

Both biological and cultural factors contribute to the development of sex differences in aptitudes and personality traits. The influence of biological factors may be relatively direct, as in the effect of male sex hormones upon aggressive behavior. Or it may be indirect, as in social and educational effects of the developmental acceleration of girls....

From a purely descriptive point of view, certain sex differences in aptitudes and in personality traits have been reliably established under existing cultural conditions. Males tend to excel in speed and coordination of gross bodily movements, spatial orientation, and other spatial aptitudes, mechanical comprehension, and arithmetic reasoning. Females tend to surpass males in manual dexterity, perceptual speed and accuracy, memory, numerical computation, verbal fluency, and other tasks involving the mechanics of language. Many sex differences in interests and attitudes have been found in studies.... Of particular interest are sex differences in social orientation and in achievement motivation. Other important personality differences have been reported in sexual behavior, emotional adjustment, and aggressiveness....

In school achievement, girls consistently excel. They seem in many ways to be more successful than boys in a typical academic situation. In later vocational activities, on the other hand, men achieve distinction in much greater numbers and to a much higher degree than women....

From all that has been said, it is apparent that *we cannot speak of inferiority and superiority, but only of specific differences in aptitudes or personality between the sexes* [emphasis added].[24]

Along with "equal representation," the biggest issue in the contemporary women's movement is differential earnings. Yet male/female ratios in income show a really amazing improvement in women's income relative to comparably situated men in recent years. The best single measure of the male/female earnings differential is to compare single, never married women in year-round, full-time employment with their male counterparts. The reasons for this comparison are two: first, it removes part-time workers from the comparison, the majority of whom are women, and, second, it removes marriage and parenthood (partially) from the comparison, both of which have a negative effect on women's earnings.

Here is a fact that deserves to be italicized: *In 1992 the 6.7 million single, never married, women who were year-round, full-time workers achieved median income parity with their 9.6 million male counterparts.*[25] These women had a *median income* of $21,011 compared with a men's *median income* of $20,914, resulting in a male/female ratio of 1.00. Eleven years earlier, in 1981, the comparable male/female ratio was .91.[26] This is truly remarkable progress, particularly in light of these years having been a time of *increasing* income differentials throughout the American economy.

When the measure of mean income is used, the male/female income ratio *declines* to .93, indicating a somewhat higher proportion of males than females in the higher income categories. Below are male/female earnings ratios for median income and mean income for single and married, year-round, full-time workers for the year 1992, by race and Hispanic origin:

		Single/Never Married	**Married**
Total	Median	1.00	.65
	Mean	.93	.62
		(N=9.6 million males)	(N=34.8 million males)
		(N=6.7 million females)	(N=20.3 million females)
White	Median	1.00	.64
	Mean	.92	.61
		(N=7.9 million males)	(N=31.0 million males)
		(N=5.2 million females)	(N=17.5 million females)
Black	Median	1.05	.76
	Mean	.96	.75
		(N=1.3 million males)	(N=2.5 million males)
		(N=1.2 million females)	(N=2.0 million females)
Hispanic	Median	1.10	.80
	Mean	1.06	.76
		(N=.9 million males)	(N=2.6 million males)
		(N=.5 million females)	(N=1.3 million females)

Marriage and parenthood have opposite consequences for men and women. Married men work more and earn more than do single men. Fathers work still more and earn more than married men who are not fathers. Married women, in contrast, work less and earn less than do single women, and mothers earn still less and work less than do non-mothers. By "work" here, let me assure the reader, I mean only conventionally defined "gainful employment."

Married working women (more precisely, married women "with income") earned 46 percent as much as married working men in 1992, but only 37 percent of these women were year-round, full-time workers (comparable figure for men, 62 percent). Among married women, 6.7 percent had no income (for men, 3.1 percent); by race the figures are 6.6 percent for white, 8.5 percent for black, and a stunning 35.7 percent for Hispanic origin women who have, by far, the highest fertility of the three populations. Marriage and children, and to a lesser extent the occupational areas women choose, are the major culprits engendering the huge differentials in the earnings of women and men in present-day America.

From around 1970, as the sex differentials in earnings have declined, income differentials in most sectors of American society have increased at a galloping rate.[27] This is a social problem of the first rank, unlike the petty issue of sex differentials in earnings, which detracts from it. These disparities have declined precipitously and are now largely a consequence of the individual choices women make. Women, married women, still have greater choice than do men as to whether to work and how much to work.

The increase in the proportions of women in what were traditionally male occupations, most notably the professions, has been enormous. In 1970, 5 percent of law school graduates and 8 percent of medical school graduates were women; by 1993 these percentages had increased to 42 percent and 38 percent, respectively.[28] According to American Medical Association data, in 1991 30.2 percent of all doctors under age 35 were women; among those aged 55–64, 8.3 percent were women.[29] All of the professions in the United States have seen similar increases. In 1993, 65 percent of degrees in pharmacy went to women, 63 percent in veterinary medicine, 49 percent in optometry, and 34 percent in dentistry. The increase in the proportion of doctorates going to women more than tripled in the three decades between 1961 and 1991; in 1993 38 percent of doctorates went to women. Professional occupations are those most dependent on success in school and hard work, and where for women, mainly white women, unlike blacks and Hispanics, the practice of affirmative action has been negligible.

The proportion of women in the professions is now about the same in the United States as it is in Sweden. This Scandinavian country was the first Western European country to become devoted to the diminution of sexual segregation in occupations and the achievement of full equality between the sexes. Gender equality and minimal gender differentiation were everywhere the official ideology in Sweden at least as long ago as the early 1960s.[30] Overall, there is virtually no difference between the two countries in the magnitude of sexual segregation in occupational life. Still, in both countries 99 percent of automobile mechanics are male, just as 99 percent of dental hygienists are women.

How persistent and intractable sexual segregation in occupational life is, and will continue to be, in the United States and elsewhere is suggested by the Swedish experience. Consider this matter-of-fact summary statement from an official publication:

> The sexes are equally balanced in upper secondary school as a whole, but not so within the various lines of study, which in this respect mirror the segregation of the labour market into predominantly male and female preserves. The largest proportion of girls (90%) is to be found in upper secondary school study programmes for the caring sector, social services and consumer education. More than 80% of students in the industrial trades and crafts sector are boys.[31]

This is the sex segregation situation in Sweden, more than a third of a century after the introduction of the great egalitarian school reform of 1958, a central aim of which was the minimization of sexual differentiation in work and life.

Also like Sweden, the United States has a higher proportion of women than men in higher education. In 1993, a remarkable 54 percent of bachelor's degrees awarded went to women. However, there are great differences in what the two sexes study. Women heavily predominate in education, health care (nursing), psychology, foreign languages; men in the physical sciences, engineering, and computer and information sciences. Near similarity is found in business management, the largest undergraduate major, biological/life sciences, and mathematics. At the doctoral level the gender differences persist and, in the aggregate, are greater.[32]

Within professions there is great sex differentiation. In medicine women and men make very different choices of specialties. Women tend to chose the personal/interactive areas of medicine and those that deal with women and children—pediatrics, obstetrics/gynecology, psychiatry—and they tend to shy away from the instrumental and technical areas such as cardiology and specialized surgery. Among physicians under age 35 in the early 1990s 30.2 percent were women, but 56.6 percent of pediatricians were women, and only 5.3 percent of orthopedic surgeons were. (See Appendix 1.) This same pattern prevails in Sweden.

Just as in academic disciplines, in medicine women tend to choose the "softer," the less technical, the more people-oriented areas of work. These are, throughout the professional labor market at least, the less remunerative areas. These data tip the balance in favor of the view that women *choose* occupational areas that are less remunerative and not the other way around, that the areas of work that pay less do so because women tend to choose them, the central argument of the comparable worth theorists.

A major exception to what I have said about gender similarity in Sweden and the United State is politics. Here we are very different from Sweden and many other industrial societies in the proportion of women elected officials. In 1994, 41 percent of those elected to the 349-member Swedish parliament were women. But there is a catch: the Social Democrats mandated that every other name on their election lists be that of a woman. So it was a foreordained result. This is a kind of affirmative action that has been commonly practiced at all levels of the Democratic Party in the United States since the 1972 election, but we don't have a proportional representation (PR) electoral system to enhance the election of women. In the United States after the 1994 election, 11 percent of the Congress were women, the highest ever. (The percentages of women elected to state legislatures are mostly in the 10 to 20 percent range.) After the 1992 election Gloria Steinem depressingly claimed it would take three hundred years at the current rate of change for women to achieve their "rightful" 50 percent representation.

My prediction is we will never even approach the Swedish level with our system. This is because we have representation by single-member constituencies rather than by PR, as do Sweden and all non-Anglo-American modern democracies. In PR systems people vote for party lists, not for individual persons. Parties from left to right all make sure that active women from their ranks are on their lists. In our system of elections, from state legislator to governor to senator to president, the whole dogged and compulsive process of getting nominated and getting elected is dependent on just those nature/nurture characteristics found in greater abundance among males: aggressivity, single-mindedness, achievement orientation. Those characteristics found in greater abundance among females hinder electoral success in our individualistic political system: nurturing, responsibility toward children, personal caring, domesticity.

A prototypical case of the implicit acceptance of the *rightness* of proportionality—in the case of women, half—is a *New York Times* report of a study of women in state and local government.[33] "Few Women Found in Top Public Jobs," read the misleading headline, followed by "Study Sees 'Glass Ceiling' at State and Local Agencies." In the text of the article we read that "only" 31.3 percent of the "high-level" jobs in state and local government are held by women across the nation. (Can 31.3 percent of anything be called *few?*) Toward the end of the piece it is noted that women made up "40 percent of all top level positions filled in 1990." Comparatively, this is a very high figure for women in "high-level jobs," and worthy of celebration. But an impatient, utopian, mindless devotion to the inexorable rightness of proportionalism triumphs over common sense: "At the rate it's changing, it's going to be a very long time before women reach equity," says Sharon Harlan, director of research for the Center for Women in Government of the Rockefeller College of Public Affairs and Policy, which did the study.

My point here is that to argue "rightness" on the grounds of proportionality for women makes even less sociological sense than to argue it for minorities or different ethnic groups. All cultural groups, any of which contains members of the two sexes, and the sexes themselves, each have different cultural experiences and different aspirations, qualities, and modes of mobility in our multiethnic, two-gender society. This makes the whole idea of gender and ethnic proportionality intellectually untenable as any kind of social or moral goal, because it assumes uniformity and plasticity of categories of people which just don't exist. Moreover, it is a goal statistically impossible to achieve without an impermissible degree of authoritarian social engineering; it would mean going well beyond garden-variety affirmative action.

A beautiful example of a nature/nurture, sex/ethnic pattern is provided by the 1994 graduating class of the New York City Police Department's police academy.[34] Of the 2,003 graduates, 84 percent were men, two-thirds of whom were non-Hispanic whites, far higher than desired by a police department striving for more *diversity.* Most are of Irish, Italian, and German background, fed to the department by an "enduring cultural pipeline." The 16 percent of women graduates, a long way from 50 percent, of the police academy, by contrast, were "almost two-thirds" black and Hispanic. Is there anything seriously wrong with these "imbalances"? Should vigorous efforts be made to change the sex and ethnic balance of the New York City Police Department beyond widely advertising openings for the police academy and ferreting out any discrimination? I think not.

A *reductio ad absurdum* of feminist proportionalism was achieved at a National Lesbian Conference where "parity" was called for at all conference events.[35] Conference guidelines specified that half the committee members were to be "lesbians of color," 20 percent lesbians with disabilities, and at least 5 percent "old lesbians," defined as "over 50 with a history of ageism activism."

Interestingly, there is slight public concern from any quarter in reducing sex segregation in traditionally female occupations, and changes here have been much less over the past generation than in the traditionally male occupations, mainly at the upper levels. Large majorities of secretaries (increasingly, administrative assistants), clerical workers, grade-school teachers, nurses, social workers, and librarians continue to be women, and I predict, will continue to be women. This is simply because more women than men *choose* to follow these occupations. They are all occupations in which it is less difficult than in many of the traditionally male professions for women to balance their *perceived* obligations of marriage and parenting, which are certainly greater than the *perceived* obligations for men. More important, they are all occupational areas attractive to persons who wish to help, nurture, and educate and where, also, women can make use of their greater verbal fluency and memory. These are all areas which, for the most part, have been exempt from gender-based affirmative action.

Gender-based affirmative action exists only for upper-level positions and for administrative, managerial, and supervisory positions at all levels. The expressed rationale is always the benefits of diversity (i.e., proportionality). The unexpressed reasons are pressures from the top and to avoid hassles and legal action. The pressures in universities, corporations, and law firms to hire and promote women, for no reason other than gender, i.e., promoting diversity, are often intense.

Gender-based affirmative action has slight relevance for the educational and occupational opportunities of women—and men—in present-day America.

Class and Affirmative Action

For all this [race-based affirmative action], the left has paid a tremendous price. On a political level, with a few notable exceptions, the history of the past twenty-five years is a history of white, working-class Robert Kennedy Democrats turning first into Wallace Democrats, then into Nixon and Reagan Democrats and ultimately into today's Angry White Males. Time and again, the white working class votes its race rather than its class, and Republicans win. The failure of the left to embrace class also helps turn poor blacks, for whom racial preferences are, in Stephen Carter's words, "stunningly irrelevant," toward Louis Farrakhan.

—Richard Kahlenberg[36]

As opposition to race-based affirmative action has increased, the call for a class-based replacement is being heard. "Class, not race," is the cry. Martin Luther King is invoked in its favor; he usually did not favor programs to help blacks alone, but programs for "the disadvantaged." Newt Gingrich, along with Clarence Thomas and Dinesh D'Souza, conservatives all, oppose race-based affirmative action, but do favor special help for "the disadvantaged" that boils down to class-based affirmative action.[37] Even Bill Clinton, who has been on many sides in the affirmative action debate, has hinted his support. In reference to his 1995 call for a review of federal affirmative action programs, he said he wanted to see "whether there is some other way we can reach [our] objective without giving a preference by race or gender."[38] What other way is there but class! "Class" in the context of affirmative action always means "the disadvantaged." The American proponents of an institutionalized class-based affirmative action have invented it quite independently of similar practices in the Communist regimes of Eastern Europe and the old Soviet Union.

It's really not a new idea, just its prevalence is new. Some colleges and universities have practiced it for years. "Need-blind" admissions is a sort of class-based affirmative action. The University of California admission policies have for some years given some small weight to socioeconomic background. More emphasis will be given to socioeconomic backround now that race- and gender-based affirmative action is apparently no longer to be practiced.

At first glance there is much that is appealing about a class-based affirmative action. It removes the obsessive focus on race. Class preferences are acceptable in a way race preferences are not. Everyone agrees that a hard-working and ambitious individual from a poor and disadvantaged background deserves a leg up. Giving a preference to a poor Appalachian eighteen-year-old in getting into Yale is certainly more acceptable than giving a preference to Hazel O'Leary's son only because he is black. Nor are there any bars in the Constitution or civil rights laws to such preference. Class is not a suspect category under the Fourteenth Amendment.

Using class rather than race, so goes the argument, will have the same consequences, only in a more palatable way. Because blacks are disproportionately among the poor they will disproportionately benefit from a class-based affirmative action. They are 12 percent of the population, but 30 percent of the poor.

How would it work?

There are three ways it might work according to Richard Kahlenberg, who is writing a book on the subject.[39] He has a simple, a moderate, and a complex way of defining class for purposes of admission to selective colleges and universities. First is simply family income, which is taken as a crude proxy for a number of disadvantages such as poor schools and a poor learning environment. Second is to use the Big Three determinants of opportunity: parental income, parental education, and parental occupation. Third, and preferred by Kahlenberg, is to consider the whole bag of measures of class and disadvantage. In addition to the three parental determinants, he would consider net worth ("for a long-term view of relative disadvantage") and quality of high school; family structure would be taken into account—for example, having grown up in a single-parent home. He would also factor in census tract and zip code data to get at measures of "neighborhood influences," i.e., poverty.

All of these measures would provide pluses without taking race or ethnicity into account. It is truly a color-blind program in all its details, if not in its purpose. The third and complex measure would most benefit blacks because they, more than poor whites, live in areas of concentrated poverty, come from single-parent households, and go to poor schools.

My guess is that such a program would have little effect in increasing the proportion of blacks in selective colleges, universities, and programs. Few of the poorest Americans of any color or ethnicity—say, those who grew up in households below the poverty level—ever get to the most selective institutions. Blacks and whites alike who make it to Stanford, and similar institutions, are heavily from middle- and upper-income families. And, how is the problem of the vast black/white chasm in SAT scores to be dealt with in a color-blind, class-preference system? Nathan Glazer, a proponent of black-only affirmative action, has asserted, but without evidence, that such a system would have the opposite effect of that intended by Kahlenberg: "The only effect of preference on grounds of class [rather than race] could be to increase the number of poor whites and Asians in institutions of higher education, and to reduce the number of blacks."[40] Whether this would be the case would depend on the relative emphasis given to, on the one hand, grades and test scores, and, on the other, the "class pluses." If the emphasis were heavily on the latter, it would *increase* "the number of blacks."

The whole obsession with getting more blacks into the most selective colleges, with or without a race-based affirmative action, is an issue that deserves to be laid to rest. It is not true as is often asserted that they would re-segregate, become "lily white," without some form of affirmative action, though for a while there would certainly be fewer blacks admitted. But *So what!* America is a country oversupplied with institutions of higher education, with ample educational opportunity for those willing to work hard, and no barriers of race itself in admissions exists anywhere. Rather than giving "class pluses" to the amazing high school graduate from a horrid ghetto high school, who worked to support her family through high school and got a combined SAT score of 1100, to gain admission to Princeton, she should go to SUNY Stony Brook where she would be admitted without the need for any class pluses. And she'll probably be more comfortable and do relatively better there than at Princeton.

And imagine the paperwork needed to determine the magnitude of one's socioeconomic disadvantage. Imagine the new competition to claim disadvantage. Imagine the opportunities for fraud.

The world of work is where any plan of a class-based affirmative action completely breaks down. Would individuals be given a degree of disadvantage score that would be part of their resume? Would law firms give preferences to law-school graduates who came from disadvantaged backgrounds? Would they try to promote to partnerships lawyers from such backgrounds as they now do with women and minorities? Would universities seek out faculty from disadvantaged backgrounds? Would the civil service give points for coming from a disadvantaged background as they do for veterans?

To be fair to Kahlenberg, he has qualified his views based on the writings of his critics:

> These criticisms point to two basic rules about class-based preferences in employment: the preferences should be based on quantifiable and verifiable indices [like government student loans and the Earned Income Tax Credit]; and consideration of economic background makes most sense in entry-level positions for those starting off in life, rather than in subsequent lateral moves or promotions of older workers.[41]

Still, how would people of modest background seeking to be electricians, plumbers, police, firefighters—all occupational areas with strong race-based affirmative action traditions—react to preferences being given to individuals with more disadvantaged backgrounds than themselves? Very negatively, I would think.

Class-based affirmative action is a last ditch and perhaps futile attempt to keep affirmative action operative at a time when the abolition of its race- and gender-based form is being threatened. It is not a feasible alternative.

Chapter 16

The People and Affirmative Action

Ancestral identities are important—so important, in fact, that every American should have several of them. At the same time, Americans should think of themselves as belonging to only one race—the human—and to only one nationality—the American.

—Michael Lind[1]

Neither the State of California nor any of its political subdivisions or agents shall use race, sex, color, ethnicity, or national origin as a criterion for either discriminating against, or granting preferential treatment to, any individual or group in the operation of the state's system of public employment, public education or public contracting.

—1996 California Civil Rights Initiative

With affirmative action, any slight change in the wording of an attitudinal question, or using one word or phrase rather than another, say, "giving preference" rather than "expanding opportunity," can dramatically change results. One can choose among polls to support the view that the public is strongly opposed to affirmative action or that the public has some degree of support for it.

Many times, from the 1970s through the early '90s, the Gallup poll has asked a national sample:

Some people say that to make up for past discrimination, women and members of minority groups should be given preferential treatment in getting

235

jobs and places in college. Others say that their ability, as determined in test scores, should be the main consideration. Which point of view comes closer to how you feel on the subject?

Each time it has been asked only 10 or 11 percent responded to the "give preferential treatment" alternative; huge majorities responded to the "base on test scores, ability" alternative. Small minorities, less than 10 percent responded to the "no opinion" choice.[2] Note that this often-asked question has a bias: "preferential treatment" is opposed to "ability." Phrasing a question on affirmative action this way gets the largest majority to oppose it.

An April 1991 *Newsweek* poll on differential attitudes of whites and blacks asked a better, more qualified question about preferential treatment.[3] Here we have a toss-up situation between "equally qualified" whites and blacks. The question asked in phone interviews with 619 whites and 305 blacks, was: "Do you believe that because of past discrimination against black people, qualified blacks should receive preference over equally qualified whites in such matters as getting into college or getting jobs?" The results were these: ("Don't know" and other responses were not given.)

	Whites	**Blacks**
Blacks should receive preference	19 percent	48 percent
Blacks should not receive preference	72 percent	42 percent

Even in this more restrictive case where whites and blacks are "equally qualified," the great majority of whites reject preferential treatment for blacks and so do a large minority of blacks.

When a similar question is asked about blacks "and other minorities" the percentage opposed to preferential hiring increases. An *NBC-Wall Street Journal* poll (released 29 June 1991) based on a telephone sample of 1,006 reported that "78 percent of the public (and 84 percent of whites) said they thought blacks and other minorities should not receive hiring preferences to make up for past discrimination against them." Fifty-three percent "said Democrats favored such preferences...only 18 percent said Republicans did." Perhaps inconsistently, when asked, "Which party represents your views on civil rights?" 48 percent of the total sample answered Democratic and 33 percent, Republican. Among blacks, the percentages were 85 and 6 percent, respectively. Even in this more restrictive case where whites and blacks are "equally qualified," the great majority of whites reject preferential treatment for blacks and so do a large minority of blacks.

Even where there are affirmative-action policies in effect which give hiring and promotion preferences to blacks and other minorities, relatively few employees claim to have been affected by them, one way or the other. According to the June 1991 Gallup poll, only "about three in ten employed Americans" say they work in places which give preferences to blacks and other minorities. There is little difference by race: 28 percent of employed whites and 31 percent of employed blacks claim to work in such places. Twenty percent of these whites say they have been "hurt" by minority preference programs, while 23 percent of the blacks say they were "helped" by them. This translates into about 6 percent of all employed white Americans claiming to have been "hurt" by minority preferences, and about 7 percent of all employed black Americans claiming to have been "helped" by them.

This same Gallup poll reported that "considerably less than a majority of Americans—black and white—actually encounter discrimination in their daily lives." The question is, "Have you ever been a victim of discrimination in getting an education, a job, a promotion, or housing?" Twenty-one percent of whites and 36 percent of blacks responded in the affirmative. Note that this question asked whether the respondent had "ever" been a "victim of discrimination."

An interesting, if rather crude, question on how people *felt* (this is the appropriate word) about "the civil rights" of eight disparate categories of people was asked in the Gallup poll of December 1989. The question was: "For each of the following groups I read, please tell me whether you think there has been too much or not enough attention to the civil rights of this group." "The elderly" received the highest percentage of "not enough" answers (84 percent), "black people" received the lowest (40 percent). Below is the rank order of the eight categories in terms of percentages responding "not enough" to the question.

	Not enough	Too much	Right amount	No opinion
The elderly	84	4	10	4
Disabled & handicapped people	81	6	11	2
People with the disease AIDS	51	31	13	5
Women	49	29	18	4
Hispanics	46	28	15	11
Asian Americans	45	25	17	13
Jewish people	43	20	22	15
Black people	40	39	17	4

The most notable observation from these data is that there is greater sympathy for the elderly and disabled than for women, persons with AIDS, and members of ethnic groups. They differ from the other categories in that all people can contemplate themselves becoming old and disabled.

How little the general population follows civil rights (affirmative action) issues was revealed by a June 1991 Gallup poll taken at a time when the Congress had been involved in months of political debate over amending the Civil Rights Act of 1964 (which resulted in the Civil Rights Act of 1991):

> Despite extensive coverage by the national press, a majority (59 percent) of Americans claim not to have heard or read anything about the civil rights bills. Blacks are more likely than whites to say they have paid attention, but even among blacks awareness is fairly low (49 percent vs. 40 percent of whites). Although it has been posited as a women's rights bill, relatively few women have heard about it (36 percent vs. 45 percent).

Perhaps now (spring 1996) there is more knowledge in the general population about so-called civil rights issues, but I wouldn't bet on it.

The September 1995 Field Poll asked 1,008 Californians about awareness and support for the California Civil Rights Initiative (CCRI), a 1996 initiative to abolish all governmental preferences based on race, sex, color, ethnicity, or national origin.[4] The poll found 76 percent of those queried had heard about the CCRI. At first, only a narrow plurality of 28 percent said they favored it, but after the respondents read the CCRI text support

escalated to 58 percent, with 33 percent opposed and 9 percent unde-
cided. Californians supported the CCRI by almost 2 to 1. Race or ethnicity
and political party affiliation were important factors. Sixty-five percent of
whites said they would vote for the initiative, and 26 percent said they
would not, "almost exactly the reverse of black respondents." Hispanics
more narrowly opposed the initiative, 50 percent to 44 percent.

By political party affiliation, the results were these:

	Favor	**Oppose**
Republicans	78 percent	15 percent
Democrats	41 percent	49 percent

The most authoritative and detailed study of the attitudes of Americans
about affirmative action is a *USA Today/CNN/Gallup* poll taken in March
1995.[5] The poll found that 55 percent of the public favors "expanding
opportunities" for women and minorities; 37 percent want such programs
[not defined] decreased, 31 percent want them increased, and 26 percent
want them kept at the same level. "[T]here is no clear front line between
white and black, male and female, Republican and Democrat," though
blacks, females, and Democrats are far more supportive than are whites,
males, and Republicans.

Gallup analyst David Moore divides the public into four opinion groups
which cut across racial, gender, and political categories. He calls them the
"true believers," the "antagonists," the "floaters," and the "dubious. "

The "true believers," 28 percent of the population, are the hard core
supporters of government affirmative action programs. They believe that
without such programs businesses and schools would not provide "equal
opportunity" for women and minorities. They tend to believe there is still
significant discrimination against blacks and Hispanics. Eighteen percent
of "minority" women fall in this category, a figure that translates into the
great majority of black and Hispanic women, who total around 21 to 22
percent of the population. A less overwhelming majority of "minority"
males are in this category: 15 percent. Almost double as many white
women as white men fall in this category, 45 to 24 percent. About a third
of *all* white women are "true believers." More than twice as many Democrats as Republicans are in this category, 63 to 29 percent—and a third of
them minorities.

The "antagonists," 24 percent of the population, are those who believe affirmative action means quotas and reverse discrimination, and they are against it. These people would be firm supporters of the CCRI. They are predominantly white and Republican. The percentage of minority women in this category approaches zero. However, 2 percent of this category is made up of minority males, not a negligible percentage. Forty-three percent of the category is made up of white women and 55 percent of white men. Republicans predominate over Democrats by more than 3 to 1, 71 and 20 percent, respectively.

The "floaters," 21 percent, make up "the great muddy middle." These are people who back some principles of affirmative action, but their commitment is lukewarm. While they tend to support quotas and special programs, only one in ten believes that discrimination is a major problem for women and minorities. These people have a more complex view of affirmative action than do the "true believers" and the "antagonists." This group breaks down as follows: 9 percent of it is minority women, 4 percent minority men, 47 percent white women, and 40 percent white men. Equal numbers are Republicans and Democrats, 44 and 45 percent, respectively.

The "dubious," 27 percent, are a second intermediate group between the "true believers" and the "antagonists." On the one hand, they oppose quotas, set-asides, and special scholarships for minorities; on the other, they support outreach programs, job training, and special education classes to aid them. They are divided on how much job discrimination there is. This category breaks down as follows: minority women, 4 percent, minority men, 3 percent; white women, 45 percent, white men, 48 percent, by political affiliation, Republicans, 49 percent, Democrats 41 percent.

The complexity, contradiction, conventionality, ill-informed and stereotypical nature of attitudes surrounding affirmative action can be demonstrated by recasting the data of what may be the most detailed attitudinal investigation of the subject.[6] Bron Taylor, a college teacher of religion and social ethics, studied the attitudes toward affirmative action of a sample of management and rank-and-file employees of the California State Department of Parks and Recreation, where he had been a state park ocean lifeguard for fifteen years. Part of the data he collected consists of 435 completed questionnaires (66 percent male, 34 percent female; 59 percent white, 41 percent non-white, i.e., black, Asian, Hispanic, American

Indian) in which the respondents were asked to "strongly agree, agree, disagree, and strongly disagree" to sixty statements with relevance to affirmative action.

I have arranged thirty-three of the sixty statements—those most directly and unambiguously pertaining to affirmative action—in rank order according to the percentage of agreement by nonwhite women, the ethnic/ gender category most supportive of affirmative action. (See Appendix 2.) White men, at the other pole, are the least supportive of affirmative action; nonwhite men and white women fall in between, both closer to nonwhite females than to white males. For each statement I listed the percentage agreement ("strongly agree" and "agree" combined) for each of the four ethnic/gender categories, along with the differential between the extremes: nonwhite female percentage agreement minus white male percentage agreement.

These responses show that a substantial majority of these people believe that affirmative action in the abstract is a good thing, a desirable thing, somehow morally right. (Note, in particular, statements 4, 5, 14, and 33). This is the case even among white males, though in all matters touching on affirmative action their views are less positive or more negative than those of the other ethnic/gender categories. Favoring affirmative action, compared with opposition to it, seems to have the moral high ground among these parks department workers.

Still, there are statements which qualify the generally positive view of affirmative action. For example, consider the response to statement 19, "Affirmative action promotes equal opportunity." The percentages agreeing for the four categories are 61, 51, 41, and a mere 25 for white males. Or statement 25, "Affirmative action violates the rights of white men." Here the percentages agreeing are 46, 46, 57, and 75. Almost half of the nonwhites believe affirmative action violates "the rights of white men."

Statements about how affirmative action works in practice (17, 20, 21, 22, 29, and 32) show much lower levels of approval than the theoretical statements about it among all ethnic/gender categories. In the case of white males, responses to all the "in practice" statements turn to disagreeing majorities, sometimes huge majorities.

The most fundamental rationale for affirmative action is past and present prejudice and discrimination. Large majorities of the four categories agree that prejudice is "common in society today" (statement 2). However, agreement is lower, much lower in the case of whites, to the statement about prejudice being "common in the parks department" (statement 10).

What we see here is the acceptance of two contradictory value systems: one the conventional American belief in success through individual effort, the other the newer and pervasive group-oriented themes. Consider the responses to statement 18: "With effort, anybody can succeed." Two-thirds of nonwhite and white females agreed; three quarters of both categories of males agreed. Yet to statement 3, "With public policies, it is better to focus on groups [rather] than individuals," *still larger majorities agreed.*

We should not try to glean anything more than the grossest generalizations from these, or any attitudinal data, on affirmative action. It would be deception to find more there. It is a subject of low salience to most people, and one on which they are not clear-headed, yet it is one infused with a big dose of inhibiting moral sensibility. When people are torn by conflicting and confused sentiments on an issue of social policy, on any issue, they put it out of mind. They are not engaged by it.

Bron Taylor, himself ideologically committed to affirmative action, summarized his impressions of the sentiments held by the employees of the California state parks department in these words:

> Some people have very little idea about what moral values are important to them, let alone how to think about moral issues such as affirmative action. These people therefore do not know how to evaluate morally affirmative action policies. Many do not seem to understand what ethical issues are at stake in the controversy, and others are torn or ambivalent about competing ethical arguments about affirmative action, sometimes endorsing contradictory principles and ideas.[7]

No occupational category in American society is, or is often thought to be, more sympathetic to affirmative action, to the preferential hiring of women and minorities, than are academics. At least no institutional area in the society has practiced affirmative action more determinedly than higher education. University administrators are overwhelmingly supportive of affirmative action. Any academic not sympathetic to it and its supporting ideology of diversity is not likely to become an administrator in contemporary higher education. But what about rank-and-file academics?

A national survey of university faculty from the 1972–73 academic year found that 32 percent of men and 42 percent of women favored preferential hiring of women at their institutions.[8] The comparable figures for the preferential hiring of minority group persons was 35 percent among the men and 36 percent among the women. In two-year colleges, in the same survey, the percentages favoring preferential hiring were lower; among male faculty 20 percent favored preferential hiring of women, 28 percent for minorities. (Percentages for women faculty were not given.)

An earlier faculty survey, from the 1968–69 academic year, found that 23 percent of men on university faculties favored "relaxing" the normal academic requirements in hiring "members of minority groups" for faculty positions at their institutions.[9] The comparable figure for women was 20 [sic] percent. Even academics of the late 1960s and 1970s, putatively a category particularly accepting of affirmative action and surveyed at a time when sympathy for the cause of minorities was near its peak, failed to claim a majority for preferential hiring.

During the 1991–92 academic year I sent a questionnaire to all 979 tenured and tenure-track faculty at the University of New Mexico to determine their views on "some of the controversial issues facing higher education in general and UNM in particular."[10] Two of the questions dealt with affirmative action. Only a minority of 235 responded; 175 male faculty, 54 female faculty, and 6 from faculty who refused or neglected to specify gender.

The first question was, "Do you believe there are cases where preferential hiring of university faculty and administrators on the basis of sex or race/ethnicity can be justified?" The responses were as follows:

Frequently (N=18)	7	percent
Sometimes (N=60)	26	
It depends (N=43)	18	
Rarely (N=60)	28	
Never (N=44)	18	
No response (N=6)	2	

Faculty in Arts and Sciences were more likely to choose the first two categories, "frequently" and "sometimes," than were faculty in other colleges of the university. More significant, however, was the difference between male and female faculty. For example, 22 percent of the males answered "never" to this query compared with 6 percent of the females.

A second, open-ended, question was: "Make any comments you wish on the theory and practice of affirmative action at UNM." The responses frequently nullified answers to the first question. Attitudes were generally more positive to the theory than to the practice of affirmative action, just as in Taylor's study of the California Parks workers. The responses can be forced into three categories which might be called the "moderate," the "proportionalist," and the "meritocratic."

The largest category is the moderates. They mention the importance of "merit" or "competence" or "quality" or some similar idea, but also mention that when two persons are "about," "nearly," "similarly," etc. equal in these regards and one belonged to an underrepresented category, *that* individual should be recruited first. The second category, numerically the smallest, is the proportionalist, much more commonly women than men. These are those with an allegiance to the ideology of diversity. Their responses stress that employment preference should be extended to women and minorities to achieve "fairness" or "equality," i.e., something like proportional representation, with no mention of merit or some reasonable facsimile thereof. The third category, in between the other two in frequency, is the meritocratic. They are devoted to *merit only;* to them affirmative action has no role to play in the hiring of faculty and administrators.

Here is a sampler of the three categories of thought about the theory and practice of affirmative action at UNM (and probably elsewhere). First the moderates, who have less passion than the proportionalists or the meritocrats:

- When candidates [are] of the same overall quality and where there is serious underrepresentation of the minority group in the type of position being filled, it is acceptable to engage in preferential hiring. (Male, A&S)
- When academic credentials and quality of scholarship are equal then hiring on the basis of sex & race/ethnicity is justified. But it should *never* be the primary factor. This is disastrous for the person, the department, and the university. (Male, A&S)

Even the authors of *The Bell Curve,* so opposed to preferential affirmative action, would fall in this category of moderates: "In the case of two candidates who are fairly closely matched otherwise, universities should give the nod to the applicant from the disadvantaged background. This original sense of affirmative action seems to us to have been not only reasonable and fair but wise."[11]

Some voices of the proportionalists:

- Until fair representation of women of all races and of men and women of color is achieved, every hiring needs to be an affirmative-action hiring. (Female, A&S)
- Quite frankly, the academic deck is stacked *against* women and minorities. Affirmative action is necessary at all levels, especially in the recruitment and retention of graduate students (to produce more equity in the *pool* of qualified candidates for academic positions). However I do not believe that most affirmative action could be described as "preferential" hiring. Preferential hiring has long existed and continues to pervade the university; the preference is given to white men (due to structural factors and subtle considerations). Affirmative action serves as a corrective. Rarely have I seen an *un*qualified candidate hired through affirmative action. (Male, A&S)

The meritocrats, more numerous than the proportionalists but fewer than the *moderates*, responded this way to the question on the theory and practice of affirmative action at UNM:

- Affirmative action violates the norms of achievement. It allows for the hiring of incompetents who are likely to be propagandists pushing for ethnic or gender nationalism. Affirmative action is inherently unjust/unfair. (Male A&S)
- Reject it as both unconstitutional and unethical. (Male, A&S)
- It seems that a "good old boy (person)" Hispanic network would like to function instead of a "good old boy" Anglo network. Actually affirmative action should guarantee *equal opportunity* for all, regardless of sex or race/ethnicity. (Male, Medicine)

The faculty from which these responses were elicited are employed by a university, administratively, in word and deed, committed to race- and gender-conscious affirmative action. A number of administrative positions are unofficially designated for women and minorities, yet there is no *public* criticism of these practices from any quarter.

The most sophisticated attitudinal study relating to affirmative action has been done by Paul M. Sniderman and Thomas Piazza in their study of race relations, *The Scar of Race*.[12] Their data from a number of studies demonstrate that America is a land of few hard-core bigots and a huge majority, tolerant and open to persuasion on matters of race. This is a very different reading from those psychologists and social scientists who see America as a society pervaded by racism.

The authors show that opposition to affirmative action does not at all imply prejudice toward blacks. The psychologists who wrote in a 1989 volume published under the auspices of the Society for the Psychological Study of Social Problems, that "White opposition to affirmative-action programs grows, in part, from subtle but pervasive racism...comparable to that of old-fashioned racism" were dead wrong.[13] While it is of course true that bigots are opposed to affirmative action, most opposition to it is on ideological grounds, because of a disdain for preferential treatment of categories of people, past discrimination notwithstanding. They show in fact that whites are "open to persuasion to a striking degree on issues of the social welfare agenda, resistant to a remarkable degree on issues of the race-conscious agenda."

More than that, the authors show that the relation between being prejudiced and affirmative action works just the other way around. Even the "mere mention" of affirmative action before asking a sample of people on their attitudes toward blacks *increases* prejudiced responses. *A dislike of affirmative action prompts a dislike of blacks!*

Sniderman and Piazza take random samples of whites, divide each sample randomly into halves. One group is asked their view of affirmative action, then their views of blacks. The control group is asked exactly the same questions, except in the opposite order. If opposition to affirmative action "provokes" dislike of blacks, then the group first asked about affirmative action should be more negative on blacks than the control group. "And," the authors write, "if the two halves [groups] are observed to differ in this way, the reason must necessarily be that the *mere mention* of affirmative action encourages dislike of blacks." The affirmative action question the authors used in the experiment was this:

> In a nearby state, an effort is being made to increase dramatically the number of blacks working in state government. This means that a large number of jobs will be reserved for blacks, even if their scores on merit exams are lower than those of whites who are turned down for the job. Do you favor or oppose this policy?

The impact of the affirmative action question on whites (N=236) *agreeing* with negative stereotypes of blacks were these statistically significant percentages:

Blacks are irresponsible:

Previous mention of affirmative action question	43 percent
No previous mention	26 percent

Blacks are lazy:

Previous mention of affirmative action question	31 percent
No previous mention	20 percent

Blacks are arrogant:

Previous mention of affirmative action question	36 percent
No previous mention	29 percent

Here is the suggestion of a final and quite unanticipated reason for abolishing race/ethnic affirmative action from our society; in and of itself affirmative action appears to enhance prejudice!

Appendix One

Distribution of Women, Under Age 35, by Medical Specialty, 1991

	N	Percentage Women	Ratio
Pediatrics	11,952	56.6	1.87
Dermatology	1,461	49.0	1.62
Obstetrics/Gynecology	7,409	48.5	1.61
Child Psychiatry	514	47.7	1.58
General Preventive Medicine	177	42.4	1.40
Psychiatry	5,675	41.6	1.38
Radiology	221	40.7	1.35
Pathology/Anatomy	2,791	38.3	1.27
Public Health	65	36.9	1.22
Forensic Pathology	23	34.8	1.15
Pediatric Cardiology	175	33.7	1.12
Allergy/Immunology	296	32.7	1.08
Family Practice	4,104	32.4	1.07
Physical Medicine, Rehabilitation	1,255	31.7	1.05
Nuclear Medicine	132	31.1	1.03
All Specialties	**133,718**	**30.2**	**1.00**

	N	Percentage Women	Ratio
Internal Medicine	31,859	30.1	1.00
Radiology	321	28.0	.93
Unspecified	5,053	27.2	.90
Neurology	1,737	26.7	.88
Occupational Medicine	2,888	24.7	.82
Diagnostic Radiology	4,796	24.2	.80
Radiation Oncology	658	23.9	.79
Emergency Medicine	3,331	23.7	.78
Other	475	23.4	.77
General Practice	478	23.2	.77
Ophthalmology	2,888	22.3	.74
Anesthesiology	6,787	20.2	.67
Pulmonary Diseases	892	16.4	.54
Plastic Surgery	411	14.4	.48
General Surgery	11,360	14.3	.47
Colon/Rectal Surgery	54	13.0	.43
Aerospace Medicine	118	12.7	.42
Otolaryngology	1,631	12.6	.42
Gastroenterology	1,176	11.6	.38
Cardiovascular Diseases	2,133	9.9	.33
Neurological Surgery	838	6.3	.21
Orthopedic Surgery	4,284	5.3	.18
Urological Surgery	1,411	5.0	.18
Thoracic Surgery	157	4.5	.15

Source: Calculated from AMA data, *1995 World Almanac,* p. 966.

Appendix Two

Agreement with statements about affirmative action, by race and gender, California Parks Department workers N=435

	N-W F	N-W M	WF	WM	N-W F – WM
1) Equal opportunity is a very good moral principle.	96	92	94	97	−1
2) Prejudice is common in society today.	90	88	85	76	14
3) With public policies, it is better to focus on groups than individuals.	90	85	82	81	9

		N-W F	N-W M	WF	WM	N-W F – WM
4)	Affirmative action is morally right.	89	82	85	62	27
5)	On balance, affirmative action benefits society.	87	82	81	64	23
6)	Affirmative action is needed to remedy the effects of discrimination	86	73	73	47	39
7)	Affirmative action is needed to ensure that women and nonwhite men get serious attention.	86	71	63	34	52
8)	White men have benefited from past discrimination.	83	83	77	71	12
9)	[The Department's] goals have become quotas, mandating the hiring of precise numbers of women and minorities.	80	73	65	71	9
10)	Prejudice is common in the parks department.	77	66	57	37	40
11)	I approve of supplemental certification.	76	60	64	40	36
12)	I approve parity hiring goals.	74	69	68	46	28
13)	It is morally right always to hire the best qualified.	71	65	70	74	–3
14)	Compassion and caring tend to lead to support for affirmative action.	70	55	72	68	2

	N-W F	N-W M	WF	WM	N-W F – WM
15) It is usually possible to identify who is best qualified.	69	63	75	82	−13
16) I approve of focused recruitment.	68	66	66	58	10
17) Overall, the workplace is better because of affirmative action.	67	67	60	40	27
18) With effort, anybody can succeed.	65	74	63	75	−10
19) Affirmative action promotes equal opportunity.	61	51	41	25	36
20) Affirmative action reduces tensions among different racial and gender groups.	59	64	56	38	21
21) It is especially hard to dismiss affirmative action candidates.	57	58	58	76	−19
22) Affirmative action helps many who do not need help.	55	48	54	63	−8
23) Prosecution is a better response to discrimination than affirmative action.	47	48	37	53	−6
24) Preferential treatment of victims of discrimination is appropriate compensation.	47	39	30	25	22
25) Affirmative action violates the rights of white men.	46	46	57	75	−29

	N-W F	N-W M	WF	WM	N-W F – WM
26) Affirmative action should be broadened to include all disadvantaged persons.	43	50	26	27	16
27) Money used on affirmative action should be spent elsewhere.	31	34	43	57	–26
28) Preferential treatment is unfair—other groups have overcome discrimination without it.	30	30	26	48	–18
29) Affirmative action reduces employee quality in the parks department.	26	40	48	69	–43
30) White men should accept fewer opportunities so that others may have a chance to succeed.	22	20	21	15	7
31) Affirmative action is wrong and should be changed.	20	28	26	53	–33
32) Affirmative action harms the mission of the parks department.	19	33	37	57	–38
33) Affirmative action is wrong and should not be obeyed.	2	9	3	7	–5

Source: Adapted from Taylor (1990), pp. 116–119

Notes

Section One
Prologue

1. Cohen, *Naked Racial Preference*, pp. 11, 53–54.
2. *Albuquerque Journal*, Associated Press (6 June 1995).
3. Kull, *The Color-Blind Constitution*, Chapter 10.
4. Clark, "An Integrationist to This Day, Believing All Else Has Failed," *The Week in Review, New York Times* (7 May 1995), p. 7; P. Applebome, "Keeping Tabs on Jim Crow," *New York Times Magazine* (23 April 1995), pp. 34–37.
5. Kull, *The Color-Blind Constitution*, pp. 184–185.
6. Wilson, *The Truly Disadvantaged*, p. 110.
7. *New York Times* OP-ED (1 March 1995).

Chapter 8

1. Mansfield, *National Review* (4 May 1984), p. 29.
2. Graham, *The Civil Rights Era*, p. 33.
3. Goodwin, *No Ordinary Time*, p. 249.
4. Graham, *The Civil Rights Era*, p. 28.
5. Ibid., p. 28.
6. Ibid., p. 134.
7. *Legislative History*, pp. 1004–1008. All quotes in this chapter from the debate prior to the passage of the Civil Rights Act of 1964 are from this source.
8. Graham, *The Civil Rights Era*, pp. 134–139.
9. Ibid., p. 152.

10. Thernstrom, *Whose Votes Count?*, is the basic source on the Voting Rights Act of 1965 to the mid-1980s.

11. Graham, *The Civil Rights Era*, p. 188.

12. All quotations in this paragraph from Graham, *The Civil Rights Era*, p. 174.

13. Belz, *Equality Transformed*, p. 30.

Chapter 9

1. *Handbook for Academic Recruitment*, pp. 3, 20.

2. Oppenheimer, *Five Models*, pp. 42–61.

3. "The Week in Review," *New York Times* (6 October 1991), p. 8.

4. Memo to Donald Dewey, Dean, School of Natural and Social Sciences, California State University, Los Angeles (12 July 1991).

5. Letter from David R. Buckholdt to Richard M. Coughlin (11 January 1978).

6. Jaschik, "U.S. upholds legality of affirmative action plan for admission to U. of California at San Diego," *Chronicle of Higher Education*, vol. 40 (13 April 1994), p. A27.

7. Ibid., p. A27.

8. *The Lobo* (UNM student newspaper) (3 March 1994).

9. Memo "Continuation as Chair," to Hobson Wildenthal, Dean, College of Arts and Sciences (4 June 1992).

10. Oppenheimer, *Five Models*, pp. 49–50.

Chapter 10

1. Hill, "*Johnson v. Santa Clara County*," p. 452.

2. Quoted by Donald L. Doernberg in a letter to the editor, *New York Times* (21 June 1991), p. A14.

3. Rosenfeld, *Affirmative Action and Justice*, p. 2.

4. *Paul E. Johnson, Petitioner v. Transportation Agency, Santa Clara County, California, et al. [March 25, 1987] 480 U.S. 616 (1987).* I also made use of Urofsky, *A Conflict of Rights*, and "The Supreme Court—Leading Cases," *Harvard Law Review*, vol. 101 (1987), pp. 300–310 in my discussion of *Johnson*.

5. Urofsky, *A Conflict of Rights*, pp. 80–81.

6. Ibid., pp. 48, 156–159.

7. Minow, *Making All the Difference*, p. 64.

Chapter 11

1. "Let Affirmative Action Die," *New York Times* OP-ED (23 July 1995).

2. *South Africa and the Rule of Law*, International Commission of Jurists, Geneva (1960), p. 37. Cited by Cohen, *Naked Racial Preference*, p. 204.

3. Supporting organizations are listed in the *Chronicle of Higher Education*, vol. 41 (12 May 1995), p. A34.

4. Rosenfeld, *Affirmative Action and Justice*, p. 2.

5. Quoted by Lieberman, *Public Education*, p. 199.

6. Cited in Belz, *Equality Transformed*, p. 198.

7. Dobrzynski, Judith H., "Some Action, Little Talk: Companies Embrace Diversity, but Are Reluctant to Discuss It," *New York Times* (20 April 1995), pp. D1, D4.

8. Glazer, "The affirmative action stalemate," p. 107.

9. Labaton, Stephen, "Affirmative Action Dispute Embroils the White House," *New York Times*, 25 April 1995, p. A15.

10. Rosen, Jeffrey, "Mediocrity on the Bench," *New York Times* (17 March 1995).

11. Glazer, "The affirmative action stalemate," p. 102; Glazer (1992), however, takes a view closer to Belz in Glazer's endorsement of Belz's *Equality Transformed* on the back page of the paperback edition.

12. Urofsky, *A Conflict of Rights*, p. 170.

Section Two
Introduction

1. Moynihan, Daniel Patrick, *Pandemonium; Ethnicity in International Relations*. (New York: Oxford University Press, 1993), p. 171.

2. "Casting the first stone," 8-14 October 1994, pp. 17–18.

Chapter 12

1. "A class thing," *New Republic* (31 October 1994), p. 12.

2. Wright, "One drop of blood," p. 46.

3. See the discussion of OMB's Statistical Directive 15 in Lind, *The Next American Nation*, pp. 118–129.

4. This percentage, and many of the percentages in this chapter, are from Wright, "One drop of blood."

5. Reported in the *New York Times*, 7 September 1991, p. 12 (no author given).

6. Communication from John G. Gross to Walter Mignolo, University of Michigan (19 November 1990).

7. See Christopher Shea, "Queens College and a measure of diversity," *Chronicle of Higher Education*, vol. 40 (11 May 1994), p. A37. "I will use whatever [category] is of advantage to me. If I think it will help me, I'll classify myself as black. If it's better for me to have a British accent, I will use that. If I'm talking to a Jamaican, I may be a Jamaican," said University of Massachusetts student Denise Bernard.

8. Raul Hillberg, *The Destruction of the European Jews* (New York: Quadrangle Books, 1961), p. 48.

9. Charles Wagley, "On the concept of social race in the Americas." Cited from Dwight B. Heath and Richard H. Adams, *Contemporary Cultures and Societies of Latin America* (New York: Random House, 1965), pp. 540–541.

10. Mentioned by Wright, "One drop of blood," p. 54.

11. Quoted from James H. Johnson, Jr., and Walter C. Farrell, Jr.,"Race still matters," *Chronicle of Higher Education*, vol. 41 (7 July 1995).

12. John Berendt, *Midnight in the Garden of Good and Evil* (New York: Random House, 1994), pp. 326–327.

13. Sarah L. Delaney, A. Elizabeth Delaney, and Amy Hill Hearth, *Having Our Say* (New York: Dell, 1993), p. 16. Bessie, on balance, opposed affirmative action.

14. Pierre van den Berghe, *Race and Racism: A Comparative Perspective* (New York: John Wiley, 1967), pp. 42, 55.

15. Cited in Charles Sykes, *A Nation of Victims: The Decay of the American Character* (New York: St. Martin's, 1992), p. 166.

16. Cited by George Roche, *Imprimus*, 23: 10 (October 1994), p. 5. I asked a University of Massachusetts professor if it were true that pedophiles were a "protected category" at his university. He told me that a few years ago pedophiles were specifically excluded from "sexual orientation" as a protected category in the university's affirmative action statement. The following year the pedophile exception was removed from the university's affirmative action statement. Hence, the belief of some people that pedophiles are a protected category at the University of Massachusetts. The professor who told me this did not want his name mentioned in this note.

17. Advertisement (20 January 1995), p. B65.

Chapter 13

1. Quoted in Jaschik, Scott, "Battle over affirmative action gets personal," *Chronicle of Higher Education*, vol. 41 (17 March 1995), p. A27.

2. Matt Selove, "The Affirmative Action Catch-22," *The Harvard Salient* (12 February 1995). Cited as a boxed item in *Academic Questions* (Summer 1995), p. 32.

3. The statement was made by Dean James A. Blackburn in 1988. Cited in Lind, *The Next American Nation*, p. 167.

4. Richard Harwood, "The New Elite in American Society," *Cosmos 1995*, pp. 13–19.

5. Jeffries, *Powell*, p. 471.

6. Klitgaard, *Choosing Elites*, p. 27; Jake Lamar, "Whose legacy is it, anyway," *New York Times* (9 October 1991), p. A15.

7. Exceptions are Sowell, *Preferential Policies* and *Race and Culture*, and Lind, *The Next American Nation*, pp. 165–171.

8. Chavez, *Out of the Barrio*, p. 120.

9. From a picture of the staff in the *Chronicle of Higher Education*, vol. 41 (28 April 1995), p. A19. The quotations in this paragraph are from the article in which the picture appears, "Private Colleges Try to Keep a Low Profile," by Stephen Burd.

10. See the voluminous evidence for the superiority of statistical vs. clinical prediction in Herrnstein and Murray, *The Bell Curve*.

11. Carter, *Reflections*, pp. 15–16.

12. SAT scores are from various articles in the *Chronicle of Higher Education* under the rubric "Affirmative Action on the Line" (28 April 1995).

13. Vincent Sarich, "The Institutionalization of Racism at the University of California at Berkeley," *Academic Questions*, vol. 4 (Winter 1990–91), pp. 77–78.

14. See Bunzel, *Race Relations*, for one such report.

15. Quoted by John Ellis, "Present at the Uncreation," *Heterodoxy*, vol. 3 (September 1995), p. 11.

Chapter 14

1. *Newsweek* (December 25, 1995/January 1, 1996), p. 79.

2. "Short guys finish last," *The Economist* (December 23rd–January 5th, 1996), pp. 19–22.

3. When 3,119 Ivy League undergraduates were asked in a survey about religious background, 24 percent said Roman Catholic, 25 percent Protestant, and 27 percent Jewish. "Big gaps found in college students' grasp of current affairs," *New York Times* (18 April 1993), p. 36.

4. In an article dealing with the living "Economic Greats," 47 names were mentioned; the majority were Jews, three were women—Irma Adelman, Claudia Goldin, and Anne Krueger. The Week in Review, *New York Times* (17 October 1993), p.12.

5. David Briggs, The Associated Press, in *The New Mexican* (17 December 1994).

6. Lipset and Raab, *Jews*, p. 2.

7. Lipset and Raab, *Jews*, p. 26. Supporting data are in footnote 48, p. 212.

8. Herrnstein and Murray, *The Bell Curve*, p. 275. A genetic explanation of the Jewish "tradition of learning" is given by Norbert Wiener (1953) in his biography *Ex-Prodigy*, pp. 11–12:

> Let me insert a word or two about the Jewish family structure which is not irrelevant to the Jewish tradition of learning. At all times, the young learned man, and especially the rabbi,...was always a match for the daughter of the rich merchant. Biologically this led to a situation in sharp contrast to that of the Christians of earlier times. The Western Christian learned man was absorbed in the church...and actually tended to be less fertile than the community around him. On the other hand, the Jewish scholar was very often in a position to have a large family. Thus the biological habits of the Christians tended to breed out of the race whatever hereditary qualities make for learning, whereas the biological habits of the Jews tended to breed these qualities in. To what extent this genetic difference supplemented the cultural trend for learning among Jews is difficult to say. But there is no reason to believe that the genetic factor was negligible. I have talked this matter over with my friend, Professor J. B. S. Haldane, and he certainly is of the same opinion. Indeed, it is quite possible that in giving this opinion I am merely presenting an idea which I have borrowed from Professor Haldane.

9. Lipset and Raab, *Jews*, p. 13. Significantly, many (most?) scholarly and journalistic critiques of affirmative action have been written by Jews. John Jeffries, Jr., in his fine biography of Justice Lewis Powell writes, p. 462: "Opposition [to reversing Allan Bakke's lower court victory in his case against the University of California] was led by prominent Jewish groups, including the American Jewish Committee and the Anti-Defamation League of B'nai B'rith." Most establishment opinion lined up behind the university, in other words, supported race-based affirmative action.

10. Sociologists now do little research on the comparative mobility of different ethnic groups.

11. "The ruling class," *The Economist*, 17–23 September 1994.

12. "Report Links Retardation to Poverty"; *New York Times* (31 March 1995), p. A14.

13. Henry, *Elitism*, p. 69.

Chapter 15

1. "An Integrationist to This Day, Believing All Else has Failed," The Week in Review, *New York Times* (7 May 1995), p. 7.

2. Quoted in Lipset and Raab, *Jews*, p. 174, but from Lipset, "Two Americas, Two Value Systems, Blacks and Whites," *Tocqueville Review*, 13:1 (1992), pp. 159–164.

3. Ezorsky, *Racism and Justice*, p. 1.

4. Steele, *Our Character*, p. 119.

5. Horowitz, *Ethnic Groups*, and Sowell, *Preferential Policies*, and *Race and Culture*.

6. See Chapter 6, "*Bakke* and beyond," in Jeffries, *Powell*, for a superb account of what went on among the Supreme Court justices in dealing with this case.

7. Rawls, *A Theory of Justice*, pp. 14–15.

8. Cited in *The Economist* (8-14 October 1994), p. 53.

9. "Affirmative action and immigration." In Mills, *Debating Affirmative Action*, p. 301.

10. Chavez, *Out of the Barrio*, p. 5.

11. Lind, *The Next American Nation*, pp. 126–127.

12. See "Population of the states, breakdown by race, Hispanic origin and sex," in Sam Roberts, *Who We Are: A Portrait of America Today Based on the Latest United States Census* (New York: Random House, 1993), Appendix C, pp. 266–271.

13. *Items,* SSRC newsletter (June/September 1994), p. 55.

14. Zeitlin to Tomasson (9 December 1994).

15. Buss, *Human Mating*, pp. 25.

16. Sommers, *Who Stole Feminism?*, p. 96.

17. This is the conclusion of Fuchs (1988) and others.

18. These organizations supporting the University of Maryland are listed in a boxed item in the *Chronicle of Higher Education*, vol. 41 (12 May 1995), p. A34.

19. King, Florence, *The Florence King Reader* (New York: St. Martin's Press, 1995), p. 45.

20. See the next chapter.

21. Jill Johnston, "Why Iron John is no gift to women," *New York Times Book Review* (23 February 1992), p. 31.

22. Bergmann, *The Economic Emergence of Women*, p. 164.

23. Ibid., p. 172.

24. Anastasi, *Differential Psychology*, p. 497.

25. All income percentages are calculated from data in *Current Population Reports, Consumer Income*, Series P60-184, "Money Income of Households, Families, and Persons in the United States: 1992," Table 28 (September 1993).

26. Sowell, *Civil Rights*, p. 92.

27. For an account of growing income inequality in the U.S., see the chapter on income differentials in Paul Krugman, *Peddling Prosperity: Economic Sense and Nonsense in an Age of Diminished Expectations* (New York: Norton, 1994).

28. These percentages and other 1993 percentages were calculated from "Earned Degrees Conferred by U.S. Institutions, 1992–93," *Chronicle of Higher Education*, vol. 41 (9 June 1995), p. A37.

29. "Physicians by Age, Sex, and Specialty," American Medical Association data, from *1995 World Almanac*, pp. 966–967.

30. See my "The Swedes Do It Better," *Harper's* (October 1962).

31. Swedish Institute, "Facts and figures about youth in Sweden," *Fact Sheets on Sweden* (Stockholm: Swedish Institute, 1991).

32. See Note 28.

33. "Few women found in top public jobs," *New York Times* (3 January 1992), p. A12.

34. Kilborn, Peter, "A try for more diversity in police force bumps into the same old ethnic profile," *New York Times*, 10 October 1994, p. B12.

35. Boxed item, *Time*, 27 May 1991.

36. Kahlenberg, Richard D., "Class, not race," *New Republic* (3 April 1995), pp. 21–27, p. 24.

37. Kahlenberg, Richard D., "Equal opportunity critics," *New Republic* (17 & 24 July 1995), pp. 20–25.

38. Kahlenberg, "Class, not race," p. 21.

39. Ibid., p. 25.

40. "Race, not class," *Wall Street Journal* (5 April 1995).

41. Kahlenberg, "Equal Opportunity Critics," p.22.

Chapter 16

1. Lind, *The Next American Nation*, p. 296.

2. In the June 1991 response to this question, the results were 11, 81, and 8 percent to the three alternatives mentioned.

3. 4 July 1991.

4. Data on the Field Poll of the CCRI are from an Associated Press release (15 September 1995). In *New York Times* (15 September 1995).

5. *USA Today* (24-26 March 1995), pp. 1–4. The poll was done 17-19 March 1995, 1,220 adult respondents. The margin of error was 3 percent overall, 4 percent for whites, 6 percent for blacks.

6. Taylor, *Affirmative Action at Work.*

7. Ibid., p. 111.

8. Lester, *Antibias Regulation*, p. 2.

9. Ibid., p. 2, footnote 1.

10. Unpublished report (1992) available from Tomasson.

11. Herrnstein and Murray, *The Bell Curve*, p. 475.

12. Sniderman and Piazza, *The Scar of Race*, especially pp. 102–104.

13. Dovidio, Mann, and Gaertner. *Resistance to Affirmative Action*, p. 85. In Blanchard and Crosby, *Affirmative Action.*

References

Altschiller, Donald, ed. *The Reference Shelf: Affirmative Action*. New York: H.W. Wilson, 1991.

Anastasi, Anne. *Differential Psychology; Individual and Group Differences in Behavior*. 3rd ed. New York: Macmillan, 1958.

Belz, Herman. *Equality Transformed; A Quarter-Century of Affirmative Action*. New Brunswick, NJ: Transaction, 1991.

Bergmann, Barbara R. *The Economic Emergence of Women*. New York: BasicBooks, 1986.

Bickel, Alexander M. *The Morality of Consent*. New Haven, CT: Yale, 1975.

Bunzel, John H., and Jeffrey K.D. "Diversity or discrimination? Asian Americans in college." *The Public Interest* (Spring, 1987): pp. 49–62.

Bunzel, John H. *Race Relations on Campus: Stanford Students Speak*. Stanford, CA: Stanford Alumni Association, 1992.

Buss, David M. *The Evolution of Desire; Strategies of Human Mating*. New York: BasicBooks, 1994.

Carter, Stephen L. *Reflections of an Affirmative Action Baby*. New York: BasicBooks, 1991.

Chavez, Linda. *Out of the Barrio*. New York: BasicBooks, 1991.

Cohen, Carl. *Naked Racial Preference: The Case Against Affirmative Action*. Lanham, MD: Madison Books, 1995.

Combs, Michael W., and John Gruhl, eds. *Affirmative Action: Theory, Analysis, and Prospects*. Jefferson, NC: McFarland, 1986.

Cose, Ellis. *The Rage of a Privileged Class.* New York: HarperCollins, 1993.

Dovidio, John F,. and others. "Resistance to Affirmative Action: The Implications of Aversive Racism." Pages 83–102 in F. A. Blanchard and F. J. Crosby. eds. *Affirmative Action in Perspective.* Published under the auspices of the Society for the Psychological Study of Social Issues. New York: Springer Verlag, 1989.

D'Souza, Dinesh. *Illiberal Education; The Politics of Race and Sex on Campus.* New York: Free Press, 1991.

D'Souza, Dinesh. *The End of Racism.* New York: Free Press, 1995.

Epstein, Richard A. *Forbidden Grounds: The Case against Employment Discrimination Laws.* Cambridge, MA: Harvard, 1992.

Ezorsky, Gertrude. *Racism and Justice: The Case for Affirmative Action.* Ithaca, NY: Cornell University Press, 1991.

Faludi, Susan. *Backlash: The Undeclared War against American Women.* New York: Crown, 1991.

Fish, Stanley. *There's No Such Thing as Free Speech and It's a Good Thing, Too.* New York: Oxford, 1994.

Fuchs, Lawrence H. *The American Kaleidoscope: Race, Ethnicity, and the Civic Culture.* Hanover, NH: University Press of New England for Wesleyan University Press, 1990.

Fuchs, Victor R. *Women's Quest for Economic Equality.* Cambridge, MA: Harvard, 1988.

Fullinwider, Robert K. *The Reverse Discrimination Controversy: A Moral and Legal Analysis.* Totowa, NJ: Rowman & Littlefield, 1990.

Fullinwider, Robert K., and Claudia Mills, eds. *The Moral Foundation of Civil Rights.* Totowa, NJ: Rowman & Littlefield, 1986.

Glazer, Nathan. *Affirmative Discrimination; Ethnic Inequality and Public Policy.* New York: BasicBooks, 1975.

Glazer, Nathan. "The Constitution and American diversity." *The Public Interest* (Winter, 1987): pp. 10–21.

Glazer, Nathan. "The affirmative action stalemate." *The Public Interest* (Winter, 1988): pp. 99–114.

Goodwin, Doris Kearns. *No Ordinary Time.* New York: Simon and Schuster, 1994, p. 249.

Graglia, Lino A. "Racial preferences in admissions to institutions of higher education." In Howard Dickman, *The Imperiled Academy*, New Brunswick, NJ: Transaction, 1993, pp. 127–151.

Graham, Hugh Davis. *The Civil Rights Era: Origins and Development of National Policy, 1960–1972.* New York: Oxford, 1990.

Hacker, Andrew. *Two Nations: Black and White; Separate, Hostile, Unequal.* New York: Scribner's, 1992.

The Handbook for Academic Recruitment and Hiring at the University of New Mexico. Albuquerque: The University of New Mexico, 1992, p. 3, p. 20.

Henry, William A., III. *In Defense of Elitism.* New York: Doubleday, 1994.

Hentoff, Nat. *The New Equality.* New York: Viking, 1965.

Herrnstein, Richard J., and Charles Murray. *The Bell Curve; Intelligence and Class Structure in American Life.* New York: Free Press, 1994.

Hill, Herbert. "Johnson v. Santa Clara County." In *The Oxford Companion to the Supreme Court,* edited by Kermit L. Hall. New York: Oxford University Press, 1992, pp. 451–452.

Horowitz, Donald L. *Ethnic Groups in Conflict.* Berkeley: University of California, 1985.

Jeffries, John C., Jr. *Justice Lewis F. Powell, Jr.* New York: Charles Scribner's Sons, 1994, Chapter XIV.

Klitgaard, Robert. *Choosing Elites.* New York: BasicBooks, 1985.

Kull, Andrew. *The Color-Blind Constitution.* Cambridge, MA: Harvard University Press, 1992.

Lester, Richard A. *Antibias Regulation of Universities.* A report prepared for The Carnegie Commission on Higher Education. New York: McGraw Hill, 1974.

Lieberman, Myron. *Public Education: An Autopsy.* Cambridge, MA: Harvard, 1993.

Lind, Michael. *The Next American Nation.* New York: Free Press, 1995.

Lipset, Seymour Martin, and William Schneider. "The Bakke Case: How would it be decided at the bar of public opinion?" *Public Opinion.* 1:1 (March/April, 1978): pp. 38–45.

Lipset, Seymour Martin, and Earl Raab. *Jews and the New American Scene.* Cambridge, MA: Harvard, 1995.

Lynch, Frederick R. *Invisible Victims: White Males and the Crisis of Affirmative Action.* New York: Greenwood, 1989.

Mansfield, Harvey C., Jr. "The underhandedness of affirmative action." *National Review.* May 4, 1984.

Massey, Douglas S., and Nancy A. Denton. *American Apartheid; Segregation and the Making of the Underclass.* Cambridge, MA: Harvard, 1993.

Mills, Nicolaus, ed. *Debating Affirmative Action: Race, Gender, Ethnicity, and the Politics of Inclusion.* New York: Dell Bantam, 1994.

Minow, Martha. *Making All the Difference: Inclusion, Exclusion, and American Law.* Ithaca, NY: Cornell University, 1991.

Oppenheimer, David Benjamin. "Distinguishing five models of affirmative action." *Berkeley Women's Law Journal* (1988-89): pp. 42–61.

Paglia, Camille. *Sex, Art, and American Culture*. New York: Vintage Books, 1992.

Rawls, John. *A Theory of Justice*. Cambridge, MA: Harvard, 1971.

Rosenfeld, Michel. *Affirmative Action and Justice: A Philosophical and Constitutional Inquiry*. New Haven, CT: Yale, 1991.

Roth, Byron M. *Prescription for Failure; Race Relations in the Age of Social Science*. New Brunswick, NJ: Transaction, 1994.

Rushton, J. Philippe. *Race, Evolution, and Behavior; A Life History Perspective*. New Brunswick, NJ: Transaction, 1995.

Schlesinger, Arthur M., Jr. *The Disuniting of America; Reflections on a Multicultural Society*. New York: Norton, 1992.

Sniderman, Paul M., and Thomas Piazza. *The Scar of Race*. Cambridge, MA: Harvard, 1993.

Sommers, Christina Hoff. *Who Stole Feminism? How Women Have Betrayed Women*. New York: Simon and Schuster, 1994.

Sowell, Thomas. *Civil Rights: Rhetoric or Reality*. New York: Morrow, 1984.

Sowell, Thomas. *Preferential Policies: An International Perspective*. New York: Morrow, 1990.

Sowell, Thomas. *Inside American Education: The Decline, the Deception, the Dogmas*. New York: Free Press, 1993.

Sowell, Thomas. *Race and Culture: A World View*. New York: BasicBooks, 1994.

Steele, Shelby. *The Content of Our Character: A New Vision of Race in America*. New York: Morrow, 1991.

Sullivan, Kathleen M. "Sins of discrimination." *Harvard Law Review*. 100 (1986): 78–98.

Taylor, Bron Raymond. *Affirmative Action at Work: Law, Politics and Ethics*. Pittsburgh: University of Pittsburgh Press, 1991.

Taylor, Jared. *Paved with Good Intentions: The Failure of Race Relations in Contemporary America*. New York: Carroll & Graf, 1992.

Thernstrom, Abigail M. *Whose Votes Count? Affirmative Action and Minority Voting Rights*. Cambridge, MA: Harvard, 1987.

United States Equal Employment Opportunity Commission. *Legislative History of Titles VII and XI of Civil Rights Act of 1964*. Washington, DC: Government Printing Office, 1968.

Urofsky, Melvin I. *A Conflict of Rights: The Supreme Court and Affirmative Action.* New York: Scribner's, 1991.

Wiener, Norbert. *Ex-Prodigy; My Childhood and Youth.* New York: Simon and Schuster, 1953.

Wilson, William Julius. *The Truly Disadvantaged; The Inner City, the Underclass, and Public Policy.* Chicago: University of Chicago, 1987.

Wright, Lawrence. "One drop of blood." *The New Yorker.* 25 July, 1994.

Index

269

About the Authors

Richard F. Tomasson is Emeritus Professor of Sociology at the University of New Mexico. He is the author of books and articles on modern Swedish society (*Sweden: Prototype of Modern Society*); eleven centuries of Icelandic history (*Iceland: The First New Society*); and the social security systems of the rich nations and their patterns of mortality and fertility. He has been the recipient of three Fulbright grants and was a Senior Fellow of the National Endowment for the Humanities. He has a particular concern with curriculum reform in the universities and the restoration of the liberal arts and required core courses.

Faye D. Crosby is Professor of Psychology at Smith College in Northampton, Massachusetts, and has been on the faculty since 1985. A leading researcher on gender roles, Prof. Crosby has published widely in both the scholarly and popular press. Her bestselling book *Juggling: The Unexpected Advantages of Combining Career and Home for Women and Their Families* demonstrated that balancing work and family is beneficial—not detrimental—to women. The book garnered national attention, and she has discussed her research in a number of media outlets including the *Wall Street Journal*, the *New York Times*, *Glamour*, and *Working Mother*. She has received a number of grants and fellowships. She serves on four editorial boards and acts as an ad-hoc reviewer for a variety of professional journals. She is active in the Ameri-

275

can Psychological Association and is on the Board of Directors of the Eastern Psychological Association. Her current work focuses on affirmative action. She has written and lectured extensively on the issue. Prof. Crosby holds an A.B. degree from Wheaton College and a Ph.D. from Boston Univeristy.

Sharon D. Herzberger is Professor of Psychology at Trinity College in Hartford, Connecticut. She received her B.A. from The Pennsylvania State University and her M.A. and her Ph.D. degrees from the University of Illinois. She taught at Northwestern University before coming to Trinity in 1980. There she served as Assistant to the President for Affirmative Action for four years. Prof. Herzberger teaches courses in social psychology, personality, criminal justice, and discrimination. Her research interests center on family violence. Her recent book, published by Brown and Benchmark, is entitled *Interpersonal Violence within the Home.* She also does research on criminal justice decision-making.